ART & ANGER

Miami University, through an arrangement with the Ohio State University Press initiated in 1975, publishes works of original scholarship, fiction, and poetry. The responsibility for receiving and reviewing manuscripts is invested in an Editorial Board comprising Miami University faculty.

ART & ANGER

✝✝✝✝

Reading

Like A

Woman

✝✝✝✝

JANE MARCUS

Published for Miami University by the
Ohio State University Press
Columbus

Library of Congress Cataloging-in-Publication Data

Marcus, Jane.
    Art and anger.

    Bibliography: p.
    Includes index.
        1. English literature—History and criticism—Theory,
etc. 2. Women and literature. 3. Feminist criticism.
4. Feminism and literature. 5. Woolf, Virginia, 1882–1941
—Criticism and interpretation. I. Title.
PR119.M37   1988   820'.9'352042   88–1223
ISBN 0–8142–0453–8
ISBN 0–8142–0460–0 (paper)

Printed in the U.S.A.

for Jason

Su describes her anger as "a little femina, two centimeters tall"
who claps inside her head every time she speaks out. "I'm dedicat-
ing my life to her, whatever the trends of the times. No more anger-
sitters. No more camps or schools. No more lollipops. She's going
to get all the advantages my expanse of years can provide, every
opportunity to become whatever she wants to become, even if she
wants to get married and have lots of little angers."

—June Arnold, *Sister Gin*

Hatred of baseness
Also distorts the features,
And anger at injustice
Makes the voice hoarse.

—Bertolt Brecht

Feminist criticism begins in negation.

—Susan Stanford Friedman

"Women's anger is pervasive, as pervasive as our oppression, but it frequently lurks underground. If we added up all of woman's depression; all her compulsive smiling, ego-tending, and sacrifice; all her psychosomatic illness, and all her passivity, we could gauge our rage's unarticulated, negative force." In a feminist revision of *Frantz Fanon's* The Wretched of the Earth, *we can imagine: "Feminist revolution never takes place unnoticed, for it influences individuals and modifies them fundamentally. It transforms passive femininity crushed with inessentiality into privileged agency under the flood-lights of history. A new kind of woman brings a new rhythm into existence with a new language and a new humanity; combatting women's oppression means the veritable creation of new women who become fully human by the same process by which they freed themselves. . . . At the level of individuals, anger is a cleansing force. It frees the woman from her inferiority complex and from despair and inaction; it makes her fearless and restores her self-respect."*

—Julia Lesage, "Woman's Rage" in *Marxism and the Interpretation of Culture*

Contents

Acknowledgments

Earlier versions of these essays appeared in *The Bulletin of the New York Public Library, New Feminist Essays on Virginia Woolf* (Nebraska University Press, 1981), *Signs, Women's Studies, The Bucknell Review, Feminist Studies, Tulsa Studies in Women's Literature, Marxist Perspectives,* and *Critical Inquiry.* The most substantial addition is a long section on *To The Lighthouse* called "Reading as Desire II" in "Still Practice." Without David Erdman's encouragement, helpful advice, and severe criticism these essays would not exist. I would like to thank the staffs of the Newberry Library, Chicago, and Northwestern University Library for many years of courteous help, the editors of the above journals and their feminist readers, the members of the Newberry Library Feminist Criticism Seminar, Portia, my students at SUNY, Stony Brook and the University of Texas, the American Council of Learned Societies, the National Endowment for the Humanities, the lupine critics, the University Research Institute of the University of Texas, my patient family, Alice Fox, who first suggested that these essays should be collected as a book, and the anonymous readers for the Miami University Editorial Board for their helpful critiques.

Introduction

Changing the Subject

There is only one subject
and it is impossible to change it.
—Laura (Riding) Jackson

For several years readers, students, and colleagues have urged me to collect these essays, which appeared in earlier forms in academic and feminist journals. "What do they have in common?" I asked. A book has a thesis, a sustained argument. And while there is certainly a polemical tone to these pieces, I was reluctant to name the argument inherent in the history of their writing: the wish to change the subject of literary study. In rereading and rethinking these essays I have looked at the growth of feminist criticism, specifically at attempts to "change the subject" of an academic training in American New Criticism and intellectual history from the study of canonical texts to those of feminist male writers and Virginia Woolf, the thesis topic expressly forbidden by my mentor. These essays are clearly marked as written by a member of the generation of self-trained American materialist feminist critics in that they are innocent of contact with contemporary theory. Such theoretical statements as they do provide, and it is surprising to see that they do, were entirely derived from the texts under discussion in relation to their historical context, as well as to a problematizing of the issue of reading by gender gained from reading Virginia Woolf's fiction. In view of the remarkable production of literary theory over the last decade, both feminist and other, to revitalize our discipline, it is embarrassing to explain that the notions of "the collective sublime" and the performative role of the reader demanded by Woolf in "Thinking Back through Our Mothers" were arrived at without benefit of Barthes, or Wolfgang Iser, or any of the reader-response critics. Like much feminist scholarship in the seventies in America, these essays seemed to situate themselves in a sociology of literary criticism, a literary version of the British empirical E. P. Thompson school of social history. But they had changed the subject of that discourse, which concentrated on working-class writers, and did not fit standard patterns. Hence their air of "homelessness." For the British at that point found Woolf impossibly elitist and lacking working-class credentials; Wilde was decadent and Meredith too dense. Feminists were gynocritically studying women, not male feminists, and Woolf was rejected as elitist.

It may be difficult in these days of dazzling theory, with so many brilliant new ways to analyze texts being produced, to imagine a practice without theory (though, of course, not produced outside of ideology). Recently, in fact, so many competing theories have been announced that the practice of literary criticism has hardly caught up with them. There aren't enough readings to enable a student to see if they work. In rereading these essays I begin to see that specifically female trope of prolepsis at work. Certainly in the ten years since " 'No More Horses' " and "Art and Anger" were written, their aims have been accomplished. Readers are paying attention to Woolf's politics. *A Room of One's Own* has been read in classrooms all over the country, and *Three Guineas* has become the bible of a new generation of pacifists. The particular conjunction of socialism, feminism, and pacifism which so attracted me to her role as a theorist and model for my own kind of feminist criticism has become a subject for serious discussion. Little about " 'No More Horses' " strikes me now as radical or worth the uproar it caused at the 1975 MLA. It seems too polite and well-mannered, now that Woolf *is* the subject of so much critical debate.

Now that Nina Auerbach's *Woman and the Demon* has been published, these studies of the heroines of Ibsen, Meredith, and Wilde do not seem so far-fetched. Because Auerbach has so radically "changed the theoretical subject" regarding Victorian women, my own practical readings seem proleptically vindicated. Meredith has been reinstated in the canon by Judith Wilt, but he still deserves more feminist analysis. If I were to rewrite the essay on Oscar Wilde, I would use not only the arguments of Nina Auerbach, but also the feminist revision of the Freudian concept of fetishism recently undertaken by Naomi Schor. Deconstruction and feminism should ensure a revival of Oscar Wilde, because in *Salomé* he destabilizes the project of critical exegesis itself. The Christian practice of reading the Old Testament only as a prophecy of the New appears ridiculous when Salomé is created as the precursor of the Precursor. The narrative of desire is similarly unsettled as we read Wilde's identification with Salomé as like Flaubert's with Emma Bovary, with the lesbian position of woman.

The essay on Elizabeth Hardwick and Ibsen is included within the section on reading men because of the particular problem to feminist criticism of prominent antifeminist women critics. Her cultural role on the editorial board of the *New York Review of Books* deserves careful study. The journal's policy of choosing a well-known woman to attack a feminist (Helen Vendler on Adrienne Rich, for example) or the periodic demolishing of a feminist work (Germaine Greer's *The Obstacle Race* or Judy Chicago's *The Dinner Party*) while maintaining a general policy of ignoring feminist debate as the major vitalizing force in American intellectual life, is worth a full investigation. *The New York Review of Books* has its own causes. If the historian of the future takes it as an index of American thinking, it will assume that the plight of Soviet dissidents was the most important issue in the U.S. in the 1980s. Female defense of patriarchy is not a new problem at either the intellectual or political level. Elizabeth Hardwick has an ancestress in Mrs. Humphry Ward.

The last essays in this volume constitute a decade-long dialogue with Virginia Woolf scholarship, the literary estate, and the editors of her diaries and letters, from a feminist perspective. They are a written historical record of opposition and objection to the official view of her work. But it is necessary to point out that these review essays are also separate from the "Virginia Woolf cult" which has flourished at the same time in the U.S., where she has become uncritically sainted almost because of her suicide and supposed madness. Because of the nature of their origin as essays, these pieces sometimes repeat points for different audiences.

"Still Practice" is offered here as a step toward a definition of a feminist aesthetic as materially grounded in process rather than exclusively concerned with the work of art as a finished product. It also discusses gender and reading and the idea of a specifically socialist feminist criticism.

Something ought to be said here about the distinguishing features of my own practice. I am concerned about the formalist element in most European-born theories, which does not consider the text to be a text until it is published and pays little or no attention to drafts or revision, or contextualizes, as in some Marxist theory, only the moment of production of the text. Derrida holds that the text constantly interacts with culture and so is changed with each reading, by translation, in new contextualizations and revisions of literary history. Why aren't the changes made in the author's conception and gestation equally important?

Deconstruction, even feminist or Marxist deconstruction, with its exclusive reliance on the published text, its religious adoration of the word, can become a new formalism which fails to account for the extremely important role of censorship and self-censorship in the work of women, radicals, blacks, homosexuals, and lesbians. There is no sacred text in these cases to which the critic can be priest or priestess, bowing and praying over it in a mysterious language which only initiates can understand. As in the case of Virginia Woolf's first novel, *The Voyage Out,* the drafts were more radical than the published version. She succumbed to her critics and her own fears. If we study only the final version, we perpetuate for our students the elitist notion of genius and discourage the writers in their midst.

I owe a great deal to teachers who trained me in British social history and American studies. Like most feminist critics of my generation, I had no female mentor beyond wistful memories of the term the distinguished Helen White taught at Harvard and tried to be a role model for innumerable literary young women. My colleagues in Woolf studies, feminist "lupine critics," have acted as mentors; the work of Adrienne Rich, Tillie Olsen, Alice Walker, and other feminist writers has meant a great deal. The Newberry Library Feminist Criticism

Seminar was a crucible for this work. Lillian Robinson's *Sex, Class and Culture* made it clear what the position of socialist feminist criticism is, and the work of others—Julia Lesage, Judith Kegan Gardiner, Moira Ferguson—has continued it. But from a historical perspective one can see that this line of specifically *socialist* feminism was "the road not taken," as many American critics turned to French models and psychoanalysis. Annis Pratt's feminist myth criticism has had a similar lack of followers. The work of Kristeva, Irigaray, and Spivak has enormously enriched the practice of feminist criticism. But we are not reduced to a choice between formalism and romanticism, psychoanalysis or politics in feminism criticism, despite this development, and we ought to encourage eccentricity in our writers and critics.

What, in any case, is a socialist feminist criticism? The answer is a simple one. It wants to change the subject. The critic is committed to social change in her workplace, the university, as well as to political activism in the world. Her perspective on literature brings those concerns to scholarly practice and teaching. She wants to reinterpret the "classics" from the perspective of ordinary people and women. She wants to make the canon of great books elastic enough to include those who have been excluded or labeled minor, and she insists on seeing literary labor in its social context. She has no ideological commitment to any one critique of phallocentric culture. Having been denied opportunity herself, she will, one hopes, not deny others the means of expression. Literary criticism is inescapably political, often when it most vigorously denies its politics. A socialist feminist position openly affirms its values while keeping a weather eye out for formalism, essentialism, or any totalizing systems.

I have shared with my feminist colleagues the excitement of a decade of work in theory and practice. So much has been done that one can hardly do justice to the pioneers. These essays are a contribution to our common practice, the result of struggles not entirely intellectual, with enormous debts to other workers in the field, especially when their work has caused me to argue with them: Elaine Showalter, Martha Vicinus, Carolyn Heilbrun, Annette Kolodny, Ellen Moers, Kate Millett, Lillian Robinson, Sandra Gilbert and Susan Gubar, Nina Auerbach, Louise De Salvo, Shari Benstock, Blanche Cook, Catherine Stimpson, Nancy K. Miller, and many other feminist critics whose work is a historical necessity for my own.

Art and Anger is in part concerned with the curious origins of one kind of modern feminism in the writings of nineteenth-century men: Wilde, Meredith, and Ibsen. Yet the feminist need not apologize for studying men. Nina Auerbach has recently very wittily asserted her right to read men, that feminist practice should be decided by what she determines is worth study and not by "gynocritics" alone. They are the literary fathers and uncles of Virginia Woolf (and also of Olive Schreiner, Katherine Mansfield, Rebecca West, and several other modern feminists). In her argument in *A Room of One's Own* that "we think back through our mothers" if we are women writers, Woolf sought a tradition of female influence beginning with Sappho. I have explored the meaning of this female tradition in "Thinking Back through Our Mothers." *Art and Anger* is not a denial of the importance of the female tradition to Virginia Woolf. "Reading Practice I" and "Reading Practice II" are meant to act in dialogue with each other, to suggest the inside/outside position of a writer like Woolf. *A Room of One's Own* is the great example of "changing the subject," and it is arguably addressed to both men and women readers, who each read a gendered text. In a broad sense the essays collected here give a different account of the rise of the feminist novelist in twentieth-century Britain. The plays and the life of Oscar Wilde, the novels of George Meredith and his feminist essays, poems and encouragement of women writers, the English productions of Ibsen's plays which incited a revolution of manners and morals among the English intelligentsia, and, though I do not explore his contributions here, Thomas Hardy's novels—these were a coherent literary seedbed for the flowering of Woolf's genius. The struggles of male artists to deal with culturally accepted notions of sex roles, the ambiguities of sexuality — including homosexuality, lesbianism, androgyny, and friendship — were important not only to the suffragettes of Woolf's generation who marched behind Mrs. Pankhurst, went to jail, and hunger-struck for the cause of their sex. They were also important to women like herself who licked envelopes for the Cause but couldn't risk the physical abuse of public demonstrations. Wilde's life and work were important to the notions of sexual freedom championed by Bloomsbury. He also made it clear that aestheticism could be seen as morally and politically radical against the background of earnest Victorian philistinism. Meredith's philosophy of comedy was based on an acute analysis of sex roles. His feminist attempt to educate the conservative Julia Stephen in the raising of daughters has a poignant irony. From Louise De Salvo's detailed study of the manuscript drafts of *The Voyage Out,* we now know how important Ibsen was to the young Virginia Stephen. Her half-brother, Gerald Duckworth, was the treasurer of the avant-garde theater group which produced the Ibsen plays to ferocious reviews and the enormous excitement of feminists, Fabians, and intellectuals.

Ibsen, Wilde, and Meredith were the literary fathers of much modern early feminist writing. Rebecca West shed her real name, Cicily Fairfield, which would have been suitable for a sweet young thing in a Shaw play, or even a Wilde comedy, for the name of the heroine of Ibsen's *Rosmersholm.* Virginia Woolf's life seems modeled on Meredith's *Diana of the Crossways.* Forster's rejection of Meredith's demand for political commitment seems part of the reason his novels read so thin and watery compared with Woolf's. Oscar Wilde's comedies are the perfect illustration of Meredith's dictum that comedy depends on the author's belief in the equality of the sexes. That is why they still amuse audiences, while the topical "New Woman" plays are lost in oblivion. It seems to me now, rereading my essays on Salomé and the Ibsen heroines, that feminist scholars might begin to look at Salomé and Hedda Gabler in terms of Freud's concept of hysteria, using the exciting revisionist work of feminist psychoanalytic criticism.

The repression and suppression of anger was an absolute condition of the Victorian female's life. Sensitive male writers could, with less fear of reprisal, express that anger of their women characters in more open ways than women writers. Even Wollstonecraft and the Brontës would not have publicly defended woman's right to rage. What license was provided by the door-slamming of Nora, the fury of Hedda, Hardy's Tess stabbing Alex, Salomé's demand for John's head on a platter,

Diana's uncontrolled revelation of state secrets! The men were, in a sense, outsiders, and Woolf would clearly have welcomed them several decades later to the Outsiders' Society of *Three Guineas*. Ahead of their times in expressing women's rage, Meredith, Wilde, and Ibsen offered an expanded range of heroines to young women artists, as well as sincere social criticism.

I came to understand the powerfully subversive nature of the woman artist's sense of a female literary tradition only by studying the ideas and characters of nineteenth-century feminist men. The theater and the novel of the 1880s and 1890s set the stage for the new women, human beings, and writers of the twentieth century. It does the feminist cause no harm to acknowledge the antipatriarchal art of the other sex.

Woolf belongs, in my script for changing the subject, in the role of the literary daughter of the great Victorian male feminists, Ibsen, Meredith and Wilde, at the center of the study of literature and politics. By virtue of her continuance of the reforming role of her Clapham Sect ancestors who abolished the slave trade, and her secure niche in the radical feminist transition from Mary Wollstonecraft through Olive Schreiner, she plays two other roles.

"Tintinnabulations," "Storming the Toolshed," and "Quentin's Bogey" are notes toward a practice of criticism of criticism. They record the birth and growth of American "lupine" critical work in this field as we alternated between our own work and the necessity to evaluate the work of other critics, as we wrestled with the subject. The polemics, a historical necessity, are meant to give courage to a new generation of feminist critics. Despite the anger of these essays, they cannot begin to challenge the authority of the official introductions to Woolf's diaries and letters. Their collection here will alert the next generation of historians that there was a feminist critique as these works were published, an attempt to "change the subject" in Woolf studies from the study of madness and suicide to a concentration on her pacifism, feminism, and socialism. My repeated insistence on these points throughout these essays is testimony to how stubborn the resistance is and to the fact that in many places the subject remains firmly unchanged.

In 1985, after a decade of practice, I began to "theorize" socialist feminist criticism in "Still Practice." The theory grew out of the practice. It seems to me now that the arguments made in Gilbert and Gubar's influential *Madwoman in the Attic* and Nina Auerbach's powerful *Woman and the Demon* give a theoretical context to my readings which was not available to me at the time these essays were written. They become far less eccentric as readings in the context of feminist critical theory. I had been writing like a woman and reading like a woman, when to do so was consciously to court marginality. But feminist critics have built a community in the margins and together have pushed back the borders of the academy. Black and Chicana critics as well as lesbian critics have made serious inroads in changing the subject. Their anger, like women's anger, is a vital source of intellectual energy in changing the subject of literary discourse.

My concern with Woolf's anger clearly grew out of my own anger and the anger of my generation of feminist critics, who were trying to change the subject without yet having developed a sophisticated methodology.

Now that the subject has been changed, we can record the history of that process. Nowhere is it more clear than in the change over one decade in feminist perceptions of who owned the cultural subject we were trying to change. This is articulated here in the problem of address. The early essays address the establishment with a clenched fist, fishwife criticism, cursing the literary hegemonic fathers. The later essays address a discursive community of feminist readers engaged in the same project. Now, like June Arnold's Sister Gin, we look forward to the work of the "daughters of anger."

The essays in *Art and Anger* are intertextual readings of Virginia Woolf with Ibsen, Meredith and Wilde, performing a critical act of thinking back through one's feminist fathers while also establishing a trajectory for Woolf's conception of female tradition in "thinking back through our mothers." Versions of vulgar feminist and socialist criticism, they are marked with that vulgarity in the subtitle, "Reading *Like* a Woman." Unlike the "reading *as* a woman" of Jonathan Culler and others, which is a masquerade, a willed choice away from other reading roles, the "like" signals an inside "natural," though not biologically essentialist, woman's reading position.

READING PRACTICE I

†††††

The Feminist Critic Reads Men:
Wilde, Meredith, Ibsen

1

Salomé:
The Jewish Princess
Was a New Woman

Salomé[1] was the icon of the ideology of the decadents. She fascinated many artists, most notably Moreau and Beardsley, but also many lesser-known painters. Flaubert, Heine, Mallarmé, Huysmans, and Laforgue recreated her image and that of Herodias as well. Why? Mario Praz says, "It is curious to follow the parabola of the sexes during the nineteenth century: the obsession for the androgyne type towards the end of the century is a clear indication of a turbid confusion of function and ideal. The male, who at first tends towards sadism, inclines, at the end of the century, towards masochism."[2] He says of Wilde's *Salomé,* "It is childish, but it is also humoristic, with a humor which one can with difficulty believe to be unintentional, so much does Wilde's play resemble a parody of the whole of the material used by the decadents and of the stammering mannerism of Maeterlinck's dramas—and, as a parody, *Salomé* comes very near to being a masterpiece." But then he remarks on her "vampire passion," her "sensual cruelty," and her "monstrous passion."[3]

In view of recent discussions about androgyny, one wonders why there is so little mention of the androgyne in nineteenth-century painting. Visually it is evident in the paintings that the androgyne is a feminized male; furthermore, this figure is often the suffering artist and is usually being tormented by a sphinx or a witch or some form of the wicked woman.[4] John and Salomé in Wilde's play can be viewed as types of these figures.

But the most important point to be made concerns the social relevance of the androgyne. The late nineteenth-century revival of this figure reflects not simply a psychological change in the male self-image

3

from sadistic to masochistic, as Mario Praz suggests. It is a fearful response to woman's desire for political equality. It is really not merely a coincidence that an interest in androgyny has arisen twice in recent history, at times when women were actively seeking equality and power. As Oscar Wilde said, "Just as it is only in art-criticism and through it that we can apprehend the platonic theory of ideas, so it is only in art-criticism and through it that we can realize Hegel's system of contraries. The truths of metaphysics are the truths of masks."

The contrary most clearly demonstrated here is that Wilde's Salomé bears very little resemblance to the Salomé of Beardsley's drawings, Moreau's paintings, or the description of them in Huysmans' *Au rebours.* Late nineteenth-century painting, from the Pre-Raphaelites to the decadents, mannerists, and symbolists, had presented either the virgin or the whore as its image of woman. There are some interesting variations, of course, but in either guise, she is usually associated with death. The revival of all the mythological, historical, and royal figures of perverse and powerful women from Sappho to the sphinx, at a time when the social, legal, and political position of women was at a low ebb, is more than ironic.

Wilde deliberately creates a contrary image of Salomé. Or rather, he demystifies the image and makes her into a real person. The image making process itself was a way of dehumanizing woman. Wilde's Salomé is not exactly a wholesome heroine, but then John, Herod, and Herodias are not exactly "healthy" human beings. What he has done in his play is to revise the Bible so that Salomé shares equally in John's role as precursor to Christ. The idea of a female precursor is antithetical to traditional Christianity; it touches on such a sensitive nerve of patriarchal religion that the superb wit of Wilde's joke was lost on his contemporaries.

The fact that this was indeed Wilde's intention is most clearly revealed in his presentation of Salomé's death. His stage directions include the curious demand that she be "crushed by the shields of the soldiers."[5] One is rather distracted in the reading of the text by the Beardsley illustration in which a bald Pierrot (in black pajamas) and Satan are tucking a naked Salomé with an androgynous Medusa-like head and a perfect female body into a coffin made from an eighteenth-century powder box.[6] The point of Wilde's instructions is the attempted annihilation of Salomé's body by the defenders of the state's power. Their shields crush her[7] as if she were the attacking enemy, as if they are defending themselves against her. This bold stroke of genius on Wilde's part is most often ignored in productions of both the play and the opera. But it is the most important piece in the puzzle of the meaning of the play. (Roman shields were also offensive weapons used against barbarians. Zoe Caldwell's 1982 interpretation of Medea as an Eastern barbarian witch plays on the same theme.)

Richard Ellmann, in his provocative and interesting essay "Overtures to Salomé,"[8] quotes Gomez Carillo as saying that Wilde originally intended the play to be called *La Décapitation de Salomé,* "thus slighting John by precisely equating the two deaths."[9] The battering of Salomé's body by the soldiers' shields is as much a fitting punishment of her perverse sensuality as the severing of Iokanaan's head is a punishment for his perverse spirituality.

This reading is in keeping with Ellmann's "Iokanaan is not Ruskin, but he is Ruskinism as Wilde understood that pole of his character—It is Salomé, and not Pater, who dances the dance of the seven veils, but her virginal, yet perverse sensuality is related to Paterism."[10] But his assumption that Herod is made the hero of the play because he survives them both does not do justice to Wilde's rewriting of the biblical story. Wilde's deliberate setting of the play so that the rise of Christ will coincide with the fall of Rome, and Salomé's demand for John's head as an act of revenge for her father's death and for Herod's treatment of her as an object of lust suggest that Herod, as the representative of old decadent Roman authority, will be destroyed by Christianity.

Wilde's *Salomé* is a historical myth as well as a morality play. We are as sure that Herod and what he represents are to be destroyed as we are that the old gods are destroyed and Valhalla with them after the deaths of Siegfried and Brünnhilde in *Götterdämmerung.*

Some critics think that Wilde identified himself with Herod, but this is another case of the Beardsley drawings (which make the same identification) distracting us from the text of the play. Herod is such a barbarian, so nouveau riche, greedy, voluptuous, superstitious, so eager to impress his Roman guests, that a good actor can make him comic and tragic at the same time. Strauss found him much easier to deal with than Iokanaan. Certainly his catalogue of the treasures he will give Salomé is both an attack on corrupt materialism and a joke at the expense of the fetishism of the decadents. (He offers her an emerald larger than Caesar's, fifty white peacocks fairer than Caesar's, topazes yellow as the eyes of tigers, onyxes like the eyeballs of a dead woman.) What pleasure could a virgin derive from the head of the prophet, Herod asks Salomé, unless it were his downfall, as has been prophesied? Herod's power, debauched as it is, still represents the authority against which both John and Salomé struggle. He has made it necessary for John to be imprisoned in the celibacy of his prophet's role and for Salomé to be imprisoned in her role as sex object.

Both our eyes and our ears have deceived us about Oscar Wilde's *Salomé*. Beardsley's insolent drawings are an attack on Wilde, the person. Wilde is the voyeur, the man in the moon; Beardsley's Salomé is an eighteenth-century transvestite, a decadent Belinda from *The Rape of the Lock*. It is precisely because Beardsley's work was a satire on Wilde, because his elegant and witty lines provoke laughter or shock, not a deeper interest, that they have appealed to a public which fears the Salomé of the poet. Generations of music critics, embarrassed by what they invariably call the "nastiness" of Wilde's play, have been at a loss to explain the source of inspiration for Richard Strauss's brilliant opera. Wilde, the unknowing librettist, is dismissed as a collaborator. Phrases such as "based on" and "founded on" obscure the fact that Hedwig Lachmann's libretto is a nearly exact translation of Wilde's play, differing only in several omissions for the sake of dramatic brevity. The most notable omission is the early conversation among the soldiers which describes the twelve-year imprisonment of Salomé's father in the cistern which holds John the Baptist, and his subsequent murder on the order of Herod and Herodias by the black executioner. Strauss's omission of this vital scene robs the opera of the theme of revenge. The ring of death and the black arm of the executioner rising from the cistern with the head of Iokanaan become tragically symbolic in Wilde's play; in the opera they are picturesquely mysterious.

Strauss himself pointed out the source of his musical inspiration in the haunting opening lines of the play: "How beautiful is the Princess Salomé tonight!" The motif for Salomé's demand for the head of Iokanaan resounds similarly from the text itself. Wilde anticipated the possibilities for exact musical interpretation. In *De Profundis* he wrote of "the refrains, whose recurring motifs make Salomé so like a piece of music, and bind it together as a ballad."

My aim here is to establish the seriousness of Wilde's play. We are not at all reluctant to rank Strauss's opera with Wagner's. I believe that Wilde's play ranks with those of Ibsen. The source of tragic beauty lies in the image of woman that Wilde has created in Salomé. She transcends the visual debris of decadents, Pre-Raphaelites, and symbolists as easily as Strauss's *Salomé* transcends *Pelléas and Mélisande.* She is an allegorical Old Testament Hedda Gabler, and John and Lovborg are examples of how each woman kills the thing she loves.

Salomé was the icon of the ideology of the decadents, if they can be credited with an ideology at all. But Wilde converts her image to its opposite, transforms her from sinner to saint, and makes her a real person as well. The critics who try to place Wilde's play in the mainstream of decadent art are puzzled by its failure to fit. For Wilde may have been inspired by Moreau's "graven images," but he refused to worship them. Still less did he propose to worship false goddesses. He said that the artist's only duty to history is to rewrite it, and that is just what he did. His Salomé is a revisionist's historical figure.

For the decadent painters and poets both history and society were female. Philippe Jullian says it would be a mistake to see vice in this art because it reveals "a compulsive need to escape from a materialist society."[11] But the interesting question is, Why were history and society female for these artists? Salomé was not the only icon of this ideology. Both the poetry and the paintings abound in figures of witches, lesbians, cruel sphinxes, chimeras, sirens, vampires, Helens, Ledas, Europas, and Medusas. There were imaginary Ophelias for the sadists and imaginary Mona Lisas for the masochists—not to mention everyone's favorite androgyne, the fainthearted suffering artist. Wilde's Salomé is clearly out of place here. Beardsley may have drawn a Salomé who was ugly and perverse, but he didn't read the play. *That* Salomé is not in Wilde. It is difficult for us to think of Wilde as a "healthy" artist, but that is exactly what he was. For Wilde both history and society were corruptly masculine. His Herod is a perfect example of the way he thought about authority.

Oscar Wilde did not approach women with fear and loathing. He liked strong women. The son of Speranza, who called herself an eagle and thought of herself as Joan of Arc, wasted and out of place rocking a cradle, was attracted by heroic women. He said, completely seriously, that the women he most admired were Queen Victoria, Lily Langtry, and Sarah Bernhardt. All three women were powerful figures in the history of their time. Political, sexual, and artistic power, which these three women represent, were rare in females of their period.

The decadent artists who depicted women as either "the flower beneath the foot" or the destroying vampire (and these figures are the extreme embodiment of virgin and whore) were responding to the rumbles of discontent from European women. Women's expression of the desire for equality was met with *Sesame and Lilies,* which encouraged them to remain on their pedestals, or with Moreau's *Sphinx,* which articulated the nightmare of the destructive woman. As consciousness of women's oppression rose in the nineteenth century, artists expressed their fears of the forms woman's revenge would take. The limited imagination saw women's oppression as mainly sexual, and it imagined her revenge as violently so. It took an intelligent and sensitive man, Oscar Wilde, to see that there was a link between the suffering artist and the aspiring woman. They were bound by society's image of them in stereotypical roles, but the artist did not often recognize his sister.

The revolutionary potential of female desire is the theme of Wilde's

Salomé. It is both a history play and a morality play in which the *Liebestod* or love-death themes of Ibsen and Wagner are pushed to the extreme. John the Baptist, the poet-prophet, refuses to recognize his kinship with the adolescent young woman Salomé. She wants to share his spiritual life. Knowing no value except the physical, she sings his body's praises in a parody of the Song of Songs. (Even Richard Ellmann finds it "perverse" that a woman should praise a man's body in biblical language.) John converts her but rejects her. Salomé is in an adolescent crisis. Herod and Herodias have murdered her father; she is attracted by the spirituality of John; she wants revenge for her father's death; and she recognizes John's wish for death and her own.

Some critics have objected to Wilde's freehanded use of history. He has purposely telescoped three Herods into one. He wished to juxtapose the rise of Christianity with the fall of the Roman Empire in order to write in *Salomé* a kind of Christian *Götterdämmerung.* Salomé demands John's head in order to bring about Herod's downfall, for Herod is the hated figure representing authority and the state. Salomé is a political play in which the poet-prophet and the aspiring woman artist die in order to bring about the revolution. The radical element in Wilde's rewriting of the biblical story is his giving Salomé as much power as John in preparing the way for Christ's coming.

There is one appropriate drawing by Beardsley, done after the others as a frontispiece, in which John and Salomé are cowering in comradely innocence before Herod's face in the moon. The moon is the shaping image of the play. Salomé serves Diana or Astarte in her fierce chastity, but she has a wry sense of humor. All the characters who do not serve her fear her, and the moon is described as cold, destructive, and female. Except by Salomé. She describes the moon as "like a little piece of money." Virginity is considered Salomé's only asset, and she knows it.

Wilde's stage directions include another cold circular image, the cistern, where Salomé's father died, and from which the chaste and prophetic John rises. The womb/tomb image becomes baroquely sexual and religious when the black arm of the executioner rises from the cistern with the head of John on a silver platter (the moon has been described as silver, but now it turns blood red).

One can, of course, interpret Salomé as a kind of Jungian anima contrasted to the narrow spirituality of the poet-prophet. Iokanaan then becomes the animus against Salomé's sensuality. She is willing to become his disciple, but his narrowness of vision will not expand to include the daughter of Herodias among the worshipers in his new religion. This defines him as merely a precursor of the Christ who, when he comes, does not say "Touch me not" to Mary Magdalene. In this reading, Salomé's lecture to Iokanaan's bodiless head (balancing his earlier lecture to her while he kept refusing to look at her) that "the mystery of Love is greater than the mystery of Death" anticipates a much more human Christianity than John's ascetic, self-denying vision will allow.

But if the play is read as a parable of the woman artist's struggle to break free of being the stereotype of sex object, Salomé does succeed. Neither Herod nor John can see her as herself; to them she is only her mother's daughter. In her identity crisis, she finds appealing the Iokanaan whose voice reviles her mother and rises from the tomb of her murdered father. Her Hamlet-like concentration on death and revenge causes her to ignore her young would-be lover, who commits suicide. Overcome by the strangeness of Iokanaan's emaciated and ascetic beauty, she tentatively tries to sing of his beauty. He ignores her song. Her dance is her second attempt at artistic expression, but it also fails as art, for her motives are not pure. When she finally has John's head on a silver platter, an exact reflection of "the woman in the moon" in its bodiless chastity, she has created as object of art, a glittering image of chastity.[12] She has shown John as only half a man, but she has done more by disassociating herself from the moon-goddess.

Salomé says she has lost her virginity to John; she becomes a kind of earth mother. Yeats saw her as an embodiment of this figure. Ellmann quotes the preface to *A Full Moon in March:*[13] "the dance with the severed head suggests the central idea in Wilde's *Salomé* . . . it is part of the old ritual of the year: the mother goddess and the slain god."[14] As both virgin and mother, the Judean princess has become even more openly a primitive Christian precursor. (In a typical Wildean paradox, when the precursor of the Virgin Mary is a nymphomaniac, the precursor of Christ is a prig.)

Although Oscar Wilde's work has suffered from some unfortunate autobiographical readings, especially by those concerned with what Ellmann genteelly called his "predisposition," his life does yield an interesting approach to *Salomé*. Salomé is like Wilde's mother, Speranza, in her fiery youth, her zeal for martyrdom, and her thwarted desire for artistic expression. In his biography of Wilde, Jullian cites Speranza's love for veils and jewels. She must have seemed remarkably like the series of Salomé paintings by Moreau, which were Wilde's inspiration. José Pierre, co-author of *Gustave Moreau,*[15] speculates in it about beheading as symbolic castration "connected in the depths of the masculine consciousness with the castratory function of the mother."[16] Moreau was very attached to his mother and had difficulty relating to other women; the figure of Salomé dominates all of his work. Pierre points out that Freud "was convinced that Judith could not have beheaded Holophernes if he had not succeeded in seducing her,"[17] and in other paintings of that decapitation critics connect "her real or imaginary deflowering with the beheading of the hero-poet." In Wilde's play, Salomé believes she has been deflowered by John. Interestingly, Wilde is the only artist of the period (Baudelaire, Flaubert, Mallarmé, Moreau, and Huysmans also recreated her) who kills Salomé in the end.

In 1891, the year in which Wilde wrote *Salomé,* he had become fascinated by Ibsen, largely through the American actress Elizabeth Robins,[18] whom he had met at his mother's house in London. He helped her to raise money for her subscription performances of *Hedda Gabler* and *The Master Builder* that year, attended the performances, and encouraged her efforts. Unfortunately most admirers of Wilde have cared more for his life than his work, and, indeed, they have emphasized some details of his life over others. The fact that he admired both Ibsen and Wagner and devotedly attended performances of their plays and operas does not fit in with the picture of the aesthete and the dandy. And *Salomé* cannot be dismissed as merely decadent. The reviewers saw its connection with Ibsen's *The Master Builder.* William Archer, soon, one hopes, to be recognized again as the great critic he is, saw the influence of Ibsen at work—and how like Hilda or Hedda Salomé really is.[19] The revolutionary content and social relevance of the drama are evident. Far from being obscene, it is a social tragedy akin to Ibsen's *Ghosts.* Its biblical setting put off critics who had begun to associate revolutionary ideas with the gloomy realistic stage sets of Ibsen.

Salomé was Oscar Wilde's "New Woman." She was a biblical Hedda Gabler. The Baptist, as a principled autonomous creative artist, evoked the same fury and jealousy in her, the prisoner of a socially determined sex role, as Lovborg did in Hedda. In fact one may attribute her demand for his head, her fascination with his hair, and her symbolic rape of the prophet-artist as revenge. Rather than morbid necrophilia, it is a parallel to Hedda's wish to crown Lovborg's head with vine leaves as she drives him to a death which turns out to be a humiliating and debauched one and destroys his manuscript. Both women, condemned to spiritual death as sex objects and thwarted in artistic expression by their culture, kill the men they love. The men, who are also punished by society for breaking the stereotypes, are condemned to suffer their own humiliations. Salomé and Hedda destroy not their masters but their brothers.

The dance, with its historical connection to prostitution, is Salomé's only art form. It exactly parallels Nora's tarantella in *A Doll's House.* Both heroines are reluctant to perform their ritual obeisance to their masters, but in the end choose this degrading act rather than find no means at all of artistic expression. Here, when the women's struggle is so explicit in both scripts, one must make a distinction between the dancer and the dance. A performance of the Strauss opera in Chicago captured Wilde's intelligent spirit. Anja Silja sang and danced the role in a cold Nordic spirit of anger and frustration. Salomé was not the only English "New Woman" who was directly derived from Ibsen.

In her jealousy, revenge, and fury Salomé is as savage as Hiordis in Ibsen's *The Vikings,* as triumphant in receiving the dead body of her hero as Brünnhilde in *Götterdämmerung*. Salomé dies crushed by the shields of the soldiers of the state; and they are protecting themselves from her. Their annihilation of her is an act of defense. She is the enemy of the state. The characters of both Hiordis and Brünnhilde, derived from the Nordic myths, suggest, like Salomé, that witches were women betrayed by love, and that they were anarchists and destroyers of the men and societies which had kept them prisoners of their own bodies. The message of Wagner's *Ring*, Ibsen's plays, and Wilde's *Salomé* is that love and death are intimately connected in a repressive society. They dramatize the death of the family through murder, incest, greed, infanticide, syphilis, and hereditary insanity. The nineteenth century's greatest fear, that the family would fail as a stable and cohesive social force, is their common revolutionary theme.

Wilde disliked Beardsley's drawings. He told Ricketts:

> They are all too Japanese, while my play is Byzantine. My Herod is like the Herod of Gustave Moreau—wrapped in jewels and sorrows. My Salomé is a mystic, the sister of Salammbô, a Sainte Thérèse who worships the moon; dear Aubrey's designs are like the naughty scribbles a precocious schoolboy makes on the margins of his copybook.[20]

Beardsley was the wrong artist to illustrate *Salomé*.[21] And, although Wilde may have derived his inspiration from Moreau's paintings and Huysmans' description of them, the fact remains that *Salomé* transcends its imaginative origins. Wilde's Salomé is neither Huysmans' "incarnation of undying Lust, the goddess of immortal Hysteria" nor "a great venereal flower raised in a hot-house of impiety." She is, as Wilde said, a mystic, a saint. Beardsley's drawings are a perverse misrepresentation. Wilde said they were "flowers of evil." They do not represent the chaste and insatiable desire for spiritual transport which Salomé embodies.

When one thinks of Bernini's statue of St. Theresa and its plastic representation of sexual and religious ecstasy, and how perfectly it suits Crashaw's poem on this theme, one wishes for Wilde's Salomé the same visual image. Rodin, whom Wilde admired greatly, could have captured Salomé in sculpture. I suggest that we look at the play with the inner eye, concentrating on Wilde's own images of moon and cistern, love and death. Let us accept the image that Oscar Wilde has given us of Salomé the New Woman, the frustrated artist, who kills the thing she loves in order to bring into being a new and healthy culture.

Some questions still arise in the attempt to revive interest in *Salomé*. Despite Borges' comment that "Wilde's technical insignificance can be an argument in favor of his intrinsic greatness," one stumbling block is the language. The childishness of the language does support Praz's argument about pornography. However, the language is also incantatory, and sets a mood for the silent violence of sacrifice, much like a Martha Graham dance of a Greek tragedy. There is as much silence in the play as there is rhythmical baby talk (the young Syrian makes no suicide speech, but falls ritualistically between John and Salomé; Iokanaan has his head severed in absolute silence; Salomé's dance is silent). The quarreling of the Jews, the nagging of Herodias, the alternating prophesying and denunciations of John, Herod's whining, begging, and boasting, Salomé's lovesongs—are primitive human noises, cries and whispers about love and death. And Wilde is less a playwright than the orchestrator of these human voices, as the pitch and volume of their pain and pleasure increase and decrease.

Pornographic reification may also be the source of the repetition of the hollow, ugly word "thing," used by each character to describe the object of or the emotion of love and desire, predating the hollow thud of Wilde's most famous line, "Each man kills *the thing* he loves."

As Borges says, "his perfection has been a disadvantage; his work is so harmonious that it may seem inevitable and even trite."[22]

Alfred Douglas, its translator, was struck with the musical form of the play. "In reading one is *listening;* listening, not to the author, not to the direct unfolding of a plot, but to the tones of different instruments, suggesting, suggesting, always indirectly, till one feels that by shutting one's eyes one can best catch the suggestion."[23] William Archer was intrigued with the play's "brief melodious phrases, the chiming repetitions, the fugal effects." He felt that there is "at least as much musical as pictorial quality in *Salomé*," that it has "all the qualities of a great historical picture—pedantry and conventionality excepted."[24] Like Virginia Woolf's *Between the Acts,* Wilde's *Salomé* has revised a few scraps of a common story from the rubbish heap of history and shaped them musically and visually into a formal design which enables us to make a new interpretation of the past.

The play is both static and dramatic, more like dance-drama or opera than a contemporary English play. Berlioz' *Les Troyens* or Wagner's *Tristan und Isolde* are closer to *Salomé* than any play of Pinero or Henry Arthur Jones. Flaubert's *Hérodias* and Massenet's *Hérodiade* certainly influenced Wilde, as well as Moreau's paintings, which even moved Wilde to look for Salomé's image in Titian, Leonardo da Vinci, and Dürer. He probably also knew of Wagner's use of the Christian legend of Herodias, the wandering Jewess, as Kundry in *Parsifal.* But Wilde's conception of Salomé is truly original.

In 1903 Strauss saw the Max Reinhardt production of *Salomé* with Gertrud Eysoldt in Berlin.[25] Wilde's use of motivic words and phrases gave Strauss a ready-made libretto exactly suited to his talents. The repetition of the word "Princess," of the phrase "Do not look at him/her," of the images of the moon, Iokanaan's eyes, mouth, and hair, and Salomé's feet "like little white doves" were all motives which Strauss found waiting for him.

The opening scene is a parody of a troubadour's courtly love laments, with Narraboth bemoaning the coldness and beauty of his princess. As her knight he will be rewarded with "a little green flower"; both the artificiality and diminution of the convention are being mocked here. Strauss envisioned Salomé as a "sixteen-year-old princess with the voice of an Isolde."[26] He composed the opera all at once, except for Salomé's dance (the critics disagree on whether the music for the dance or the music for John's prophecies is the weakest section of the opera). Strauss himself said, "You know, Jochanaan is an imbecile. I've got no sympathy at all for that kind of man. I would have preferred above all that he would appear a bit grotesque."[27]

Interestingly, and much to the distress of the critics, Strauss linked

the motives of Christ's coming and Salomé's desire, perhaps unconsciously. But the linking underscores the argument first stated by Wilde
himself that Salomé is a mystic, a St. Theresa. She declares that she
has been ravished by John—and thus speaks in terms of a religious/
sexual conceit such as "never chaste except thou ravish me." As the
first nun of the new religion she brings to her conversation all the
sensuality, Jewish mysticism, and Oriental passion that we associate
with Spanish Catholicism.

Strauss's motif of the quarreling Jews, his "hubbub" theme, has
been interpreted by some as anti-Semitic. Some of my colleagues have
suggested that this might be a possible explanation for the popularity
of the opera *Salomé* in Germany and the complete disregard for the
play in England and America. But the opera is more complex than
this. The shock of the idea that Christ is the Messiah, which sends
the first Jew right out of key (as Norman Del Mar points out), is
balanced by Herod's similar response when the Nazarenes remark that
Jesus has raised people from the dead. Herod of course is frozen in
fear because he has murdered his brother, Salomé's father. While this
reaction is clearly linked to the soldier's discussion of the murder in
the first scene of Wilde's play, it is an odd note in the opera.

Strauss's motives point out to us the effectiveness of Wilde's themes:
Salomé's last soliloquy nostalgically incorporates her love for Iokanaan
as a teacher as she asks his head, "What shall I do now, Iokanaan?
Ah, wherefore didst thou not look at me?" (Narraboth has entreated
Salomé not to look at John; his page has begged him not to look at
Salomé; Herodias has insisted that Herod stop looking at her daughter;
Salomé shudders at the thought of Herod looking at her "with his
mole's eyes.") Strauss emphasizes by repetition how Iokanaan has
prophesied that Salomé will be crushed to death by the shields of
Herod's soldiers. That the opera is Strauss's most brilliant is generally
accepted; nagging moral doubts are still solved by blaming Wilde.[28]

It is interesting to note that although the Lord Chamberlain banned
a London production of the opera in 1907 (just as Wilde's play had
been banned[29]), the opera had met with great success all over Europe
(sometimes staged with a star of Bethlehem lighting up the backcloth

at the end). Maud Allan danced her own version of *The Vision of Salomé* in Vienna in 1904 and throughout the Continent until 1908 when she played the Palace Theatre in London for 250 performances. Although her dance was based on Flaubert's interpretation, she was accused of sharing Wilde's perversions. In 1918, J. T. Grein (of the Independent Theatre which had produced Ibsen's *Ghosts* and given a first hearing to G. B. Shaw) caused a furor of anti-German hysteria with his production of Wilde's *Salomé* starring Maud Allan. Noel Pemberton Billing, M.P., in a published attack on Allan, declared that her performance was encouraging perversion in women and pointed out her German training as evidence of a plot to corrupt the English. In court Maud Allan claimed that she saw Salomé's passion as symbolic of spiritual awakening. Allan's name was eventually cleared of lesbian allegations, but not before many doctors had had their say in court about the immorality of Oscar Wilde and his play.[30] Obviously what was on trial was lesbianism itself. Nothing overt in the play indicates that Salomé was a lover of her own sex. She kills a man, therefore she must be a lesbian, runs the reasoning of the trial. Beneath this fear is also a fear of women's violence. Oscar Wilde writes from the lesbian position.

Maud Allan's interpretation of Salomé was in keeping with Wilde's. Even Strauss wrote, "Anyone who has been in the Orient and has observed the decorum of its women, will appreciate that Salomé should be played as a chaste virgin, an oriental princess, with but the simplest, most dignified gestures, as if her shipwreck on encountering the miracle of a brave new world is to arouse compassion and not horror and disgust."[31] Sarah Bernhardt, in rehearsal with Wilde for the abandoned production, sensed this. Although she was over fifty at the time, she was going to wear her Cleopatra costume and dance in a static position. "It is heraldic," she said, "like a fresco, and the words should drop like a pearl in a crystal bowl. That is right, no rapid movements, and stylized gestures."[32] Sarah Bernhardt embodied the image of Salomé for the last romantics of the nineteenth century. Lorrian wrote, "Yes, she is surely the daughter of Gustave Moreau, the enigmatic Sarah, sister of the Muses, who carried the decapitated chiefs, of Orpheus and of those Salomés, willowy and bloody, the Salomé of the famous water-colour, the Salomé of the Apparition, whose triumphant and coruscating costume she wore even in *Theodora.*"[33]

The political interpretation of *Salomé,* in which the prophet and the young woman who lusts after his body are agents of the revolution and martyrs to the cause of freedom, has been made before now. In the Kamerny Theatre production in Moscow in 1917, Alexandra Exter combined this view with Constructivist technique to produce extraordinary costume designs and a curtain described by Oliver Sayler as a "bold piece of Cubist work—it sets the aggressive, tragic, passionate keynote of the play, with a sharp pointed sun-like arc in white against a black background and above it to the right three flaming banners in red—military pennons set dead against the wind."[34] This is a far cry from the Salomé of Moreau or Beardsley.

The theme of the struggle for power in Wilde's play, as well as the severed head and the passionate love song, haunted Yeats, despite his denigration of Wilde. *A Full Moon in March* is the most obvious example, but most of the other plays were influenced by Wilde as well. Yeats's static and symbolic dances and songs lack the breadth of Wilde's imagination. In Yeats's play the Queen and the Beggar-King fight each other for power. The man is killed because his love song is not powerful enough, although there is a suggestion of fertility rites and rebirth in the legend in which the drop of blood from the severed head begets a child in the woman's womb. In Wilde the man and the woman are both martyrs to a higher cause; their personal tragedy prepares the way for human happiness.[35]

Perhaps *Salomé* is now rescued from the charge of decadence, even though one may say with Thomas Mann that in Wilde's case "aestheticism was the first manifestation of the European mind's rebellion against the whole morality of the bourgeois age."[36] As Max Beerbohm said, Wilde should have rewritten the whole Bible, then there would be no more skeptics.

Why, one wonders, did Wilde ignore both the biblical blame placed on Herodias and most versions of the story, which depict Salomé as the instrument of her mother's revenge? If Salomé is a destructive

Narcissa in his play, she also represented the fear of the lesbian to a fin-de-siècle culture which witnessed the rise of public lesbianism in the salons of Paris, and the association in the public mind of dance itself (in the work of Loie Fuller, Maud Allan, and Isadora) as a lesbian art form. Wilde's play depicts woman's rage at objectification by both kinds of patriarchs, powerful kings and Christian ascetics. Only a little leap of the imagination transformed this furious girl into a suffragette with a rock in her hand.

2

"Clio in Calliope"
History and Myth in Meredith's
Diana of the Crossways

The Novel and History

When Thomas Carlyle urged George Meredith to write history, Meredith replied that he did—in the novel: "I make History sing! Clio in Calliope." He mixed his muses, his metaphors, and his myths to achieve his effect, remaining constant only to Clio and the female heart. One is tempted to say "the human heart," for a critic once remarked that *Diana*'s success was due to the ease with which men could identify with the heroine. (Virginia Woolf remarked of the author: "He does not sing only; he dissects.")

History has rewarded Meredith's faith. *Diana of the Crossways* brought him fame in 1885, a renewed reputation in 1897, a spate of hero worship from 1908 to 1911 at the height of the suffrage movement, and, most recently, a new readership of students and feminists. It is this new readership I wish to address, to meet students' objections to Diana as "an ideal of the heroical feminine type." They object to her marriage to Redworth as much as earlier critics objected to her flight from Warwick.

Meredith had anticipated such objections. The novel, he argued in his opening chapter, could never cut off its roots in social history. Once women's wrongs were righted, the example of Diana could be dangerous: "For when the fictitious creature has performed that service of helping to civilize the world, it becomes the most dangerous of delusions, causing first the individual to despise the mass, and then to join the mass in crushing the individual" (17).[1] Meredith saw that the individual struggle of the hero or heroine against society could be revolutionary or reactionary, depending on social conditions. Clearly the divorce laws have been changed, and some measure of political equality has been achieved, though not enough to deny Diana's passionate quest for personal freedom a strong basis in reality. Meredith argued convincingly in his *Essay on Comedy*—and continued the argument in his didactic introductory chapter—that absolute equality between the sexes is necessary for comedy to flourish. In the interim, he suggested, the novelist takes up philosophy, history, mythology, and psychology, until social conditions relieve him of his moral burden and he may flirt with form and dally with the comic spirit to his heart's content.

It is admittedly a little shocking to come upon this statement of alarm about the role of the revolutionary heroine once the revolution has taken place. Meredith had great faith in the power of art to change human lives. A great nineteenth-century hero like Siegfried appears to us now, as Shaw said, too Bakunin-like to bear. His anarchism and anti-intellectualism are frightening, now that some measure of democracy has been accomplished in the Western world. Yet Brünnhilde is still heroic; her struggle both to be her father's will and to break it still moves us. Meredith foresaw the day when Brünnhildes and Dianas would seem individualistic and reactionary. That day is not yet here. But political separatist feminism and certain forms of feminist criticism today might fit his pattern.

The interesting question is whether Diana, Meredith's fictional heroine, did help to "civilize the world," as Meredith put it. Caroline Norton, her historical counterpart, certainly did. She, Sheridan's granddaughter, was largely responsible for the Infants' Custody Act of 1839 and the 1857 act which provided protection for deserted, separated, or divorced wives. As a poem in *Punch* (June 30, 1877) claimed, despite gossip and scandal Caroline Norton "gave back scorn for scorn." The muse of history must have been muttering under her breath when the republication of *Diana of the Crossways* in 1897 revived the scandal of the state secret. A case was brought to court; Mrs. Norton was vindicated; her name was cleared (as it had been in the divorce suit which named Lord Melbourne); and Meredith prefaced his new edition with the cautionary note that his work must be read as fiction. But fiction and history are now inextricably interwoven. It is curious that although Meredith took as his model a woman who fought long and hard for custody of her children (and extended the battle into the political arena so that other women would benefit), he made his heroine virginal. Of course motherhood and fertility constitute a deep underchord in the novel, but they are not immediately apparent. And then Caroline Norton's husband did not die until she was sixty-seven years old. At sixty-nine she remarried. In the novel, Diana's husband Warwick is conveniently killed in an accident, and Diana is young, attractive, and chaste when she remarries.

We know that Meredith actually met Mrs. Norton at the Duff Gordons', but for his portrait of Diana he also drew upon other women he had known, among them the learned recluse Mrs. Wood, who paid Meredith to read to her; her niece Kitty O'Shea, Parnell's mistress; Meredith's first wife, who was Peacock's daughter; and Janet Duff Gordon, a young friend of the Copsham cottage period. But most important of all, I think, for the invention of Diana were the words of an anonymous reviewer in the *Westminster Review* (July 1864) who forged a literary link between "two novelists with a purpose" as "social reformers" and "social accusers." Caroline Norton's *Lost and Saved* and Meredith's *Ordeal of Richard Feverel* and *Sandra Belloni* were acclaimed together as serious novels:

> Women have especial need, as the world goes, to be shrewd, self-reliant, and strong; and we do all we can in our literature to render them helpless, imbecile, and idiotic. When Charlotte Brontë endeavoured to do otherwise, we can all recollect that a prudish scream was raised against her, and genteel virtue affected to be horrified with the authoress who drew women and girls endowed with human passion. Something of the same kind has been said against the authoress of "Adam Bede"; and there was a time when a discreet Englishwoman would have blushed to acknowledge acquaintance even with a chapter of George Sand. We are so thoroughly impressed with the conviction that art and morals alike suffer by the prudish conventionalities of

our present English style, that we are inclined to welcome rebellion against it merely because it is rebellion. We are disposed to give a friendly reception to George Meredith and Mrs. Norton, were it for nothing but the mere fact that conventionality might be inclined to shriek out against them. A Parisian critic lately, when noticing some objections urged against the numerous undraped Graces, and Bacchantes, and Nymphs, and Ledas in the season's Exhibition, drily remarked that so long as vast skirts, and hoops, and spoon-bonnets endured, it was a relief to get a glimpse of the true outlines of womanhood under any circumstances. We own to something of a kindred feeling in regard to our English fiction.

It certainly put wind into the sails of the self-styled champion of free women to be linked with a famous woman who had actually accomplished radical political goals; he was now a serious novelist like her. And it did his ego no harm (after the disastrous failure of his first marriage) to be mentioned in the same breath with a lady so sexually attractive, charming, and witty. Nor have the ironies of Clio ceased. Meredith's deliberately anachronistic novel looks more and more like Caroline Norton's deliberately anachronistic life. Both reputations rise and fall with historical waves of feminism. Caroline suffered at the hands of feminists like Harriet Martineau, who found that her personal style and evident female sexuality disqualified her for the title of disinterested feminist despite her magnificent achievements in the struggle for women's rights. The history of English feminism has yet to be written which gives Norton her rightful place. As with Wollstonecraft, the very tragedy of her life as a female caused later puritanical and intellectual feminists to disdain her actual accomplishments.

Caroline Norton's flamboyant passion and intellect recall the eighteenth century and were out of place in Victorian England. Ironically, the Reform Bill of 1832, her first political passion, actually deprived women of the right to vote. In this cause she met Lord Melbourne, and their political, intellectual, and emotional intimacy destroyed her life. "The Byron of modern poetesses" of 1840 is not remembered today as novelist or poet, or even as the champion of the Infants' Custody Act, but as the scandalous figure in a divorce trial with Lord Melbourne. No matter that the case against her was lost. She suffered for a lifetime, and the shadow of that ancient scandal still hovers to influence the reading of *The Letters of Caroline Norton to Lord Melbourne.*[2] Hoge believes he detects in the tone of the letters "the discarded mistress" rather than "the disappointed friend." To me the letters suggest an angry, reproachful woman who has been deserted by her powerful, loving friend. The letters were not known to Alice Acland when she wrote her fine biography of this romantic friendship,[3] but their discovery does not essentially alter her portrait of the relationship.

What the letters strikingly demonstrate, however, is that Meredith was psychologically unerring in his portrait of Diana and her relationship with Dacier. Indeed, Meredith may well have read these letters, so close are their passion and force, their abrupt reversals, to those he assigns to Diana. At first Caroline's epistles to her political friend are flirtatious and bold; they even allude to the acting out of roles from her grandfather Sheridan's plays. But her marriage was destroyed by her politics, not by infidelity, whatever the truth or falsehood of that still unproven charge. Her husband and his friends took revenge on the Liberals; Melbourne and Caroline were victims of a deeper anger than would have been aroused by the friendship of a powerful old man and a spirited young woman if party had not been involved. Sheridan had been passionately in love with Lady Bessborough, Melbourne's wife's mother. His wife had been Caroline Lamb, of Byronic fame. That their relationship would be passionate and tragic seemed almost predictable.

Alice Acland has shown that many of the traits of Meredith's Diana derive from his insight into the personality of Caroline Norton, and the letters reveal even more of the psychic reality of their similarity. Yet Meredith's purpose, however much he may have known about Caroline from the Duff Gordons, was to attack sentimentality about women and in women, for an audience of women who would, he hoped, by exhibiting a courage modeled on Diana's, be better mothers to a new generation.

In 1902 he was still explaining Diana to his lady friends. To Lady Ulrica Duncombe's disapproval he replied that "Goethe would have appreciated her." And he lectured her on the ignorance of brides and the necessity of coeducation: marriage can be reformed when "English girls have wiser mothers. Such donkeys are those dames in all our classes."[4] Women have no idea, he said, how strongly men desire "complete possession, down to absorption," of their wives. Diana's experience was universal except for "the frigid or the tepid." The comic spirit had the final thrust, affirming that women do indeed have sexual desires: "The happy accident of the absence of opportunity has helped to the rescue of many eminent virgins at critical moments." No wonder women liked him! A woman novelist remarked that his knowledge of women was "almost indecent," but Oliver Elton in *Modern Studies* faulted Meredith for having "reversed the order of Paradise."

Calliope took a few other liberties with Clio's version of reality. Along with transformation of Caroline Norton's sex life and her age at remarriage, fiction had uses for the actual "facts" of history. Some phrases in the novel denouncing gossip and scandal were actually lifted from a newspaper piece defending Lord Palmerston in the divorce scandal. In the incident of Diana's bringing a Tory secret to the editor of *The Times,* one wonders how much personal regret and wish were involved, for in his day as a journalist, Meredith, the supposed radical, had written leaders and editorials for Tory papers.

Clio had other tricks up her sleeve, however, and the current revival of *Diana of the Crossways* is one of them. But its revival today is much easier to explain than its vogue in 1908–11. For Meredith's heroines then were not dear to the hearts of the suffragettes, but to another, possibly overlapping group of women, described by Christopher Lasch and William Taylor as the "sisterhood of sensibility." Their essay sheds light on the relationship between Emma and Diana and a large audience of women who experienced similar intellectual friendships.[5] They describe the relationship of the American novelists Sarah Edgarton and Mrs. Case as exactly that of Emma and Diana: "an ideal of pure friendship between women, based on a shared sensitivity . . . "

> What they sought in literature was not so much craft as companionship, and their most eloquent flights—expressed in the amorous language which was the characteristic style of feminine friendship in the nineteenth century—were addressed not to the muse but to each other. But the ideal of pure friendship, given the peculiar moral atmosphere of the period, grew quite logically out of a devotion to literature. With whom, after all, could a woman converse, assuming that she was endowed with the refinement which qualified her in the first place to write of the beauties of the "spiritual" life, except with other women so endowed? [Lasch and Taylor, p. 25]

The "sisterhood of sensibility," as the social historians describe it, was founded not on reform but on a dream of "gypsy freedom," that same freedom which Diana and Emma discuss as they pore over their Latin books, the "Libertas" which Caroline Norton took as her pen name. This phenomenon, which Lasch and Taylor describe as an alternative to crumbling family and religious institutions, seems to me to be a pastoral vision in female terms of the free life dreamed by the young heroes of nineteenth-century novels. Lasch and Taylor see the myth of the purity of women as a last-ditch effort to find a unifying principle in society, as well as a "reorientation of domestic life around the ideal of privacy." They argue:

> But the cult of women and the Home contained contradictions that tended to undermine the very things they were supposed to safeguard. Implicit in the myth was a repudiation not only of heterosexuality but of domesticity itself. It was her purity, contrasted with the coarseness of men, that made woman the head of the Home (though not of the family) and the guardian of public morality. But the same purity made intercourse between men and women at last almost literally impossible and drove women to retreat almost exclusively into the society of their own sex, to abandon the very Home which it was their appointed mission to preserve. [29]

Here is the crux of the matter. One thinks of the exclusion of poor

Sir Lukin, Emma's husband, from the world of the wood nymphs and his remorse about his life with London prostitutes. But what else was possible for him? If Emma was the angel in the house, Lukin was forced to play the devil. The actual result of putting women on the pedestal was: no children. Emma as much as tells Diana that her illness is the result of sexual repression, that chastity has broken her home, not preserved it. She leads Diana toward fertility, yes, but not toward loss of freedom.

The "sisterhood of sensibility" was not unusual. Virginia Woolf, in her essay "Geraldine and Jane," describes the friendship between Jane Carlyle and the novelist Geraldine Jewsbury in similar terms. Jane thought her friend's novel *Zoe* was more "indecent" than George Sand, but they felt that their intellectual friendship would be an example as women struggled toward freedom. Their letters contain hope for the future: "I do not think that either you or I are to be called failures . . . we have looked and tried, and found that the present rules for woman will not hold us. . . . There are women to come after us, who will approach nearer the fullness of the measure of the stature of woman's nature."[6] One critic described reading Meredith as "like construing a difficult chapter in Thucydides," and often this is true. The most deeply felt passages are the scenes between Emma and Diana, when the muse of history is forgotten for the moment, and Calliope holds sway. History is better served by this arrangement, of course, and it is their friendship which lights up our memory of the novel. The conscious effort to write the historical novel, explained in the preface, shows Meredith deliberately composing flat jokes and boring witticisms be-cause his theory of comedy demands it. Women were less free then; the wit must have been less telling. This merely puts off the reader. We learn our history lesson while the teacher is out of the room. The technique of revealing the ignorance of our unenlightened ancestors through their deliberately concocted unfunny witticisms fails Meredith, the conscious historical novelist. He is nearer to both truth and comedy when he gives us Sir Lukin in remorse or Lady Wathin defending morality or the brilliantly satirical portrait of English virginity, not as historical types but as eternally frail human beings. Constance Asper, cold marmoreal Britannia, pedestaled high on the white cliffs of Dover, is surely an ancestor of Ford's portrait of Sylvia Satterthwaite Tietjens in *No More Parades*. Meredith's men get the women they deserve. Constance Asper is not satirized as herself, but as the English Tory's dream woman in the flesh:

> He had the English taste for red and white, and for cold outlines: he secretly admired a statuesque demeanor with a statue's eyes. The national approbation of reserved haughtiness in woman, a tempered disdain in her slightly lifted small upper lip and drooped eyelids, was shared by him; and Constance Asper, if not exactly aristocratic by birth, stood well for that aristocratic insular type, which seems to promise the husband of it a casket of all the trusty virtues, as well as the security of frigidity in the casket. Such was Dacier's native taste.[7]

From October 23 to November 18, 1908, a series of miniature "portraits" of Meredith heroines was exhibited in the Doré Gallery. His grand women were captured in "exquisite little paintings on ivory." Hammerton tells us that Mr. Bedford had spent many years "searching out fair sitters who already possessed many of the physical charms of the heroines" (Hammerton, p. 380). Shortly afterward, Hodder and Stoughton published a large and luxurious "birthday book" lavishly done, the plates interspersed with two types of quotations from the novels, physical description of the heroines and scenes of female friendship.

Now, what is one to make of this? At the height of the suffragette movement, the book was obviously not aimed at an audience of "the shrieking sisterhood." Meredith had deliberately left out of his novels the standard romantic descriptions of his heroines, and Bedford had to work hard to dig up his material. That he painted miniatures says something about his response to the social fear of strong women, and also about an audience which clearly wanted to be reminded, through Meredith, of an ideal woman decidedly not of the heroic type. The book, large enough for two laps, was the perfect gift for those women who were not concerned with reform but shared a wish for freedom.

A portrait of Diana is on the cover and is very like the real Caroline Norton. She has the profile of a Greek goddess, a "noble brow," and white drapery around her shoulders.

The idea of a Georgian miniaturist painting the literary heroines of an earlier generation at the height of the suffrage movement is curious in itself. The miniatures reinstate a view of womanhood whose omission was deliberate on Meredith's part. One cannot imagine two ladies poring over a book of paintings of Jane Austen's heroines, or George Eliot's. The "sisterhood of sensibility" responded to a vision of the ideal, while their less sensitive sisters fought in the streets. One suspects that Meredith's Diana had indeed become dangerous, but not for the reasons he had anticipated. The format of this book domesticates his Diana and uses her to reinforce ideals of passivity.

Feminism and the Novel

Virginia Woolf was born at the same time *Diana* was. Meredith and Julia Stephen wrote to each other about the difficulties of bringing to birth their respective "children." The daughter of Julia Stephen, growing up to be a novelist and an intellectual, accepted the influence of her spiritual godfather, his feminism and socialism, and rejected her mother's wifely role as "princess to a patriarch." She inherited Meredith's belief that the novel belongs to the middle-class imagination, is upwardly mobile, and struggles against even the most sincere author's attempt to move downward. She praised his "brisk, inquisitive and combative" efforts to deal with class distinctions even though he knew he would fail. There is still great resistance to reading *Diana* in the class terms which Meredith made so explicit. Plainly, however, Diana is shown to achieve identity only after rising in London society and then rejecting it. Giving up her luxurious London flat as well as her inherited Crossways, she buys a cottage and assumes the class identity of a cottager, comfortable at last with herself as Mrs. Warwick, widow. From this position her marriage to Redworth, "the rich Radical," is possible. The reader is pleased with the comic author's pleasure in reversing the course of the sentimental heroine. But it is by no means downhill all the way (as with *Tess of the d'Urbervilles* or *A Mummer's Wife,* where the class values are held rigid).

In a letter to Virginia Woolf's mother, Meredith described the process of creating Diana as "traversing feminine labyrinths." "Traversing" suggests the switchbacks in descending a mountain trail, as well as a troubled voyage into unconscious motivation (Diana says, "The black dog of consciousness refuses to be shaken off"). There is a spot part way down the mountain where Diana finds her own level. In mythological terms it is like the sacred grove at Nemi, where Diana Nemorensis haunts the woodland glade. E. M. Forster described this perfectly, despite his distaste for the "suburban roarer" in Meredith: "A Meredithian plot is not a temple to the tragic or even the comic Muse, but rather resembles a series of kiosks most artfully placed among wooded slopes, which his people reach by their own impetus, and from which they emerge with altered aspect."

In her perceptive "glass box" essay, "The Niece of an Earl," which deals so well with class in English fiction, Woolf notes the "tremendous strain" on Meredith to struggle with class distinctions despite the resistance of the novel as a genre. The comic spirit relishes these distinctions and keeps English fiction from Russian pitfalls, "the immensity of the soul and the brotherhood of man." Forster was annoyed with Meredith's "We live but to be sword or block," and Forster's refusal of the sword has led to our present view of him as part of the block. (His liberal antifascism looks rather timid today.) Woolf (brandishing her own sword as feminist, socialist, and pacifist) praised Meredith as "a great innovator" and answered the critics' charges against his style: "The English language is naturally exuberant, and the English character full of humours and eccentricities. Meredith's flamboyancy has a great ancestry behind it; we cannot avoid all memory of Shakespeare."[9] Woolf, we can see now, armed herself with the same sword as Meredith and his heroines. Their blows were aimed at patriarchal institutions, as much in the cause of freedom for artists as for women.

I often think how much Woolf's poet Carmichael in *To The Lighthouse* is Meredith. He is the only character who sees how much of

Mrs. Ramsay's earth-mother pose is humbug. How Virginia Woolf must have enjoyed Meredith's letters to his "stout Angel," her mother. Many of them were written during the composition of *Diana* and record his progress and his agonies. The name of Mrs. Leslie Stephen was prominent on Mrs. Humphry Ward's antisuffrage petition in *The Nineteenth Century,* which, like *The Athenaeum,* took a strong anti-feminist stand. Many prominent women, led by the well-known novelist Mary Ward, opposed giving political rights to women. Meredith's thrust (in comic fury) was this mocking letter: " 'Enough for me that my Leslie should vote, should think.' Beautiful posture of the Britannic wife! But the world is a moving one and will pass her by."[10] Meredith was clearly ambivalent about the Stephens. He admired Sir Leslie's manly virtue as a mountaineer and mental giant—Stephen was the model for Vernon Whitford in *The Egoist*—but when Stephen died, Meredith wrote to his daughters that his chief virtue had been his worthiness to be the husband of Julia Stephen.

In August 1884 Meredith wrote wishing he could join the Stephens at St. Ives to "observe Thoby's first recreancy! [Thoby was Virginia's brother]—before his father has taught that he must act the superior, and you have schooled the little maids [Virginia and Vanessa] to accept the fact supposed:—for it is largely (I expect you to dissent) a matter of training. Courage is proper to women, if it is trained, as with the infant man.—My *Diana* still holds me; only by the last chapter; but the coupling of such a woman and her man is a delicate business. She has no puppet-pliancy. The truth being, that she is a mother of Experience, and gives that dreadful baby suck to brains—I have therefore a feeble hold of her; none of the novelist's winding-up arts avail; it is she who leads me" (743).

Meredith enjoyed the role of feminist and teacher to many bright and beautiful women, both young and old, throughout his life. This is perhaps why Diana playing Egeria to a series of great men is so realistic and so highly charged with felt experience in the novel. He nagged away at "Mrs. Leslie" to educate her daughters and, although she didn't, they educated themselves in a way in which he would have approved. He wrote to her (March 1884) as if her own experience of childbirth could rouse sympathy with his artist's pangs at the "delivery of the terrible woman afflicting me (a positive heroine with brains, with real blood, and demanding utterance of the former, tender directions of the latter)." (732). In May 1884 he wrote that Diana "keeps me still on her sad last way to wedlock. I could have killed her merrily, with my compliments to the public; and that was my intention. But the marrying of her, sets me traversing feminine labyrinths, and you know the why of it never can be accounted for" (737). Meredith's writing as worried mother to worried mother makes one think of Mrs. Ramsay in *To the Lighthouse* marrying everyone off. The metaphor which links artistic production with childbirth has been part of our culture since the Greeks, but few artists have been so openly sisterly about their "pregnancies" to actual women. As Meredith grew more aware of how his creative processes mimicked nature, his respect for women deepened. There is some measure of experience behind his portrait of Diana's "involuntary twitch" at the thought of motherhood, which concludes the novel on a realistic note. The wedding bells of Diana's marriage to Redworth signal not a happy ending but the beginning of physical sexual life and the dangers of childbirth.

Meredith identified the middle class as the enemy of comedy and urged "cultivated women to recognize that the comic Muse is one of their best friends. They are blind to their interests in swelling the ranks of the sentimentalists. . . . They will see that, where they have no social freedom, comedy is absent; where they are household drudges, the form of comedy is primitive; where they are tolerably independent but uncultivated, exciting melodrama takes its place, and a sentimental version of them."[11] Caroline Norton's grandfather, Sheridan, had mocked the sentimental muse as well in the prologue to *The Rivals,* which gives some rather vivid examples of what happens when women are deprived of education. Meredith is thus firmly in the tradition of feminists who, from Mary Wollstonecraft through Olive Schreiner and Sylvia Pankhurst to Virginia Woolf, have argued that women are often their own worst enemies and have raised their voices against middle-class mothers who refuse to educate their daughters, and instead of freedom as a goal, provide the image of "angel in the house." In Schreiner's phrase, these girls go from ignorance to "married prostitution." Later, the feminist movement under Emmeline Pankhurst made an explicit alliance between upper-class and working-class women. The enemy to whom "the cause" was to be brought was the middle class. Suffragette propaganda plays had stock characters, the brave and determined lady and her servant, who successfully win over the "nice" suburban couple. Meredith was in league with these feminists—all of them, by the way, leftists in politics—and even on his eightieth birthday championed women's intellectual powers and their "combative spirit."

As a publisher's reader Meredith was chiefly responsible for the publication of Olive Schreiner's remarkable feminist novel, *Story of an African Farm.* The heroine, Lyndall, like Diana, is proud and free. As a "New Woman" she is unable to find a fit mate and dies after childbirth, having refused marriage to a man who asserted his superiority over her. She is nursed by Gregory Rose, who dresses in women's clothing to be near her. Meredith must have recognized the novel's psychological depth, which reveals a kind of bisexuality in all of the characters. Its biblical pastoral vision of the evolution of the New Woman on the ancient African desert is akin to his own vision of Diana's mythological namesake haunting the woodland glades, more hunted than huntress.

Meredith himself was ambivalent about Diana. How "feminist" was her search for freedom? And women critics have felt ambivalent about her as well. The feminist novelist Adeline Sergeant was critical of Meredith's apparent views, for, she felt, "no amount of intellectual training will obliterate these distinctions of sex . . . we shall more closely follow nature's lead if we emphasize rather than seek to lessen the differences between men and women." She queried:

> But what, on analysis, is this heroical feminine type? Its pro-
> genitor seems to hold the view that the natures of women have
> been differentiated from those of men simply through man's
> agency, by man's tyranny and oppression acting on woman's
> physical weakness; that woman's highest aim is to reinstate

herself by his side, to become his equal—"the mate of man, and the mother of a nobler race"; and that she may some day attain to this proud position of likeness and equality, but only by man's aid and man's consent. If this be Meredith's theory, it seems to me to be founded on a wrong view of the physical nature, the mental weaknesses, and the moral capacities of both women and men.

But, she went on to say:

There is scarcely a woman in his books who is not, righteously and grandly, in revolt, at war with herself, or with society; at war with the ignorance, the cowardice, the want of candour, want of judgment, want of sense, which a bad education, rather than a bad disposition, has made characteristic of woman; at war with society for its narrowness, its harshness, its want of humour and tolerance, and its impenetrable stupidity. With these the best among us are constantly at war; and we owe thanks to George Meredith for his pictures of women nobly at odds with themselves and with the world.[12]

Harriet Preston felt that Meredith was simply a new kind of chivalrous crusader:

The emancipation which he invokes for the suffering fair is in no sense an intellectual one. It is anything and everything rather than an affair of sciences, languages, courses, and careers. And still less is it what is quaintly called by a certain class of agitators "economic." It is purely moral, and can be achieved only through the moral regeneration of woman's natural master. A champion of Woman's Rights—even with capitals—Mr. Meredith stands confessed; yet with the clearly defined proviso that a woman has no rights, under the present dispensation, save such as may accrue to her through the righteousness of man. No other author ever gauged so accurately all that a high-spirited woman feels, as none, surely, ever exposed so relentlessly the dastard quality that may shelter itself within the clanging armour of your imposing masculine bravo. Nevertheless Mr. Meredith takes his text quite frankly from "Paradise Lost," "He for God only, she for God in him."[13]

At the end of the novel Diana does fear some curb to her freedom, but not from Redworth. It is childbirth that frightens her. And although she does think of him as Apollo and the "captain of her ship," she makes sure her marriage ceremony is free of romantic and sentimental cant. She insists that there will be no kneeling, he to her or she to him. Her view of marriage and childbirth is that it is "sailing in the dark," though with Emma's love and Redworth's devotion at least she will not be alone. Hardly a chivalrous view—but it is one that declares the female's struggle for identity to be as painful as the male's. ("I have not studied women more closely than I have men, but with more affection, a deeper interest in their enfranchisement and development.") As Meredith saw it, one could create a very individual and rebellious heroine and still be on the side of progress, though history would frown on a Byronic or Shelleyan hero of the other sex and condemn the author as an enemy of the common man.

One can say with some certainty that *Diana of the Crossways* is a feminist novel and that Meredith was a feminist. Diana's marriage and her fear of the danger of marriage are real to women who are afraid of loss of personal freedom as well as the physical and emotional terrors and responsibilities of bearing children. Meredith's experiences as artist and husband gave him a sympathetic awareness of woman's desire for power and identity in the world. His sense of social justice led him to attack those institutions which most militated against the freedom of the middle-class woman: the marriage and divorce laws and bourgeois marriage itself.

The Novel and the Myth

Why did Meredith choose the mythological method, and why the myth of Diana? The myth presupposes a time in which women were physically and mentally brave and free; it gave weight to the argument of the nineteenth-century feminists that women were struggling to regain lost power. Meredith, because of his erratic education and his difficult childhood, did not share the educated Englishman's belief in the superiority of Greek culture. He was not a purist, and the ancient Near East and late Roman adaptations of myth were intriguing to him. His Diana is never associated with the moon and frigidity but rather with the later Hecate, the huntress but also the nurse, the watcher at deathbeds and childbirth. One might say that *Diana of the Crossways* was to nineteenth-century art what Frazer's *Golden Bough* was to anthropology. While Frazer concentrates on the rituals of Diana's priests at Nemi, their death and rebirth to celebrate the fertility of the earth mother, Meredith shows modern women restricted by patriarchal institutions, marriage, and the law. Emma is childless; Diana fears childbirth, but in the end sacrifices her freedom for fertility.

Meredith dined with his friend Andrew Lang, the cultural anthropologist and collector of folktales and myths, while writing *Diana,* and he ordered Lang's *Custom and Myth* and *Helen of Troy* from his bookseller. (Lang had also written a preface to Marian Roalfe Cox's *Cinderella* in 1893, and the story of Cinderella influenced Diana as well.[14]) The last chapter of *Custom and Myth* is on the early history of the family; Lang here enters the controversy, rife in the new science of anthropology, on the side of those who posited a matriarchal or matrilineal society preceding patriarchy (Morgan and Engels). The Germans were posing the same thesis, and August Bebel used their arguments in *Woman under Socialism*[15] to prophesy a future in which women would be returned to their former power. The discovery of the layers of cities under Troy spurred the imagination of many intellectuals. These became indeed Freud's constant metaphor for his own search for the unconscious and the human need to come to terms with the mother. Meredith's genius was at work in recognizing that the search for the mother was a necessity for females as well as males, and often a more difficult psychic journey. The process of discovering Diana is for the reader somewhat like the discovering of Troy. Under the layers of social criticism, the obvious dialectic between gossip and scandal, between art and politics, London and the country, Ireland and England, between money and social climbing and respectable poverty and deliberate self-declassing, we come at last to Diana's rebellion, her psychic death and rebirth in the discovery of her feminine self.

Her terrible pre-oedipal struggle into female identity is dramatized deftly in chapter 36, "Is Conclusive as to the Heartlessness of Women with Brains." Meredith had stopped the novel with chapter 35 in its serial form in *The Fortnightly Review*. Yet he shows no signs of strain in the extraordinary scenes in which Emma feeds Diana from her own spoon, sleeps with her, and brings her back to life, although when he added this final chapter his wife was on her deathbed, willing her death.

The use of myth in Wagner's operas fascinated Meredith. While he was writing *Diana* his letters were full of allusions to them, and he attended performances of *Lohengrin* and *The Flying Dutchman*. Hearing of Wagner's death, he wrote to Louisa Lawrence, "He is gone and it grieves me," and urged her to see *Parsifal*. Lady Butcher (the Alice Brandreth of the *Letters*) recalled that Meredith had met Wagner at the Dannreuthers' and had looked up to the man as well as his work. He admired Cosima Wagner too, inevitably, as did his good friend Frederick Jameson, who translated *The Ring*. The man who wrote *Diana of the Crossways* manifestly respected both Brünnhilde and Isolde.

There is an anonymous critic for the *Times Literary Supplement* who persists in calling Brünnhilde a "female hero." Odd as the phrase is, and inappropriate for Brünnhilde, it seems to suit Diana. As a protagonist she is torn between art and politics the way many nineteenth-century heroes are. And neither concept of herself, as artist or as politician, has anything to do with her sexual identity as a female. The same critic complains that Brünnhilde has usurped the role of the hero in *The Ring,* that she completes the action that Siegfried "was meant" to do. Exactly. It is Brünnhilde's capacity for action, her intellect and her will, her strengths physical and spiritual, that define her as a great revolutionary heroine, a woman worthy of the title. She dies for love of Siegfried, as well as in the hope of a new world—whose birth she makes possible as an act simultaneously political and artistic. Some, like the aforementioned critic, find these qualities unfeminine, threatening. Brünnhilde seems a "man-eater." The implication is, I think, that she has eaten a piece of the hero's action—and that action is a male prerogative. A similar threat is represented in Diana's mystifying act of betrayal of a political secret, that her timid friend Dacier's party was planning to repeal the Corn Laws. In the first place, of course, Percy Dacier betrayed his party by telling its secret to a woman, and it was not just a casual telling. He sold his government for her caress; yet she—who ostensibly sells the secret out of hurt pride and for money—is the one punished. However, although Brünnhilde was very much in Meredith's mind as he wrote *Diana of the Crossways* (he describes Diana as a "splendid brune"), I think it is more appropriate to define Diana as a "female hero"; she is not a heroine with Brünnhilde's self-knowledge and strength. Diana is divided as "The Woman of Two Natures," her definition of herself as the author of *A Man of Two Minds*. The divisions are deeper than she knows, and Meredith's narrator only increases her distance from the reader with his several cloaks of gossip, scandal, diaries, myth, and history.

Opera and music were not the only arts to participate, with Meredith's, in the search for an understanding of women through myth. Certainly painting in the last twenty years of the century, from the academic and salon painters to the decadents, abounds with figures of both historical and mythological women. Louisa Lawrence, who shared with Meredith during this period both Germanophilia (as they called it) and a love of Wagner, sent him a copy of Alma-Tadema's painting "Lesbia Listening to Catullus." Meredith had written in chapter 23 of *The Egoist:*

> Women have us back to the conditions of primitive man, or they shoot us higher than the topmost star. But it is as we please. Let them tell us what we are to them; for us, they are our back and front of life: the poet's Lesbia, the poet's Beatrice; ours is the choice. And were it proved that some of the bright things are in the pay of Darkness, with the stamp of his coin on their palms, and that some are the very angels we hear sung

of, not the less might we say that they find us out, they have
us by our leanings. They are to us what we hold of best or
worst within.

Meredith deliberately yokes Catullus and Petrarch as representatives
of poets and cultures who define women as devils or angels, never
comrades or equals of men. But Emma Dunstane, "deeply a woman
and dumbly a poet," regards Redworth as a fitting comrade for Diana.
She describes her to him as "one of Shakespeare's women. . . . I dream
of him seeing her with that eye of steady flame. The bravest and best
of us *at bay* in the world [my italics] need an eye like his to read
deep, and not be baffled by inconsistencies." Diana is both historical
and mythological in that she exemplifies the deterioration of the huntress into the hunted.

   Sometimes Meredith abandons Clio and Calliope for the comic spirit;
the wonderful scene describing the pig is a tribute to Diana, patroness
of the slaughter of animals. When Lord Larrian gives Diana a guard
dog, myth is again invoked for its humor and irony. Diana says later,
"Our weakness is the swiftest dog to hunt us." (When Yeats met Maud
Gonne with her dog, he felt she was consciously living the role of
Meredith's Diana.) The traditional Diana of the crossroads has a triple
face; not until the end of the novel does Diana recognize her third
visage. She warns Dacier that her Christian name is Pagan and that
she is also Hecate, full of magic and witchery and a bringer of death.
In reality she has many faces and names: Diana Merion (Irish feminine
Meredith?), fiery daughter of Celtic poets; Princess Egeria to great
statesmen; "Antonia" (appropriately bisexual pseudonym for a lady
novelist), gallant Tony to her Emmy; Mrs Warwick, wronged wife,
then widow; finally she is Diana Redworth, Artemis to Redworth's
Apollo.

   "George Verimyth," as a *Punch* burlesque called him, rather overdoes
Redworth as Apollo. (One critic suggested that a Welsh pronunciation
of "Meredith" would accent the "red.") Frazer said that Roman kings
reddened their faces with vermillion, both to impersonate the sungod
and to emphasize their descent from Diana's priests. Emma calls Redworth "Sol in his moral grandeur"; Diana compares him to Apollo and

the sun: "He is Roman, Spartan, Imperial; English if you like—the pick of the land" (379). We always see the worthy red man (noble savage) riding westward into the sunset, historically and silently pursuing Diana's honor. Emma's vision of the marriage not only unites brother sun and sister moon but restates one of the novel's political themes; it stands for "Old Ireland transforming Old England."

The first myth which Meredith evokes in the novel proper is that of Cinderella. Diana, beautiful penniless orphan, is summoned to the ball by her fairy godmother. She ignores Prince Charming (Redworth) and attaches herself to the most powerful man present, Lord Larrian.[16] This is only the first of a series of attachments to great men, father figures, in which Diana plays Egeria—without the physical marriage which was Diana's nymph's role in the Roman legend. The ball ends in a great debacle over Diana's virtue (image of prospective priests fighting for the golden bough), to which Diana herself is oblivious. Analogous to Cinderella's glass slipper is a series of nautical images which do not return until the end of the novel, where Redworth is described as rescuer and captain of the ship *Diana*. While Meredith mixes his myths as well as his metaphors, the Cinderella story is kept up through the novel as Emma plays godmother, protecting Diana from dame gossip and dame scandal and finally presiding over her marriage to Prince Charming. But the Cinderella myth, besides being a story of the older woman who helps the younger through the perils of adolescence into womanhood, is a rags-to-riches story. And Meredith turns this story upside down. In the novel's critical scene, Diana rejects "The Crossways" and its aristocratic heritage, buys a cottage, and completely identifies herself by class with the cottagers. She names herself Mrs. Warwick, widow, demystifying that ancient necessity, the virgin bride. She rejects her past by class and sex roles and is her own woman, free and independent, when she marries Redworth.

The comradely coolness with which they plight their troth is remarkable. In a glade reminiscent of Diana's sacred grove, she asks the name of a trailing vine, and Redworth tells her it is clematis. "It drags in the dust when it has no firm arm to cling to," sermonizes Diana

(406). It is a measure of Meredith's art that the reader is reminded of the earlier scene in the mountain meadow at Rovio where Diana in a self-assertive spirit sermonizes and botanizes at her two- minded but fancied hero, Dacier.

The Italian alpine scene, as rich and allusive, fluent and descriptive as the later scene is bare and subdued, chronicles an important moment in Diana's psychic development. We see the action from Dacier's confused and sleepless point of view. All night the bells have tolled Diana's name; he gazes at the campanile as a roysterer would at Aurora and climbs the Generoso, "where the waters whispered of secrecy to satisfy Diana herself. . . . They conjure classic visions of the pudency of the Goddess irate or unsighted. The semi-mythological state of mind, built of old images and favoring haunts, was known to Dacier" (151). Meredith, skilled dramatist, has led us to expect the unfolding of the myth of Diana and Actæon. We expect him to surprise her in her bath and be punished, if not as a stag devoured by his own dogs, in some equally horrible way. But the author has tricked us. He switches myths in midstream. We are astonished not by a description of a naked Diana but by the materialization of a clothed one (read: a lavender lesbian Diana).

The description is also retrospectively astonishing, as the only direct one of Diana's outward appearance in the whole novel (only diarists' descriptions having been quoted in the introductory essay). "She was dressed in some texture of the hue of lavender. A violet scarf loosely knotted over the bosom opened on her throat. The loop of her black hair curved under a hat of grey beaver. Memorably radiant was her face" (153). Meredith once wrote: "Every man who is not a milliner in spirit" desires the end of the crinoline. "The introduction of the crinoline has been in its effects morally worse than a *coup d'état*. It has sacrificed more lives; it has utterly destroyed more tempers; it has put an immense division between the sexes. It has obscured us, smothered us, stabbed us."[17] Meredith, perhaps like the mythological painters, has here aroused his readers and then attempted to purify their minds. History and reality return; no nineteenth-century Englishwoman would have dared to strip and bathe in the mountain stream.

We are moved to nostalgia for a lost innocence and a lost health.

Diana asserts that she has not heard the bell which so disturbed her companions. Dacier at once falls into the background, "as he did only with her, to perform accordant bass in their dialogue," and for the rest of the scene plays Echo to her Narcissus. They engage in a dialogue in which she praises her beloved Emma, and by implication herself, and he echoes her praise. When Dacier asks her for some of the "pale purple meadow-crocus," she lectures on the rarity of colchicum and describes the flowers as a sacrifice for the woman who is "the next heavenly thing to heaven," the "*coeur d'or* of our time." Dacier echoes these remarks by naming Emma "a bit of a bluestocking" and the friends "the Damon and Pythias of women." Diana treats Dacier as a fellow youth, hearing only his praises of her beloved. He is puzzled and annoyed when she twice declares her wish to be a man, for she is deep in her fantasy of herself as the gallant Tony paying court to the ideal woman, Emma. Dacier breaks the spell by comparing a half-wilted crocus to a ballerina. Diana grows confused, upset, angry, for in her narcissistic trance she has become Tony, and the budding crocus is her own phallic image of herself. The crocus is the flower which Persephone picks before she is abducted in the powerful mother/daughter myth of Demeter-Persephone. But Dacier also reminds Diana, in the figure of the wilted ballerina, of the fate of women who perform as artists. Dacier now becomes an enemy. She feels "wounded, adverse, armed. He seemed somehow to have dealt a mortal blow to the happy girl she had become again" (157). His news of Lord Dannisburgh's impending death reminds her of the role of princess Egeria which caused her social downfall, and evokes the desire to be Diana, nurse and healer. And Meredith ends the chapter by calling her "wife and no wife, a prisoner in liberty, a blooming woman imagining herself restored to transcendent maiden ecstasies—the highest youthful poetic" (160).

It is these transcendent maiden ecstasies, their narcissism, desire to court and please the mother, to be son and lover to the mother, which Meredith has recorded so faithfully in his portrait of a female egoist. Diana's unconscious struggle through the stages of a prolonged adolescence is subtly and dramatically rendered, and Meredith is at his best in these scenes with Dacier and with Redworth.

The resourceful and complex use of myth in *Diana,* both conscious and seemingly unconscious on Meredith's part, reveals a "woman of two natures," as Diana recognizes herself to be. The outer struggle to be free from personal and legal assault, the arrows of scandal and gossip, financial need, and social constraints on her artistic and political desires is matched by a fiercer inner struggle to become a whole woman. *Diana* is no case history, but a work of art. We know Diana by her actions, which neither she nor Meredith can explain in rational terms. The psychic reality of Meredith's portrait of the development of an independent woman is uncanny and magnificent, mystifying even its maker. He attempted to explain or condone her most controversial actions in economic terms—and their inadequacy forced him to relate that Diana, once created, sought her own truth and would not be held down.

Epic in size and structure, *Diana of the Crossways* is the living daughter of the nineteenth century. Efforts (like Jan B. Gordon's brilliant essay)[18] to explain the novel in purely structuralist terms must fail ultimately, because even if Meredith had been wholly committed to the building of the novel into a dialogue between "gossip" and "scandal," which he was not, his moral, social, and psychological intentions were often far stronger than his sense of design. As an architect he was eclectic. But even if the novel cannot be forced to fit the modern desire for intellectual and formal perfection, with its values of neat equations with standard myths and a shaping symbolist imagination, *Diana* claims our attention on a deep psychological level.

Why Did Diana Do It?

Diana's odyssey is the story of the prolonged and difficult adolescence of a freedom-loving girl voyaging to her final acceptance of the responsibilities of womanhood. Fraught with dangers both personal and social, her journey begins and ends with a trip across the Irish Channel. The first crossing is stormy and troubled, as the motherless child crosses the sea alone. In the second, Redworth is firmly in command of the ship *Diana*. The woman Diana has learned that his captaincy does not deprive her of her freedom but gives her a secure base for her independent pursuits—as well as the unmentioned but implied satisfaction of physical needs. The geography of the novel links the sea and the land, Ireland and England, the majesty of the Alps and the mystical peace of the Nile, the city of London and the South Downs. The critical center, the eye of the storm, is always "The Crossways" itself, and Diana haunts its graveyard like her namesake's alter ego, Hecate. Her inner journey is marked by a pattern of alternating flight and rest, testing her powers and recouping her losses. "The Crossways" rouses guilt, a sense of death and despair, and a need to meet the high standards of action and speech of her forefathers.

But Diana's actions have a feminine universality. Why does Diana flee from Sir Lukin's advances into an unhappy marriage with the first man to present himself? While in actuality she has not seduced Lukin, she feels guilty because she has unconsciously wished to. She can never confess to Emma, her "mother," that she has desired Lukin, her "father." Why does she flee again when scandal and divorce link her name with Lord Dannisburgh? She is innocent, but feels guilt and shame because of her repressed desires. Meredith describes her confusion, her despair, and we are sympathetic. As Diana says, the artist in her relating language to life: "We women are the verbs passive of the alliance, we have to learn, and if we take to activity with the best intentions, we conjugate a frightful disturbance. We are to run on lines like the steam-trains, or we come to no station, dash to fragments."

Some critics have attributed these actions to Diana's highly emotional nature, but that is not her character at all. The most difficult problem in the novel for Meredith's contemporaries as well as for students today is Diana's impetuous rushing to the editor of *The Times* with Dacier's party secret, the decision to repeal the Corn Laws. Meredith fails to convince us, either in the novel or in his letters, that Diana's real or fancied financial difficulties are such as to warrant her action. She does not herself understand why she acted or why she was blind to the consequences, but these frighten her into falling in love with "King Death" (as she tells Emma), into a desire for self-annihilation so strong that only her substitute mother's "magic" forgiveness can save her. Diana has spent months creating Percy Dacier as her male self. She has written his speeches, entertained his friends, passed on all the political knowledge she gained from his uncle and the other great men to whom she has played Egeria. The young Diana whom we first meet declaring her wish to be a soldier becomes a woman who has transferred her dearest wish to be a politician to Dacier as her puppet. Her other wish, to be an artist, inadequately fulfilled in her writing of romans à clef, she has enfleshed in Arthur Rhodes, whom she has created as a poet. What that episode reveals is her secret desire to wield the power of the editor.

The great newspaper editor, Tonans, combines the artist and the politician. His taunting Diana with a lack of fresh news has touched a nerve, and she realizes, as she is stricken with writer's block in the crucial scene between her hero and his mistress in *The Man of Two Minds,* that her actual situation is that of a woman writing for a living, unsuccessfully. Tormented alike by having had to sell the "The Crossways" and by Tonans' taunt, she is shaken by Dacier's use of his political news as a weapon of seduction and a means to demonstrate to her that he is a separate person and a man. In shame and heightened anxiety she goes "like a bullet" to Tonans. She is angry, and the expression of anger by women is the great Victorian taboo. Meredith delves into her mind to show her working herself up to believe both that she has been sexually assaulted and that she has been acting like an adventuress and deserves his disrespect, then convincing herself that her financial plight is desperate. But her irrational need to rush off in the night to *The Times* springs from a deeper source than she can acknowledge. It is not that, as some critics have claimed to exonerate her, as a woman she does not understand the political import of the secret. She does. Politics has been her life's blood. It is not even that as a woman she has a weaker sense of justice, a less stringent conscience than a man. On the contrary. As an experienced woman of the world, she could and did handle Dacier's advances with grace and firmness. Her

shame sprang from the realization that she had used him as an extension of herself, since she was forbidden by sex from acting in a male
world. In a way he was her child, and his lovemaking shocked her,
broke a taboo of her own making. Released, she resolves for once to
act like a man, and she does. Anger is a "masculine" emotion.

"The tremendous pressure upon our consciousness of the material
cause, when we find ourselves cast among the breakers of moral
difficulties and endeavour to elude that mud-visaged monster, chiefly
by feigning unconsciousness, was an experience of Diana's, in the
crisis to which she wrought," writes Meredith calmly in the center of
the most emotionally charged scene in the novel. Here Diana, having
lost "The Crossways," is at the real crossroads of her psychic development, and the chapter is called "A Giddy Turn at the Spectral Crossways." The passage in which the "unmasked actress" imagines a
fantasy of power after being numbed into a realization of her femaleness and her powerlessness is worth quoting in full, for in terms of
feeling, it is the strongest in the novel:

> The visionary figure of Mr. Tonans, petrified by the great news,
> drinking it, and confessing her ahead of him in the race for
> secrets, arose toweringly. She had not ever seen the Editor in
> his den at midnight. With the rumble of his machinery about
> him, and fresh matter arriving and flying into the printing-press,
> it must be like being in the very furnace-hissing of Events: an
> Olympian Council held in Vulcan's smithy. Consider the bringing
> to the Jove there news of such magnitude as to stupefy him!
> He, too, who had admonished her so sneeringly for staleness
> in her information—. [310]

"Diana Victrix" as she arms herself for battle, already feels dread and
guilt; the news is "throbbing like a heart plucked out of a breathing
body" (310). Promethea will challenge the gods. This daughter dares
a rebellious act of identification with and contempt for the father.

The scene throbs to a climax more intense than any love scene.
"Diana Victrix" imagines a duel with Tonans, herself the winner; she
shivers as her imagination turns the cab she drives in with Danvers

into "a funeral convoy without followers." She says, "You are not an Editor of a paper, but you may boast that you have been near the nest of one" (315). Diana herself boasts to her companion, in exhilaration and relief, after she has told Percy's secret. She has entered the male world which has so long excluded her and "sprung a mine." Diana has signified both her desire to be a man and her contempt for all the values of the patriarchal world. No more vicarious political action behind the scenes: she walks boldly on stage and thumbs her nose at the audience. She has finally entered the male world and simultaneously violated it. She has conjured up a near-rape scene by Percy and then countered with a similar act. Diana acts in anger.

To Percy, Diana claims temporary insanity, says her excuse is that Tonans "railed at me for being 'out of it,' " her inability to write, her lack of money (325). But Meredith reminds us that Tonans and his paper are Radical; we are aware that Diana had allied herself disastrously with a man and a party whose class interests she did not deeply share. We have some suspicion that in her psychological identity crisis her true radical instincts have also come out. Her later insistent self-definition as a cottager comes as no surprise. The internal radical challenge to authority is a revolutionary act in the outer world of politics as well. And the expression of anger is a feminist act.

The struggle to bring herself to birth as a new woman almost kills Diana. Meredith's respect and sympathy for a woman's struggle to gain sexual and political identity are clearly stated in the novel. He takes seriously her conscious and unconscious desire for power, and her guilt. Most significantly, he strikes bare a rock of psychic truth in Diana's relationship with Emma, that the strongest bond of the human condition is with the mother, so strong that young women as well as young men must work their way to psychic freedom by competing with the father for the mother's love. Every reader is aware that apart from the scene just described, the most deeply felt passages are in the scenes between Emma and Tony. The last lines of the novel reveal Meredith's awe of woman. The "involuntary little twitch of Tony's fingers" with which she greets Emma's last demand that Diana bear a child and make her a real godmother is as moving as it is realistic,

according to what we now call, after Nancy Chodorow, "the reproduction of mothering." Diana's internal history does meet Meredith's
demands of the novel as "the brainstuff of fiction." He has created
"an ideal of the heroical feminine type" (16, 17). But Meredith would
be the first to agree that Diana's three-selved identity is not enough.
The leap from hunted to huntress is a baby step in the progress of
humankind until all the newly freed Dianas (as he says in *The Ballad
of Fair Ladies in Revolt*) "be tamed to say not 'I,' but 'we.' "

3

Nostalgia Is Not Enough
Why Elizabeth Hardwick Misreads Ibsen, Plath, and Woolf

Elizabeth Hardwick's *Seduction and Betrayal,* subtitled "Women and Literature," might deceive the unwary reader into thinking that Hardwick is a feminist or that the book contains some theoretical ideas about heroines of literature or female writers. The title essay (also the most serious) is fascinating. In a high elegiac style (and style is Hardwick's forte), she mourns the loss to literature of all the seduced and betrayed heroines as subjects or objects of the reader's pity, now that sex is no longer considered a tragic subject. While most critics seem considerably cheered by this prospect, Hardwick is saddened. Were the author's name absent, the reader might assume, with some justification, that the book is a pastoral elegy by a Southern gentleman-scholar for the good old days when seduced and abandoned women aroused the reader's sorrow and pity. The book is an exercise in nostalgia for woman as victim.

Hardwick's essays are personal, subjective, and ahistorical, if not antifeminist, to a surprising degree. Both literary criticism by women and feminist literary criticism have histories; the latter category, for example, contains a recognizable subgenre of social or socialist feminist literary criticism. Hardwick's writing is a rearguard pretense that one can write outside ideology, from some pure objective position, about a literature that was composed outside ideology. The vigorous defense of Hardwick by Susan Sontag might lead one to believe that Hardwick thinks of her own work as a contribution to the some form of feminist debate, even to its subgenre of socialist feminism; but she is mistaken. For Hardwick, the essential problem is power, and she finds abhorrent the search for it, even when power simply means the quest for identity

49

by a fictional heroine or an actual female writer. She blames the wives and sisters of great writers (e.g., Jane Carlyle and Dorothy Wordsworth) for not themselves becoming great; yet the women writers who do become powerful are therefore frightening. Heroines of the benighted past, on the other hand, are "interesting"—because they have been betrayed (Donna Elvira, Hester Prynne). "Seduction and Betrayal" contains this statement:

> For us now, the illicit has become a psychological rather than a moral drama. We ask ourselves how the delinquent ones *feel* about their seductions, adulteries, betrayals, and it is by the quality of their feelings that our moral judgments are formed. If they suffer and grieve and regret, they can be forgiven and even supported. If they boast or fall into an inner carelessness, what they are doing or have done can seem to be *wrong*. Love, even of the briefest span, is a powerful detergent, but "destructiveness" is a moral stain.[1]

At the risk of sounding very unfashionable and conservative, I beg to differ. The capacity for moral judgment has not changed simply because Freud has given us tools for understanding human motivation. Even the problems of sexual "sins" have moral solutions, whether Hardwick recognizes them or not. The literary critic's potency is weakened by Hardwick's refusal to accept the critical role of making moral as well as artistic judgments. The refusal of this power, by arguing that one can no longer make moral judgments about literature, is irresponsible. That a woman critic who writes about heroines in novels and about women writers should abjure moral power at a time in history when she has a chance of being heard is puzzling to say the least.

"The idea of sexual responsibility for the passions of youth cannot be understood as an ethical one," Hardwick writes of *An American Tragedy*. She argues that modern readers do not share Tolstoy's characters' view in *The Kreutzer Sonata* that "real debauchery consists in freedom from the moral bonds toward a woman with whom one enters into carnal relations."[2] Stoicism in the face of sexual betrayal is the quality Hardwick most values in women. It is no wonder that Tess of the d'Urbervilles is her favorite heroine. "Transcendent stoical suffering" at the hands of men and fate have made Tess too impossibly passive for many modern readers; yet Hardwick mourns her passing. Sex is no longer a serious subject; alas, the victim can no longer claim our pity. Anyone who was equally nostalgic about the loss to literature of the subject of slavery or child labor would appear ridiculous.

Yes, we do need female literary critics of authority and perception. But let Hardwick put her pearls away, and hang around her neck a magnifying glass, a pair of scissors, and a pen with a very sharp point. Let her take the long historical view and ask the right questions. Virginia Woolf did it; her essays on Jane Carlyle and Dorothy Wordsworth praise the writing and power of observation of the two. Woolf asked how it was possible for Jane Carlyle to write at all, given the demands her husband made on her time and her health. She found the answer in Jane Carlyle's relationship with another female writer, Geraldine Jewsbury, a relationship both provoking and sustaining, a clue to how many nineteenth-century women "managed" to write. Hardwick is determined to make us feel that Carlyle overpraised his wife's writing out of guilt for being a bad husband.

By placing the reader in the subject's time and social circumstances so that we may see the restrictions on her freedom, the bravery and struggle it took to be creative, Woolf set an example for the female critic. By digging up and preserving the lives and work of women writers, she called on women to write the history of women and to keep it alive in books and libraries and women's colleges. Hers was a call for alternative institutions based on the knowledge that there can be no creativity without power. She saw the female artist's struggle as economic and historical. "For masterpieces are not single and solitary births; they are the outcome of many years of thinking in common, of thinking by the body of the people, so that the experience of the mass is behind the single voice," Woolf wrote in *A Room of One's Own*. In that book she urged college women to rewrite history with women in it, and she berated earlier generations of women for giving money to Oxford and Cambridge, urging present and future generations to concentrate and collect the history and experience of women because "we think back through our mothers." *Three Guineas* warns women of the dangers of entering the male professions in very specific terms; it was as a socialist and feminist that Virginia Woolf refused the order of Dame of the British Empire. She always wrote and acted as a woman first.

The works of feminist literary criticism we learn from now (1978) are Virginia Woolf's essays, the work of de Beauvoir, of early Rebecca West, of Millett and Greer and Brigid Brophy, despite some lapses, Elizabeth Janeway, Mary McCarthy, and currently Adrienne Rich and Tillie Olsen. Patricia Spacks's *The Female Imagination* made little theoretical advance and suffers because the author condescends to her subject, to her reader, and to the students she taught. Ellen Moers in *Literary Women* brilliantly gives feminists new categories of thought and experience to analyze and takes into account women's influence on each other. Hardwick's work resembles Mary Ellmann's *Thinking About Women* in that neither author *writes* as a woman. Fearing male criticism, both writers, to avoid provoking it, conceal female identity and use the "least feminine" critical weapons, wit, irony, and intellect. They are never angry or earnest; they do not espouse causes or make moral judgments; they never say "I think," much less "I, a woman, think . . . " This technique works. Ellmann writes down to the reader. Hardwick has not, in fact, been attacked by male critics, and one does not imagine that Mary Ellmann would take Norman Mailer's wrath seriously. But they have confused their female critics and readers. This is not to say that a feminist literary critic must be personal, or that she must devote all her energies to the cause. She might take all literature as her province. But, like their distinguished forebear Virginia Woolf, feminist critics speak and write proudly as women, and as feminists they assume a female authority in tone; they never let an opportunity slip by to correct the errors of their male colleagues. They seem to like being women; they like other women. (Virginia Woolf said, "The truth is, I often like women, I like their unconventionality. I like their subtlety. I like their anonymity.") They know the history of women writers and critics and write as part of that history, acknowledging by what they do Virginia Woolf's prophecy that it will take generations of women writers and critics to develop the social conditions necessary to produce a great woman writer, a "Shakespeare's sister."

Feminism has its fellow travelers as well as veterans of its battles and scalers of barricades. *Women and Literature,* the subtitle of Elizabeth Hardwick's book, is as misleading as *Essays in Literature and Society,* the subtitle of her earlier book, *A View of My Own.* (In that title the words *My Own* invite comparison to Woolf's *One's Own*: while Woolf regards herself as the voice of silent thousands, Hardwick stresses her singularity.) Like her publishing in *The New York Review of Books,* Hardwick's subtitles imply social conscience or at least social consciousness on the part of the literary critic. There appears to be some buried wish in the author to make these essays socially useful, but the wish is not fulfilled. She really is not sure she likes women at all, not sure of what she thinks their lives should be. In the earlier book there is an extremely ambivalent essay on Mary McCarthy. Hardwick admires McCarthy—in fact, it may have been the challenge of McCarthy's essays on Ibsen in *Sights and Spectacles* that inspired her own work. She admires the "subversive soul sustained by exceptional energy." But she writes as if they did not share the same sex: "She is an odd woman, and perhaps oddest of all is this stirring sense of the importance of her own intellectual formulations. Very few women writers can resist the temptation of feminine sensibility; it is there to be used as a crutch, and the reliance upon it is expected and generally admired."

What is one to make of this? Like Shaw, Hardwick finds the intellectual and political female writer so alien a creature as to warrant the creation of a third sex to accommodate her ego. Worst of all to Hardwick is McCarthy's ruthless morality, which becomes aesthetically acceptable only if one admires the daring exploit and adventure of a woman writing from moral conviction. The critic praises by denying sisterhood under the skin with the writer. She wonders—like Dr. Johnson regarding that odd animal the passionate woman preacher—that she can do it at all. "A career of candor and dissent is not an easy one for a woman," Hardwick explains, "the license is jarring and the dare often forbidding. Such a person needs more than confidence and indignation. A great measure of personal attractiveness and a high degree of romantic singularity are necessary to step free of the mundane, the governessy, the threat of earnestness and dryness."[3] To whom, we ask, is the license jarring? If one has beauty, class, and style, one can afford to be serious, political, and moral. These words do not come from the woman's side of the fence as a friendly warning to women, but from the other side; they are exactly the words of kind male professors to their earnest female students.

Susan Sontag has come to the defense of *Seduction and Betrayal* in *The New York Review of Books* while attacking Adrienne Rich for being too earnest, "governessy," and moral. That publication, using Virginia Woolf and Adrienne Rich as scapegoats, seems to be leading a crusade against our best feminist artists and two who coincidentally have expressed strong political views and a concern for the study of motherhood as a social construction. *Seduction and Betrayal,* Sontag says, is the "most remarkable of recent contributions to the feminist imagination of history."[4] I assume from this that Sontag and Hardwick wish the book to be classified as feminist; yet it altogether lacks the imagination of history as well as of feminism.

Most feminists have read Hardwick's work as antifeminist. And rightly so. Not because we are self-righteous and anti-elitist, as Sontag asserts (although we are often both—with some historical justification), but because the sides have been drawn in these battles and Hardwick, sometimes too ladylike to fight at all, has written in defense of the view of women held by the supposed legions of men who are grieving over the loss to literature and culture of "feminine sensibility." Hardwick supposes in another essay, called "The Subjection of Women," that "there is bound to be a little laughter in the wings at the mere thought of this madly sensible and brilliantly obscure tome by Simone de Beauvoir, *The Second Sex.*" We can only assume the author of this faint praise to be among the laughers. One thing partisans of the same cause have in common is the enemy, but he must be named to be known.

Hardwick writes from an ivory tower where novels and their characters exist outside of literary history, outside of social context and social history, like well-matched pearls on a string. The effect of these pearls is superficially glamorous, charming, and ladylike, but ornamental. The book's one solid virtue is its good taste—sometimes good taste is bad form. *Seduction and Betrayal* is as well written, mannered, and gently unideological as Quentin Bell's biography of Virginia Woolf. That book, in Rebecca West's words, turned literary biography into a "blood sport," conducting its slaughter of the reputation of a great writer in tones of an aristocratic assumption of superiority; the Hardwick book elegantly deals a similar blow to women's literary criticism. In her attack on Woolf, her reviling of the great heroines of Ibsen, Hedda Gabler and Rebecca West, and her making fun of Mrs. Linde and Hilda Wangel, she reminds one of those critics of the 1890s who called *Hedda Gabler* "an open drain," "a dirty act done publicly." To praise Thea and Beata and all the self-sacrificing women in Ibsen's plays is not only to misread Ibsen but to sneer at anyone who has found joy and strength and wisdom in the "Northern Wizard's" knowledge of the human heart and of bourgeois society.

I would like to argue with Hardwick's readings of Ibsen, of Plath, and of Woolf. These writers and their works have been the subjects of much critical controversy. Are they feminists? Are their works feminist? Woolf and Ibsen are; in my view Plath is not. Hardwick's view is the opposite.

One mark of Hardwick's failure as a critic is, I believe, her use of indirect discourse, a device she shares with Mary Ellmann. In earlier times this mode and its sister modes of pseudonymity and the epistolary style were often subversive and feminist. As Virginia Woolf used them, they were. The indirect discourse of *A Room of One's Own* is balanced by the direct factual attacks in the footnotes, and by the time Woolf wrote *Three Guineas* she had transformed the polite tone of a lady writing a letter into direct and angry polemic. The past had its uses to Woolf; history armed her with facts about women. Hardwick, on the contrary, is sentimental about the past; she is nostalgic about the literature of women's oppression. Hardwick's publishers call her

"America's foremost woman of letters." This title—conferred, not won—acts as a territorial warning to other female literary critics: recognition and power are for the well-mannered noncombatants in the current ideological battles. Her recent essays praising Simone Weil show unblushingly an admiration for the brilliant martyred woman. The tragedy of self-immolation and destruction escapes Hardwick, for she does not see it in social terms. Simone Weil's life is a frightening cautionary tale, but she insists on seeing it as a romantic opera.

"That profoundly interesting subject, the value that men set upon women's chastity," would make an interesting book, Virginia Woolf wrote in *A Room of One's Own;* and "Chastity had then, it has even now, a religious importance in a woman's life, and has so wrapped itself round with nerves and instincts that to cut it free and bring it to the light of day demands courage of the rarest." One wishes that Hardwick had the courage, for she writes so well, to mock the male fetishism that made heroines into victims. Instead, she yearns nostalgically for a sentimental view of women. I wish she would write, with something like Woolf's galloping good humor and political wit, of the real heroines: Antigone, Clytemnestra, Cassandra, Medea, Rosalind and Lady Macbeth, Nora, Hedda, Hilda Wangel, and Rebecca West. Woolf names her heroines and then is struck by the historical contradictions. Why did the Greeks, she wants to know, and Shakespeare and Ibsen, who came from societies supposedly so repressive to women, produce such magnificent heroines? But Hardwick is not concerned with these questions. Let us look at her reading of Ibsen.

For Ibsen's real heroines she has nothing but reproach, and she sets about finding her own heroines, the victims: Thea, Beata, and Mrs. Solness. It would be very interesting to see her reading of *When We Dead Awaken,* Ibsen's most difficult and disturbing play, about the artist's abuse of muse, the model, the victim, and her revenge.

Hardwick says that Hedda Gabler has "no motivation whatever" and wishes that, like the Greek heroines, Hedda's destructiveness could be explained by sexual betrayal. Hardwick cannot see Hedda's social role as important. In the classroom the students will say of this praise of victims, long-suffering women, the self-sacrificers:

"Ah, but you have missed the point. The Theas, Beatas, and self-sacrificing aunts are the enemies of freedom. Hedda is all of us. She is the type of the female artist. In her despair at her lack of education and experience, Hedda kills her fellow artist, her 'brother.' She is like Wilde's Salomé, a woman, an artist, and a revolutionary. Social conditions and family life have destroyed the possibility of freedom. She makes her death a work of art, as Salomé makes John the Baptist's death and her own into art."

"Yes," they will say, "one should be afraid of Hedda. But she is not fully responsible for the evil she causes. Ibsen's genius is shown not only in Hedda's tragedy but in the details of her despair. Tesman's aunt gives her George's slippers, carefully wrapped, as a symbol of domesticity and service, the passing of the role from aunt to wife, accompanied by some teasing remarks about Hedda's pregnancy. That Hedda attacks only the aunt's hat is a miracle of restraint. Tesman has spent their honeymoon doing research on the domestic industries of Brabant in the Middle Ages. Hedda is horsewoman, free spirit, motherless daughter of a powerful father. Like all of Ibsen's heroines, she is neither industrious nor domestic. She is the class enemy of bourgeois life. Her first weapon is idleness, as upsetting to those who live by the Protestant work ethic as passive resistance was to British soldiers in India."

"We seem able to accept Russian nihilists as heroes, and even the sorrows of young Werther as social, romantic, and revolutionary. With Mann's guidance we can even see that aesthetes and dandies under the banner of art for art's sake began the revolt against Victorian values. Why can't Hedda be seen as a heroine?"

Elizabeth Robins, the great Ibsen actress who almost single-handedly produced, directed, and played the leading role in *Hedda Gabler*, and who was largely responsible for the staging of most of the Ibsen plays in London in the 1890s, came to Hedda's defense in her *Ibsen and the Actress*. No man except that wizard Ibsen could understand Hedda, she said. Men couldn't see her in their own wives and daughters. She was "a bundle of unused possibilities." But Robins rejected the temptation to make Hedda "sympathetic."[5] She never wanted to "whitewash

General Gabler's somewhat lurid daughter"; Hedda was "pitiable in her hungry loneliness," but insolent—and tragic. Robins saw that Hedda's life was constricted by fear, that she had the courage nevertheless to refuse life on certain terms, and that she did not choose to submit herself to bourgeois respectability or even to comfortable adultery. General Gabler's pistols guaranteed her the right to suicide, a right that we perhaps do not take seriously today but which those socialists or social Darwinists of the 1890s, Elizabeth Robins and Henrik Ibsen, considered one of the few rights that gave dignity to the lives and deaths of the oppressed.

"Certainly the particular humiliations and enslavements that threaten women do not threaten men. Such enslavements may seem so unreal to decent men as to appear as melodrama," wrote Robins. To create the effect of the stunted artist, the plunderer of beauty, Robins played Hedda in a feather boa. Shaw said that the blood of the slaughtered birds would load her down at Judgment Day, but the fashionable ladies of London took it up immediately. Its exotic concentration of death and sexuality persists today. Ibsen would have liked that touch, as appropriate as Hedda's treasured, rather phallic, pistols.

The feminist critical consciousness has no need to remake Hedda into a suitable propagandistic model. She exists, as Ibsen created her, as a horrifying example of the personal and social consequences of neglecting to give women useful and interesting work of their own. Hedda is the universal of the unawakened female artist. She cannot make the transition from daughter to wife because neither role has allowed her to find her own identity. She wishes that the vine leaves of her bitter jokes could crown her own head or give her some connection with the creative life of the artist. She shudders at the thought of the life in her womb because she, a dependent creature, will be responsible for another creature. The ties of marriage and motherhood will then be strengthened, and she will participate in perpetuating the very social structure that so restricts her freedom. It is interesting in this context to note that there are other objections to Hedda as heroine than Hardwick's horror. Some modern readers don't find the struggle of the middle-class artist truly universal. Meredith wrote, to mystified nineteenth-century readers, that he looked forward to the day when his individual artist-heroine, Diana of the Crossways, would be seen as reactionary because she did not represent the aspirations of all women for freedom. Perhaps we are free enough to be approaching that day in reading Ibsen.[6]

It is no accident that allusions to syphilis constitute a strong under-current in both *Hedda Gabler* and *A Doll's House,* constantly pulling us back to a realization of havoc wreaked on society by the double standard. The unseen fathers play a huge role in Ibsen's plays. They pass on syphilis, insanity, and debt to their sons, but desire for an impossible freedom to their daughters. Hedda tells Judge Brack that she wanted to jump out of the train on her honeymoon, but was terrified that her stockings would show. Ibsen dramatizes in this detail the whole conflict in her character between desire for liberty and fear of it.

Hedda thinks perhaps that women are freer in Mme. Diana's whorehouse, but her status excludes her from Judge Brack's "stag party," which brings Ibsen's concern for the separation of the sexes to a mythological climax. It is at Mme. Diana's that Lovborg, like Actæon, meets an ugly and ignominious death. Accidentally shooting himself in the bowels, he is like Actæon surprising Diana and her nymphs bathing. Did Ibsen name his whore "Diana" to make us question what has happened to the ideal of womanhood?

When Hardwick writes that Ibsen's heroines were created out of suspicion, she is wrong. "The old man" seems often to have known women better than they know themselves. When she revives the idea that Ibsen was not a feminist, one wonders what her motives are. Ibsen wanted to make it clear that he was an artist, not a politician, and his statements that he was not a socialist or a feminist must be taken in the context of a lifetime of work for both causes. Instead, Hardwick suggests that there was some misogynist motive behind Ibsen's destructive women.

Max Beerbohm explained this problem very well. He suggested that Ibsen was perhaps not a feminist in the strict sense of the word, but a poet of the human heart's longing for freedom. In Ibsen's experience it was middle-class women who embodied that desire most fully. So he took them as his subject. In our own time, somewhat the same struggle persists. In Meredith's terms (described above), it will take a great measure of psychological as well as political freedom to make the individual middle-class heroine's struggle obsolete because too individualistic. Ibsen explores the personalities of those women who hold back the freedom of others very well, the self-sacrificers and self-appointed "muses." There are fewer Theas about, but those meek girl graduate students do seem to inherit the earth. Thea found another "professor" to serve before Lovborg was cold in his grave. The future belongs to Tesman and Thea at the depressing end of the play.

There are fewer Beatas who kill themselves because of their barren-ness when it is their husbands who are impotent; there are fewer Beatas who fight with those weapons of passive aggression so well known to women throughout the centuries, the absolving letter that blames, the revenge after death. There are fewer frigid Mrs. Solnesses, clutching their childhood dolls, for whom marriage, childbirth, and death are only a long slow retreat from the promises of girlhood. But you can meet Hilda Wangel, with her knapsack and her mountain boots, in the street or in the classroom any day. She may not be a feminist, but she has no intention of ending up like Mrs. Solness. "Radiantly, unscrupulously, immorally sane," as William Archer said, she will drive her teachers to their deaths, to acts of heroism and creation that go beyond themselves—that is, unless she is given the education and training to build her own "castles in the air." Hilda is the stereotype of the "woman behind every great man" pushed to the extreme. She is Ibsen's attack on the social convention of woman as "inspiration" to the artist.

In *The Master Builder* we have a warning to men of genius to teach the next generation, not to rely on the young for new visions or potency (the climax is appropriately sexual, when Solness crowns the spire with a wreath and plunges to his death), but to provide them with the tools to make their own way in the world. *The Master Builder,* like many of Ibsen's plays, explores the male artist's need and guilt in using woman as muse for inspiration as well as the woman-as-object's intricate forms of revenge. Hilda is both angel and troll, virgin and witch. If this young artist finds no way open to her desire for power and freedom, she will find it in human relationships. She will be the siren, the muse who inspires but destroys.

The ghost of Rebecca West, radical, feminist, and "New Woman" is also still abroad. Like some nineteenth-century critics of Ibsen, Hardwick concentrates on the wronged wife, ignoring the havoc Beata's ignorance and innocence can wreak. For *Rosmersholm* is a play about how society controls its dissidents. Rebecca brings down reactionary Rosmersholm and all it stands for. But the liberals, not the radicals, benefit. It will certainly be easier for the liberals to take over the town once the purists of both right and left have been eliminated.

The revelation that Dr. West was Rebecca's real father is the climax of the play, and one need not consult Freud's brilliant essay (which Hardwick dismisses) to know that Rebecca's guilt about her sexual desires for Dr. West and her realization that her mother had been not only his servant but his mistress cause her downfall. She is Rosmer's servant and has helped to drive his wife insane. She confesses her sexual desires for Rosmer, her new father figure. But he retreats from her as he had from Beata's sexuality. Rosmer traps Rebecca's idealism and guilt in his demand that she match the self-sacrifice of Beata's love. Does she love him enough to die for him? Rebecca is converted to Rosmer's "higher love," and they go off to drown in the millrace. Whose is the victory? It is a lesson in social control. Radical idealists can be destroyed by guilt about their family and sex lives; the conscience is conservative. Think of all the young radicals following ascetic gurus. Yes, Rebecca is still with us.

Hardwick's essay on *A Doll's House* misinterprets the pivotal role of Mrs. Linde and revives the old "How could Nora leave her children?" complaint. Hardwick argues that Mrs. Linde is "dependent" and therefore cannot be the agent of "independent" Nora's liberation. But Mrs. Linde is one of Ibsen's self-sacrificing women who have changed. She now regrets the past and seeks her own happiness. She can help the dependent Nora, who is a secret self-sacrificer, to rid herself of her illusions. Hardwick says, "It drops a stain on our admiration of Nora.

Ibsen has put the leaving of her children on the same moral and emotional level as the leaving of her husband, and we cannot, in our hearts, assent to that." In the 1890s the critics were cruder, and several of them rewrote the ending. One classic of wish fulfillment had Nora return to find Torvald a drunkard, her daughter a prostitute, and her son an embezzler. Hardwick is more delicate, but just as judgmental.

For a woman in a play, Nora has caused an extraordinary century of trouble. When she slammed the door on that bulwark of patriarchal society, the middle-class family and motherhood, she aroused as much fury as if she had spat on the flag.

It seems to me that one of Ibsen's major themes is sisterhood. Nora can escape from the doll's house only with the help of her old Nanny and her childhood friend, Mrs. Linde. Hardwick has harsh words for Krogstad; she fails to see that the Krogstad-Mrs. Linde subplot functions as a Shakespearean one, as a foil to the main plot. Krogstad did exactly what Nora did; he forged to save his family. Ibsen wanted to show that the law applied only to men. Krogstad was punished. Torvald's fury was not based on fear that Nora would go to jail but on his "honor." What would have happened if the secret got out? All Christiania would have known that Mrs. Helmer had sacrificed for years to save her husband's life. As a member of the rising bourgeoisie, Helmer wanted an idle, beautiful wife as an object to remind his friends of his power, wealth, and masculinity.

In returning to Krogstad, whom she had truly loved, Mrs. Linde is recovering from the misery that self-sacrifice for her family has caused her. Nora takes courage from her friend's example. Nora has sat up at night for years, sewing to pay back the debt that saved her husband's life. She has twisted her whole personality to save his honor. She has not even the dignity of the traditional bowed head to bless her sacrifice, or Torvald's self-esteem would collapse. Those aching fingers must shake the tambourine as if their only experience has been pleasure. The body bent from "fancy work" must sway to the rhythm of the tarantella—Italian, erotic, and exotic. The "angel in the house" must dance to exorcise the devils in Helmer and his friends. Nora's dance has a witchery like a ritual of health but also, because of Helmer's schoolmasterish rehearsals, a *Red Shoes* mood of possession. She is a puppet on a string. And we are reminded of the history of women's dancing to please men in the harem. Her frivolity reflects the young banker's capital, her dance his sexual prowess. Neither gives him private pleasure; his excitement is derived from the jealousy of his friends.

As the action of the play moves from the sham reverence of a family Christmas (with Krogstad reminding Nora of debt) to the sham revelry of New Year's Eve (with Rank announcing his imminent death), both grim realities reach Nora through the letterbox, a miniature prison that is a model of the prison of her home. For all the joy, domestic and sexual, brought to this house by Nora is based on a lie. She has been acting one half of an ancient chivalric code of courtly love. But Helmer's character has been formed by capitalism; he is not her knight but her keeper. He will not lay down his life to protect her, and that is her ultimate humiliation.

The fuss over the children has obscured the issue of Nora's identity for long enough. Nora honestly believes that she is not a fit mother for Helmer's children. Since they are his "property," it would be useless to appeal to the law. Her old nanny will bring them up. There is as strong a bond between them as Nora has with Mrs. Linde. Nora's father had taken the nurse in to care for his motherless daughter when she was rejected by her own aristocratic family for refusing to reveal the identity of the lover who had brought her dishonor. In one sense Nora, Mrs. Linde, and the nurse represent a feudal morality that is being crushed by a capitalist one. Their hopes for an ideal love have been disappointed, but they have helped one another.

Since Hardwick's essays on Ibsen are written with such praise of self-sacrificing women and with such blame of destructive ones, her essay on Sylvia Plath is somehow bewildering. Plath's life and work are full of violence, self-destruction, hate, and anger. She is Hedda Gabler with a Smith College diploma. And yet Hardwick seems to admire her. She criticizes her for being too victorious a victim, un-feminine in the defiance of her poetic stance. It is not so much that the suicidal poet abandoned her children, though some blame is meted out for that; Plath's anger, "the destructive contempt for her family," upsets Hardwick. And yet, after praising Elizabeth Bishop and Marianne Moore, she expresses admiration for Plath as the abandoned wife of the poet, even if insufficiently stoical in her suffering.

Sylvia Plath made a gas chamber out of her own kitchen and became both victim and murderer, both the foot in the boot and the crushed Jews of "Daddy." Her suicide was an act of self-destruction, revenge, and, in an odd way, a "work of art" like Hedda's suicide. It and her life and the novel are inseparable from the poetry. *The Bell Jar* is so autobiographical a piece of fiction that one can hardly judge it by the rules of art or of life. Esther and her creator are so blurred that the reader is not sure what to think of an author who speaks through so self-pitying a narrator. Confessional whining in the novel makes one squirm.

Unable to accept Hardwick's view, I think *The Bell Jar* can be read only as a sociological document of the American fifties. The book is the female twin of *Goodbye, Columbus*. The reader, put off by the self-pitying and defensive tone in each case, cheers for Buddy and Brenda, bruised objects of artistic ego. It is, in fact, crucial that *The Bell Jar* opens with the execution of the Rosenbergs and later refers to Esther's shock treatment in terms of their gruesome deaths in the electric chair. The comparison is audacious, but Plath's capacity as a poet to enshrine private pain and suffering in terms appropriate to the suffering of millions appeals to that special audience which needs to feel that its private suffering is unique and colossal.

Students respond to Plath very personally. They often identify strongly with the angry victim-narrator in "Daddy." For some of the suffering young, the murder of six million Jews is exactly equal to the rage felt twenty years later at a father's death. Perhaps some archetypal experience has been articulated in the poem, for Plath has harnessed hatred, thrown a controlling net around the howling beast of rage. She has syncopated the howls, orchestrated the groans of self-destruction, revenge, and despair.

Surely one cannot demand that poetry be written by the happy and the good for the happy and the good. But one can signify one's response by the right name. I have heard Plath's poetry used for propaganda purposes. Robin Morgan whipped an audience into a frenzy of man-hating, ending by reading a poem of her own that exhorted the hearers to take revenge on Ted Hughes and save the children. The shame that I felt after this orgy of anger was based on the recognition of those emotions in myself. It is the living husband, the male poet, who intrigues Morgan as well as Hardwick, although in a different way. It is Plath's "daring," her boldness, that Hardwick admires. Plath, like Mary McCarthy, seems to have had enough "class and style" for Hardwick to admire her as a rebel. But Plath does not rebel for all of us. She offers no solutions except Hedda Gabler's. Gas ovens for mothers' daughters, guns for fathers' daughters; neither are weapons to help us make ourselves into our own women.

The hatred in the poetry is enhanced by the elegance of form, the strength of the line, irony, wit, and control (all qualities lacking in the novel). Can one allow oneself to participate in the celebration of death as revenge, to vocalize the violence of one's feelings on aesthetic grounds? No. The hatred of men is obscene. Like the fascism or the anti-Semitism of Yeats and Pound, it cannot be condoned on the grounds of the poet's style. Sylvia Plath was not a feminist; her novels and poems are not feminist. Her hatred of men was as real as Pound's hatred of Jews and must be opposed on the same grounds.

Beardsley's drawings are a case in point. The message is plain— hatred and fear of women. At the same time, elegance, wit, and extraordinary use of line and curve, expressive control of black and white spaces cannot be denied him. Beardsley had as good an eye as Plath's unerring ear. But absolute technical control is no excuse. One can admire the technique of a murderess, an artful suicide. One can even explain the act as ritual. In a way Sylvia Plath was and is a scapegoat for the anxieties and wishes of many people. But such poetry palls. In the end we weary of reading it, because we do not always wish to die. Children say in fits of angry self-destruction, "I'll be dead and you'll be sorry!" but they grow out of it. Plath is dead; we are sorry, but sorrow will not revive her.

Exaggeration of sex hatred is one of the qualities Plath shares with Beardsley. Literary historians will eventually see her poems as anticipatory to the new wave of feminism, as Beardsley's work was in the 1890s. One wonders if economic inflation has literary consequences. The proper use of the word *genocide* was recently debated in the columns of the *Times Literary Supplement,* with participants arguing over just which modern atrocities could equal Nazism. In Plath's case the images work inward to encourage private triumph over pain. Had she been a great poet, a great woman, the images would have worked outward, to explain the pain of all women.

Even so lovely a poem as "Nick and the Candlestick" ends with a frisson of horror. The mother's voice of despair and pain relieves itself with:

> You are the one
> Solid the spaces lean on, envious.
> You are the baby in the barn.

The outrageous comparison of the male child with Christ sums up brilliantly the delusions of our patriarchal culture. The lost lives of all the mothers who tried to find freedom in the lives of their sons is appallingly caught, hurled at us. "Your son may be the Messiah" are words that have imprisoned women, not liberated them.

Sylvia Plath was, let us not forget, an American poet. She wrote also as a woman and as a romantic, clothing death with negative excitement. Angst ruthlessly examines itself, exposes its wounds, calls on history's most wicked deeds as witness to the truth of her pain: "The blood jet is poetry, there is no stopping it."

One of Plath's special qualities, one that links her to the exiled writers of the twenties, is the ironic stance of the exile. She is as tough as Lauren Bacall in films or a feminine Humphrey Bogart. Brief, challenging messages, delivered straight from the shoulder, straight from the hip, mimic, mock, and simultaneously enshrine both English and American ordinary speech. The trained ear of the self-exile (imitating her father's exile in America), aware of and oversensitive to class and national distinction, captures and pins like a wriggling insect the language of the fifties. "Doing their blue dissolve" makes a noun out of a verb in the best Madison Avenue style; "Tate and Lyle . . . the refined snow" particularizes sugar, mocking a similar habit in British speech. "With holes where to hide" would never be said by an American. Like "not to worry," it is a construction of the ordinary Englishman that Plath's ear picks up. "Snazzy" is American slang from the forties given a new transatlantic life. She says of eyes, "they are no stool pigeons," and both English and American speech are exactly caught in

> With a goddam baby screaming off somewhere.
> There's always a bloody baby in the air.

She uses "cross" for angry, "glass" for mirror, "torch" for flashlight, "drawing pins" for tacks; the details catch the American reader unawares. How does the English reader respond to "blown your tubes" or "your cute decor"? The whole of "The Applicant" is interwoven with the American "backtalk" of a teenager trying out irony as a weapon against adults and the fast patter of a door-to-door salesman: "Come here, sweetie, out of the closet."

It is the ear for common speech that makes Plath a good poet. All her intelligence was spent on style. What the poems say, as the wife throws her "cloak of holes" like a net, flashes her smiles like hooks, is "don't abandon me." May the net and the hooks soon be in a mausoleum of memory of what a dependent woman's pain and anger were like, and Sylvia's Plath's name on the wall as its best recorder. Hardwick says, "There is no need to wonder whether her awful black brief was worth it," but there *is* a crying need to wonder, and to explain.

Hardwick's attack on Virginia Woolf is based on fear of Woolf's creative and critical power. In fact, the fear is so strong as to pretend not to recognize the power. "Nostalgia is the emotion most deeply felt in Virginia Woolf's novels," Hardwick writes (136). "Nostalgia is passive, the books are passive." Surely such a misstatement was not conceived in ignorance. To accuse Virginia Woolf of a fault that is unmistakably her own and utterly inconceivable as a critical response to Woolf, the least sentimental, most painfully objective, impersonal, and active of modern novelists, betrays a severe disability. The most "interesting" aspect of Virginia Woolf was her suicide note. Quentin Bell's biography and Leonard Woolf's were only sources in which Hardwick could satisfy her curiosity about the details of Virginia Woolf's mental breakdowns.

It is impossible here to deal with Hardwick's statement that Virginia Woolf's novels "aren't interesting," that they are circular and boring. It is a question of taste. Some people find *Ulysses* boring and circular and Woolf a source of endless delight. But some specific points can be dealt with. Miss Kilman is not "the object of the author's insolent loathing." She is seen entirely from the point of view of Clarissa Dalloway, who feels that "there but for fortune go I." Mrs. Dalloway, whose most intense feelings have been for other women, chose, against her instincts, to be the frigid wife of Richard. She is a little guilty. "I failed him once at Constantinople." But we see her rationalizations. She understands Miss Kilman's desire for her daughter, Elizabeth; she remembers Sally Seton's kiss. The fear and loathing are not the author's but the character's, at the recognition of her double, distanced by poverty and a superior education.

Hardwick may be right, I suspect, in her accusation of snobbery against James and Forster. But to link the writer of the "glass box" essay—the critic constantly concerned with "class in English fiction" who sought to quell her father's masculine and snobbish *Dictionary of National Biography*—with her own "Lives of the Obscure," is getting a little tiresome. It is time, however, for critics to read Virginia Woolf's novels and essays and to stop repeating the same old husbands' tales about Bloomsbury snobbery and "poetic" prose. The prose, in point of fact, is hard, concrete, and Anglo-Saxon. The intellectual position, clearly stated, is that of a committed and active socialist, pacifist, and feminist. "Exegesis about Virginia Woolf" is not "a trap." For readers of twentieth-century fiction who are concerned not only with stylistic experimentation but also with social history and the philosophy of art, reading Virginia Woolf is an education.

Hardwick's dismissal of Virginia Woolf as a snob, and the attack on the novels that claims that she despised the lower classes, deserve to be taken seriously and put into historical context. The *New York Review*-er is acting out the same role earlier played by F. R. Leavis' "Scrutineers" and by E. M. Forster in his famous denunciation of Woolf's attitude toward class.

Both Hardwick and the *New York Review,* Forster and *Scrutiny,* took that recognizable, morally self-righteous role of the liberal. Mrs. Leavis viciously attacked *Three Guineas, ad feminam,* not for its ideology, but because Woolf had no children and therefore no right to speak as a real woman. For Hardwick, Woolf's class background must disqualify her as a serious socialist. Woolf's fictional "ordinary people" are not nice. She does not romanticize or make heroic her working-class characters. That she was telling the truth as she saw it is irrelevant to the "liberal imagination." Such critics ferociously bark from the secure position of the liberal bandwagon that Woolf was morally and socially unenlightened because Miss Kilman's dirty mackintosh frightens Mrs. Dalloway.

But when the "liberal" critics cry "naughty, naughty" over the unsavoriness of Virginia Woolf's lower-class characters, they betray an utter failure to take into account her own standards of artistic honesty, not to mention the clearly radical political views stated in her essays.

Virginia Woolf wrestled her whole life with the problem, "What is the role of the intellectual in relation to the working class?"[7] Obviously, this is a question that serious socialists like Virginia Woolf took seriously then, and that serious socialists take seriously now. It is here that the liberal imagination boggles. It does not take these questions seriously and cannot understand anyone who does. (Miss Kilman is not nice; therefore Virginia Woolf was a snob.) For a radical visionary like Woolf, the solution to her artistic problem was to create a revolutionary form for the novel, since she felt that its content was determined by the limitations of its middle-class origins. She never failed to praise a novelist who could capture honestly the rhythms of working-class life. Woolf's essays on feminism, socialism, and pacifism, her lifelong work for the Working Women's Cooperative Guild, her encouragement of working women's writing, can stand by themselves as arguments for the passion of her commitment to political causes.

But she despised the reformer's temperament, the middle-class preacher in fiction or in politics who went as missionary to the masses to solve their problems for them. Because she respected her common reader she would neither lecture in her fiction nor hold her sharp tongue in her polemics. She made enemies then and, obviously, she still makes them.

It is sad to see a practicing woman critic rejecting the best in her heritage. Virginia Woolf remarked in *A Room of One's Own* that "we think back through our mothers." Through her essays on women writers and women in fiction, her analysis of feminine style, and her demand for a new feminine historical and critical consciousness and new female forms of writing, Woolf left us an example of how to be a literary critic, and a woman. The trouble with Hardwick is that she takes no risks; she seldom says where she stands, whether she is for or against an issue. Ethics is excluded from her definition of criticism. Reading Virginia Woolf, one is always sure that the feminism is socialist, that the socialism is feminist, and that the high standards of literary criticism do not exclude readers or writers because of class or fashion. It is all clearly explained. Hardwick wants us to infer from the company she keeps (*The New York Review of Books*) that she has liberal views, while abjuring the responsibility of stating them. In the June 12, 1975, issue she writes of Vietnam, "I feel some hesitation about a final statement. One's adjectival vehemence has been used up." She who hesitates is lost—as a critic of culture at any rate. While the vehemence of one's adjectives may not be a sure measure of the passion of one's commitment to truth and justice, one may still make clear, even in the gentlest of words, where one stands.

Hardwick is thinking back through the wrong mothers, the seduced and betrayed, the victims and the self-haters. But it is not too late. Her essay on Woolf ends with belated praise of "a great mind working" in Virginia Woolf's novels. Perhaps she could learn to think of this "great mind" as the mother of her own.[8]

READING PRACTICE II
†††††

The Socialist Critic
Reads Virginia Woolf

Thinking Back through Our Mothers

The Collective Sublime

Writing, for Virginia Woolf, was a revolutionary act. Her alienation from British patriarchal culture and its capitalist and imperialist forms and values was so intense that she was filled with terror and determination as she wrote. A guerrilla fighter in a Victorian skirt, she trembled with fear as she prepared her attacks, her raids on the enemy. She was so hostile to the patriarchy and felt that her anger was so present in all her efforts that no evidence of literary "success" was assurance enough of acceptance, and she collapsed after sending her books to the printer. She always feared she would be found out, that the punishment of the fathers for daring to trespass on their territory was "instant dismemberment by wild horses," as she told Ethel Smyth.[1] The violence of men's imagined retaliation was in direct proportion to the violence of her hatred for their values. Like Kafka she felt that writing was a conspiracy against the state, an act of aggression against the powerful, the willful breaking of the treaty of silence the oppressed had made with their masters to ensure survival. Language and culture belonged to *them*; to wrest it from them was an act requiring the utmost courage and daring. If language was the private property of the patriarchs, to "trespass" on it was an act of usurpation. To see herself as untying the mother tongue, freeing language from bondage to the fathers and returning it to women and the working classes, was also to cause herself acute anxiety about what *they* would do when they found out. By writing she committed a crime against the fathers, and she expected, like her beloved Antigone, to be buried alive for it. As Antigone's defiance of Creon was not simply that of the individual against the state, or a woman against men, but the assertion of old matriarchal forms against a new male legalistic and revengeful culture, so Virginia Woolf's rebellion sought not only the overthrow of male culture but also a return to the oppressed of their rightful heritage and the historical conditions in which to enjoy it. No wonder she was afraid.

When she published "A Society," in which she dared to suggest that a sisterhood of philosophical inquiry might be as necessary to women as male secret societies or brotherhoods to men, Desmond MacCarthy, as "Affable Hawk," showed his claws. She never reprinted the sketch, in which her characters decided that a way must be found for men to bear children to occupy themselves in a useful way and to prevent them from obstructing women's progress toward intellectual freedom. She answered him.

> Can he point to a single one of the great geniuses of history who has sprung from a people stinted of education and held in subjection, as for example the Irish or the Jews? It seems to me indisputable that the conditions which make it possible for a Shakespeare to exist are that he shall have had predecessors in his art, shall make one of a group where art is freely discussed and practiced, and shall himself have the utmost freedom of action and experience. Perhaps in Lesbos, but never since, have these conditions been the lot of women.[2]

Virginia Woolf's position as "daughter of an educated man," a self-styled "outsider in British society," may be likened to the position of the Jewish intellectual in Weimar Germany.[3] While the Holocaust provides historical evidence that Kafka and Walter Benjamin were not neurotic in their perception of the hatred of the Germans, British male violence against women took less murderous forms. Nevertheless, Woolf's *feelings* about women's oppression match those of her German Jewish contemporaries. Even as they felt that as Jews they were administering the intellectual property of a people who denied them the right to do so, Virginia Woolf felt as a woman literary critic that she stood in the same untenable position in relation to British culture. Rationally they could prove that hatred of them as Jews or as women was unfounded. In neither case could that lessen the sting of real and genuine contempt. Kafka regarded words as stolen property; he strove for perfection in prose style in German, as Woolf did in English, to lessen the anxiety of being found out. The products of bourgeois families, they saw the enemy within as well as without in those who pretended that Jews or women were not the hated objects of society's contempt. For the Jews the way out lay in Zionism and communism. For Virginia Woolf it was feminism and socialism.

Walter Benjamin kept notebooks full of quotations; tearing statements out of context, he felt like a robber making attacks on history. Virginia Woolf did the same thing, as the notebooks for *Three Guineas* and *The Pargiters* show us. By quotation she sought to rob history of its power over women. The quotations she used in *A Room of One's Own, Three Guineas,* and *The Pargiters,* the scholarly footnotes in which documentation is a form of possession of the truth and exorcism of evil, are the intellectual pacifist outsider's only weapons against lies and injustice. Like Bernard in the *The Waves* or the eccentric Samuel Butler, the Jewish or female notebook-keepers could, by collecting facts and insults, rob them of their power to hurt. "All notebook literature," she wrote in "Mr. Kipling's Notebook," "produces the same effect of fatigue and obstacle, as if there dropped across the path of the mind some block of alien matter which must be removed or assimilated before one can go on with the true process of reading. The more vivid the note the greater the obstruction." It was with this consciousness of creating an obstacle course for the reader that she used the technique herself. When Virginia Woolf wrote essays on women writers or collected material for her projected *Lives of the Obscure,* part of the excitement lay in her role as raider on received history. She could see herself as a redeemer of lost lives, and she described with rapture the feeling of rescuing stranded ghosts, as their "deliverer." Finding *The Mysteries of Udolpho* much better than she had been led to believe, she declared that she would lead "a Radcliffe relief party." The artist of the oppressed articulates the desire for deliverance of the stranded ghosts of her ancestresses throughout history. She seems hardly to have lived among her contemporaries but to speak directly to the future, to our generation. Leonard Woolf described his wife's peculiar walk, how people stared at her; it is the same as Hannah Arendt's description of Walter Benjamin's—a mixture of advancing and tarrying, one foot in the past and one in the future. The "incandescent death" which Bertrand Russell found alight in her novels derives from what Lukács called "transcendental homelessness" in the modern novelist and from her identity as spokeswoman for the outsiders. She was a redemptress of time, saying to her contemporaries in *Between the Acts,* with Kafka, "There is an infinite amount of hope, but not for us."

When Clive Bell compared his sister-in-law's style (in living and writing) to Constantin Guys, the Parisian painter and flaneur, he claimed a worldliness and cosmopolitanism which few others have recognized in Virginia Woolf. But a female flaneur is almost a contradiction in terms. For a woman who walks the streets of a big city aflame with curiosity can only be a streetwalker, a prostitute. A self-defined "street-haunter," Virginia Woolf knew all the awkwardness of these contradictions. While Benjamin was haunted by all the Berlin streets from which class and race prohibited him, Woolf was inhibited both by sex and by class from following her nose or her eyes wherever they longed to go. She knew not only the fright which followed Rose's experience of the pervert exposing himself on the corner of her own street in *The Years* but also the humiliating crippling of the imagination which forces Rose to give up thinking of herself as the brave, adventuring Pargiter of Pargiter's Horse. Each excursion was dangerous and debilitating, an antipatriarchal act, a storming of the citadel of male dominance. Whether the men were would-be attackers or would-be protectors, they impeded women's halting progress through the streets. And women whose interest was in maintaining the status quo were the first to stare and point at the eccentric whose relaxed insistence on being her natural self in the street violated all the taboos by which one can always distinguish a lady from a tramp. Caring so little for class distinction signified, ironically, a lack of sexual discrimination in a person so fundamentally pure.

Imagining herself a woman warrior, Virginia Woolf stormed the city of London (as she "stormed" the texts of classical male culture with her Greek teacher, Janet Case). London was simultaneously the citadel of her suffering and the space of her joy. So she enshrined it in memory, while mocking its monuments to patriarchy, imperialism, and capitalism. In her London novels, *Night and Day, Mrs. Dalloway, Jacob's Room, The Waves,* and *The Years,* as well as in her essays, all the temples to great men are desecrated and denounced: St. Paul's, Harley Street, Big Ben and the House of Parliament, the British Museum and Westminster Abbey. She felt the pulse of London all the more powerfully because she was an "outsider." As Walter Benjamin had recorded a bourgeois Jewish childhood in Berlin, she recorded a ghetto which pretended it was paradise before its members disappeared into the diaspora. Benjamin has captured a whole culture in *Paris: The Capital of the Nineteenth Century.* But Virginia Woolf has memorialized a *London: The Capital of the Patriarchy.* Her own battles for psychic and physical space in that all-male territory which restricted middle-class women to the private house are recorded in *A Room of One's Own.* The woman artist's need for privacy is there declaimed not as a retreat, but rather as a place to put on her armor for her assaults on the public world. When one is both a radical and a feminist, one must build a counterworld to that of both the fathers and the mothers. And, while she was at it, Virginia Woolf also built in her fiction a spiritual protest to the self-righteous ethics of her family.

Virginia Woolf, like Walter Benjamin, was both a "Marxist" and a mystic. It has been far easier for critics to chase the "rainbow" in her style than to knock their heads against the "granite." When forced to recognize the pervasive feminism, they have diagnosed it as a social disease which breaks out in ugly spots, branding her as a bitter ingrate. Will she ever be greeted with the sum of her attributes rather than with the partial acclaim which must exclude the content from the form or the radical message from the luminous matter? Can we see her as a scholar, a fantasist, a historian and a practical joker, a recluse and a flaneur, a poet and a propagandist, a mystical dreamer and a hardworking journalist? If she could read Proust for the social criticism as well as the poetry, we can learn to read her in the same way. Like Walter Benjamin she reads the things of the real world, the objects and spaces luminous in her own memory, both as sacred texts and as productions of dialectical historical forces.

For both of these refugees from bourgeois reality, dwellers in the diaspora of dreams, memory is the mother of muses. And she demands that, if you dig deep enough (for Benjamin she embodies the archaeologist digging the layers of Troy, while for Woolf she is the fisherwoman letting down her line into the depths of the unconscious) you can draw out of the individual memory the "illuminations" or "moments of being" which allow the artist to touch the collective memory. By her spiritual geography in the mapping of places and monuments, time is defeated by space and the remembrance of rooms and rhythms and objects (like her mother's chair in "A Sketch of the Past"). Remembrance, as in Proust, is a triumph over time, the building of a "continuing city." Recall the moment in *Mrs. Dalloway* when the airplane flies over Greenwich—an intersection of time and space. But here is no hallowed image of time the reaper. Instead, a solitary man rolling the lawn observes the scene. As in Marvell's "Mower against Time," time has been the sower of discord and war, and is demolished and rolled flat. Big Ben in her novels, particularly *Mrs. Dalloway* and *The Years,* is a great masculine bully, dominating the lives of the citizens.

Like Benjamin, Woolf works topographically against the patriarchal and genealogical imperative, the strength of whose dicta we see in her own remembrance of the inability to step over a puddle (and Rhoda's in *The Waves*). It is with fear and trembling that one crosses the thresholds of street space strictly forbidden by the fathers. In mapping the diaspora the writer takes on an enormous task, the book's last gesture of defiance before the loudspeaker and the film drown out the human voice. In both writers a fierce Marxist desire for social change is matched by visionary myths and symbols for order and community. The pacifist's passion for a violent cleansing is only just held in check. The reader trembles in conspiracy with the writer of *Three Guineas.* Will the patriarchs (pictured like police posters of the enemies of society) leap off the page en masse and imprison us, who have identified them as the real fascists? Woolf's concept of the collective sublime was Greek, operatic, Brechtian, an anti-authoritarian rational and mystical answer to individualistic, romantic, and personal traditions of European thought and action. If we see her with Benjamin and Proust, Brecht and Kafka, rather than with Forster and Lawrence, we are doing the right topographical job as critics. With the right maps we may find our way in the city of her novels.

Fascism is what they feared. Both Woolf and Benjamin chose suicide rather than exile before its tyranny. It seems oddly coincidental that they were both tormented by the same dream figure, the little hunchback of German fairy tales, the crippled figure which appears in so many of Woolf's novels. "We are Jews," she described herself and Leonard—meaning they were outsiders, oppressed critics of oppression. *Three Guineas* was the pacifist's last stand against fascism, whose origins were to be found in the family and private poverty. Women and the working classes were not responsible; let the capitalists and imperialists fight it out. In the meantime women and their working-class brothers ought to "trespass" on the private property of language and literature, educate themselves in anticapitalist colleges, and assert their own collective values. This view infuriated her own generation. Its ethical purity appeals to ours, little as we live up to it.

While she lived and wrote and battled against the fathers, she sought relief from anxiety about these attacks in the imagination of a linked history of literary and political mothers. (Her childhood, she told Ethel Smyth, was dominated and depressed by 'those 68 black books,' her father's *Dictionary of National Biography*: her *Lives of the Obscure* would slay the patriarchal ghost.) "Thinking back through our mothers," a necessary act for all women writers, would afford one maternal protection for one's own raids on the patriarchy and simultaneously raise female consciousness. For finding our mothers is no easy task (Woolf was particularly tormented about the gap between Sappho and Jane Austen). She expected that women artists would become feminists through this experience and also that they would make common cause with other oppressed groups. She herself found Joseph Wright, who wrote the *English Dialect Dictionary*, to be a brother; the witty Sydney Smith so "lovable" a man that she wished she could have married him.

All her life, Woolf sought "protection" from living women as well as from historical mothers. "What you give me is protection," she wrote to Ethel Smyth.

> I look up at you and think if Ethel can be so downright + plainspoken . . . I need not fear instant dismemberment by wild horses. It is the child crying for the nurse's hand in the dark—you do it by being so uninhibited—so magnificently unselfconscious. This is what people pay £20 a sitting to get from Psychoanalysts —liberation from their own egotism.

Woolf knew by experience how women influence each other. Far from Harold Bloom's concept of the "anxiety of influence," it is rather the opposite, affording the woman writer relief from anxiety, acting as a hideout in history where she can lick her wounds between attacks on the patriarchy. Anxious Virginia Woolf was indeed, but not out of the need to appease her ancestresses or outdo her mothers. She did desire to surpass her sister contemporaries, but laughed at Katherine Mansfield, calling her the new Jane Austen. Her own portrait of Jane is in fact a self-portrait set a century before ("She, too, in her modest, everyday prose, chose the dangerous art where one slip means death"), and *Mrs. Dalloway* is not even a new *Clarissa* except in so far as English fiction demands that chastity is woman's character.

When Virginia Woolf wrote that "we think back through our mothers," she had, as usual, a triple point to make, since her roles as artist, feminist and socialist were subtly intertwined in what she called "the triple ply," and her literary criticism is always a braided narrative with three strands of thought. She meant here, I think, to assert that fiction had long been female territory, but, more than that, that each generation of women writers influences each other, that style evolves historically and is determined by class and sex. She expected her literary "daughters" to take up where she left off; they would not be so discreet about sex, and they would not have "the shoddy fetters of class on [their] feet." "For masterpieces are not single and solitary births," she wrote in *A Room of One's Own*, still using her maternal metaphor, "they are the outcome of many years of thinking in common, of thinking by the body of the people, so that the experience of the mass is behind the single voice."[4] And her letters always maintain to her critics that if the Edwardians had been better writers, the Georgians would have been better still.

Was she trying to establish a female "canon" of great works by women as an alternative to male critical authority? I think not. She saw herself as a link in a long line of women writers; she knew just where her own work fitted and what heritage she was leaving for the women writers who would come after her. She wrote to Ethel Smyth of her

> ecstasy at your defence of me as a very ugly writer—which is what I am—but an honest one, driven like a gasping whale to the surface in a snort—such is the effort and anguish to me of finding a phrase—and then they say I write beautifully! How could I write beautifully when I am always trying to say something that has not been said, + should be said for the first time, exactly. So I relinquish beauty, leave it as a legacy for the next generation.[5]

It is interesting that Woolf characterizes women's protection as liberation from the ego. For the ego is the enemy; even in herself, where she fought fiercely to control it, she saw the ego as male, aggressive, and domineering. In the psychic triangle of mother, father, child, it was an attempt to eliminate the father. In Freudian terms, she sought to fuse the id and the superego—in *her* artistic terms, granite and rainbow—leaving the mental, the personal, out altogether. The "damned egotistical self" must be repressed, and one can even see in Marxist terms that her worship of solid objects and their spiritual reality is a fusion of sub- and superstructure, avoiding as much as possible the middle term of patriarchal society as it exists. What some readers have seen as her incapacity to create character is not an incapacity at all, but a feminist attack on the ego as male false consciousness. She will not supply us with characters with whom we may egotistically identify. This would be weakness on her part, encouragement of self-indulgence on the part of the reader. She disarms us.

We are forced to lay down our weapons as readers. All our egotism and individuality, the swords and shields of the hated "I, I, I" must be abandoned outside the doors of her fiction. Not only do her novels advance a collective idea of character, but the common reader is stripped of his individual relationship to author and text. We are to see ourselves as part of a collective audience, as in Brecht's epic theater, linked to readers of the past and future as the writer is engaged in building the structure of "literature" as a historical effort. In "How It Strikes a Contemporary" she urges us to see "writers as if they were engaged upon some vast building . . . being built by common effort. . . . Let them scan the horizon; see the past in relation to the future; and so prepare the way for masterpieces to come." (T. S. Eliot uses a similar idea in "Tradition and the Individual Talent" to enforce reactionary patriarchal ideas.)

The final apotheosis of this anti-individual "philosophy" is expressed in *Moments of Being*:

> We—I mean all human beings—are connected with this; that the whole world is a work of art, that we are parts of the work of art. *Hamlet* or a Beethoven quartet is the truth about this vast mass that we call the world. But there is no Shakespeare, there is no Beethoven; certainly and emphatically there is no God; we are the words; we are the music; we are the thing itself.

This is the final victory over the ego, the utter identification of art with human struggle, as Marx and Engels defined history as "*nothing but* the activity of man pursuing his aims." The rapture which the writer feels on perception of the collective unity of art and life in history is extraordinary. As a philosophy of art, it revives the romantic idea of literary progress while eliminating the idea of artists as a priesthood of men of genius. While the poet is still for her the legislator of morality, his authority is derived not from his individual talent but from his expression of collective consciousness. The "egotistical sublime" of the patriarchy has been replaced by a democratic feminist "collective sublime."

Her model is the opera house—Bayreuth, to be specific. Her 1909 visit had filled her with the desire to make fiction aspire to the condition of Wagner's opera: a unity of the audience and the natural world with the words and music, the nearest approach to the sublime she had experienced. It was epic theater for ordinary people, an aspiration fulfilled in *The Years* and *Between the Acts*. As in Brecht (whose essay on epic theater she may have read in Desmond MacCarthy's *Life and Letters* in 1936), there is no Aristotelian catharsis, no empathy with the stirring fate of the hero. We are educated to be astonished at the circumstances in which the characters function, and dramatic moments are caused by interruptions of daily life. The reason for the "plotlessness" of Woolf's novels is that they reverberate to the rhythm of the common life, not of the individual life. She could say with Proust, what is the plot of Ecclesiastes or the *Divine Comedy?* She wants to close the gap, to fill in the abyss which separates the players from the audience, art from life. In an age in which fascism and socialism fought for the allegiance of the masses, she sought to hold history, art, and the people in the embrace of a giant "we."

We are to play the role of the chorus in a Greek play: we share her risk—"how dangerous this poetry, this lapse from the particular to the general must of necessity be"; "the intolerable restrictions of the drama could be loosened" by the comments of the chorus, "the undifferentiated voices who sing like birds in the pauses of the wind" to capture "those ecstasies, those wild and apparently irrelevant utterances"[6] which characterize her novels from *Jacob's Room* onward. Participating in the collective sublime of Woolf's narrative voice, we share her dangerous mission, become co-conspirators against culture. In redeeming our own past we become our own redeemers.

Redemption and Resurrection

Virginia Woolf first learned to say "we" as a woman. It was not so much a liberation from her own ego, as she explained to Ethel Smyth, as a liberation from the loneliness of individual anxiety. Thinking back through her mothers gave her her first collective identity and strengthened her creative ability. Her whole career was an exercise in the elimination of the ego from fiction in author, characters, and readers. It was the expansion of the word *we* in a world of women writers past and future which grew eventually to speak for all the alienated and oppressed, as Mary Datchet's feminism expands in *Night and Day* to international socialism.

Virginia Woolf's "mothers" and aunts and women friends brought her into being as a writer, encouraging her efforts, publishing her work in the *Guardian* (a church weekly.)[7] In this circle of female friendship the members collected the letters and diaries of their mothers and aunts, wrote their biographies, shared faded photos and anecdotes of ancestresses. The first lives of the obscure which attracted Virginia Woolf's romantic vision of herself as "deliverer" were women's. She would untie their tongues—"the divine relief of communication will soon again be theirs." Her essays provide an example and a methodology for feminist critics and biographers, extending the literary and political rescue and redemption to obscure and working-class men (such as Joseph Wright) and to "the eccentrics." "Sometimes, though it happens far too seldom, lives have been written of these singular men and women, as, after they are dead, someone half-shamefacedly has put together their papers." Coming to their rescue she found them

> often so dishevelled, in such *dishabille* from their long obscurity and fantastic behavior that we are not certain of remembering even their names. Without names and so strangely inspired, leaving behind them now one line, now one word, and now nothing at all, what whim is it that bids us go seeking them round the corners and just beneath the horizons of so many good books devoted to good men? Surely the world has been right in conferring biographies where biographies are due? Surely the shower of titles and honours has not always descended on the wrong heads? That the world's estimate has been perverse from the start, and half her great men geese, are themes too vast to be disposed of in one short article.[8]

If our mothers provide us with protection, camouflage, and courage, the duties of daughters include not only redemption of their lives and

works but resurrection as well. In the "heart of the woman's republic"—
a place Virginia Woolf felt had a reality in the company of Margaret
Llewelyn Davies and her companion Lillian Harris, Janet Case, her
Greek teacher, and her sister Emphie—the lives of women would be
brought to light and life. In the women's republic all our sainted
mothers are present only by our efforts in raising them from obscurity
and reprinting their works.[9]

What Virginia Woolf sought in her intense personal and artistic
relationships with women may best be explained in mythological
rather than psychological terms. The work of the great classical scholar
Jane Harrison had a powerful influence on Virginia Woolf's imagery
and metaphors.[10] Harrison's work on mothers and daughters in preclassical Greece, her study of the transition of the powerful myths of
mother-goddess worship into patriarchal Greek thought as we know
it, was very important to Virginia Woolf's writing and thinking. The
"Hymn to Demeter" and the story of Persephone were especially
moving for a writer who always thought of herself as a "motherless
daughter." It may help us to understand what she meant by "thinking
back through our mothers." She sought in her friendships with women
both freedom and protection. The Demeter-Persephone myth affirms
eternal refuge and redemption as well as resurrection. The mother will
never abandon her daughter. She will weep and wail and search the
underworld, bring her out of the darkness of sexual experience,
childbirth, madness, back into the world of light and freedom. She
will restore her virginity.

Woolf's mother died just as her daughter reached puberty, linking
sexuality and death forever in her mind. Marrying, she added a note
of savagery to the chastity of her name and self-image. In "A Sketch
of the Past" she recalled the intense pleasure she felt when her mother
praised a story she had written: "It was like being a violin and being
played upon." Her mother's praise unleashed all the dormant creative
forces within her, untied her tongue, gave her freedom and speech.
Did she relive the experience when her women friends approved her
manuscripts? "It is true," she wrote to Ethel Smyth in 1930, "that I
only want to show off to women. Women alone stir my imagination."

She sought out people who remembered her mother, cherishing Elizabeth Robins' description of Julia Stephen as "half madonna, half woman of the world." She and her friends discussed their mothers. Early in her relationship with Ethel Smyth she wrote, "Yes, I think your mother adorable. So was mine." "Odd as it may seem to you," Ethel Smyth wrote on May 2, 1930, "I did love you before I saw you, wholly and solely because of *A Room of One's Own.*"[11] Woolf's feelings confirm Smyth's theory that

> with me and I think many women the root of love is in the imaginative part of one—its violence, its tenderness, its hunger . . . the most violent feeling I am conscious of is . . . [her ellipses] for my mother. She died thirty-eight years ago and I never can think of her without a stab of real passion; amusement, tenderness, pity, admiration are in it and pain that I can't tell her how I love her (but I think she knows). Now you can imagine how much sexual feeling has to do with an emotion for one's mother!

(About as much sexual feeling as Woolf dramatizes in Lily Briscoe's love for Mrs. Ramsay, one imagines.)

There is a poignant irony in the situation, given the real Julia Stephen's actual opposition to women's emancipation. She signed the ardent antisuffragist Mrs. Humphry Ward's petition in the *Nineteenth Century,* joining the ranks of middle-class mothers who were the worst foes of women's freedom in the eyes of radical feminists from Mary Wollstonecraft to Olive Schreiner, George Meredith to Virginia Woolf. Meredith mocked his friend, " 'Enough for me that my Leslie should vote, should think.' Beautiful posture of the Britannic wife! But the world is a moving one and will pass her by." Julia Stephen remained his "stout Angel," but he never ceased to criticize her for playing the reactionary role of "princess to a patriarch." For he knew that it was the daughters of such mothers who suffered, and he asked to see the children before their father had convinced Thoby that he was superior to his sisters, and before Julia had insisted that they accept the role of inferiors. "Courage is proper to women," he told her, "if it is properly trained." Meredith was having a difficult pregnancy with his great feminist novel *Diana of the Crossways* as she was bringing to birth her daughter Virginia. The feminist novelist wrote to the mother of his successor as feminist novelist, worried mother to worried mother. But Julia Stephen had no sympathy whatever with Diana, the fictional motherless daughter who wants both a political and an artistic career.[12]

Virginia Woolf kept her mother's copy of *Diana of the Crossways*, inscribed by Meredith, "An Emma might this Julia have been,/To love at least forgive, the heroine."[13] She did not live to love or forgive her own Diana-like daughter. And other women—Margaret Llewelyn Davies, Madge Vaughan, Violet Dickinson, Vita Sackville-West, Ethel Smyth—were able and willing to play the role of Emma. The most important relationship in Meredith's novel is between Diana and her friend Emma. The two intellectual women belong to the "sisterhood of sensibility." They play the roles of mother and daughter and of lovers to each other. In an extraordinary scene which makes "George Verimyth" worthy of his nickname and echoes with the power of the Demeter and Persephone myth, Emma brings Diana back to life by feeding her from the same spoon and sleeping with her. Diana's suicide attempt was to starve herself to death. Emma brings her back to life and into marriage with a "radical," warning her in the end of the dangers of childbirth and the terrors of the journey.

Life, of course, often imitates fiction, but seldom as accurately as Virginia Woolf lived the life of her fictional stepsister, Diana. As we know from the *Letters,* her relationship with Violet Dickinson exactly paralleled that of Diana and Emma, even down to the details of Violet nurturing the postsuicidal Virginia back to life after her disappointing sexual experiences with a man. Diana's "betrayal" of the Corn Law repeal as an antipatriarchal act is like Virginia Woolf's involvement in the Dreadnought hoax.

Violet Dickinson's wedding gift of a cradle to Virginia Woolf seems explicable in the same terms. After an apprenticeship (both literary and human) as daughter, then as lover, the young woman is sent into the world of men by the childless older woman to become a mother and an artist. But, as Persephone comes back to the woman's world of sunlight and freedom for half the year, so the daughter fears separation but hopes for protection. Their shared ideal is an ideal of freedom, and freedom is symbolized by virginity. The fear of marriage (in fiction and in life) is the fear of loss of freedom with loss of virginity. Maternal love makes one both chaste and free. In Woolf's female utopia written for Violet Dickinson (in the Berg collection), freedom is the theme in a world much like Carroll Smith-Rosenberg's "female world of love and ritual." Liberty is eroticized by the idea of the power of maternal love to redeem and rescue the daughter, who can enter the male world but return for rebirth into light and freedom, back in her mother's arms, a virgin.

Woolf sought from many "mothers," including her husband, maternal protection from her own suicidal impulses. The letters, early and late, refer to the "ethical" aspects of suicide. She demands from her sister Vanessa, and from Ethel Smyth, philosophical arguments on the ethics of suicide. That Leonard agreed to a suicide pact in case of Nazi invasion was enough "maternal" approval for her to sink herself forever in mother water.

She had demanded to know how her friends wrote, painted, composed music, thought—and she shared with them her own deepest analysis of writing. She also flirted outrageously, courted affection and then withdrew, wanting love letters more than love scenes, for words to her had as much potency as acts to other people. She explained that words, like women artists, need privacy. "Why?" she asked in *A Writer's Diary,* and answered herself, "for their embraces, to continue the race." In "Craftsmanship" she claimed, "Our unconsciousness is their privacy; our darkness is their light." Words, she wrote, "are much less bound by ceremony and convention than we are. Royal words mate with commoners. English words marry Irish words, German words, Indian words, Negro words, if they have a fancy. Indeed, the less we enquire into the past of our dear Mother English the better it will be for that lady's reputation. For she has gone a-roving, a-roving." Language can mean liberation, Woolf believed, and her image here of Mother English as promiscuous is another of those forays against patriarchal culture. Not only has she changed the sex of language and culture; she has robbed them of respectability.

In "Royalty" she wrote of Queen Victoria,

> between the old Queen and the English language lay an abyss
> which no depth of passion and no strength of character could
> cross. . . . When she feels strongly and tries to say so, it is like
> hearing an old savage beating with a wooden spoon on a
> drum. . . . But probably she owed much of her prestige to her
> inability to express herself. The majority of her subjects, knowing
> her through her writing, came to feel that only a woman immune
> from the usual frailties and passions of human nature could
> write as Queen Victoria wrote. It added to her royalty.

Here she has completely turned the tables of history: the Queen is a savage because she misuses language; commoners who can express themselves are the real aristocracy of culture. The woman who was the symbol of an age's repression of women, symbolic of their loss of freedom in politics and art, is reduced to a stone-age caricature, a primitive animal. "We begin to wish that the Zoo should be abolished; that the royal animals should be given the run of some wider pasturage—a royal Whipsnade." Then she attacks: "Words are dangerous things let us remember. A republic might be brought into being by a poem." Certainly she believed that the "woman's republic" might be brought into being by the extension of the literary franchise to "the feminine sentence"—that is, as she wrote in the original "Professions for Women," if men could be educated to stand free speech in women.

The fertile and promiscuous mother tongue is the first mother we think back through in Virginia Woolf's theory of how collective history and the collective unconscious collaborate in the female artist's mind. In "English Prose" she has robbed culture not only of its male origins but also of its princely pretensions, for she sees prose as Cinderella, occupied with "menial tasks." "She has to do all the work of the house; to make the beds, dust the china, boil the kettle, sweep the floors." And in *The Years* she has accomplished the final revolution, the creation of the artist as charwoman to the world. This is a startling concept and as radical as the New York playwright who makes God a Puerto Rican janitor. In "Men and Women" she wrote, "For the first time for many ages the bent figure with the knobbed hands and the bleared eyes, who, in spite of the poets, is the true figure of woman-hood, rose from her wash-tub, took a stroll out of doors, and went into the factory. That was the first painful step on the way to freedom," but "it will not be in this generation or the next that she will have adjusted her position or given a clear account of her powers." She quotes Bathsheba in *Far from the Madding Crowd* on having the feelings of a woman but "only the language of men" in which to express them. "From that dilemma," wrote Woolf,

> arise infinite confusions and complications. Energy has been liberated, but into what form is it to flow? To try the accepted forms, to discard the unfit, to create others which are more fitting, is a task that must be accomplished before there is freedom or achievement. Further, it is well to remember that woman was not created for the first time in the year 1860. A large part of her energy is already fully employed and highly developed. To pour such surplus energy as there may be into new forms without wasting a drop is a difficult problem which can only be solved by the simultaneous evolution and emancipation of man.

Each of her novels is an experiment in the evolution of these new forms; they are to be forms "appropriate," as she says in another essay, to women; the role of the chorus and of the reader as collaborator grows greater and greater. The gap is bridged as the prose imitates music more than speech, and the form of fiction dissolves in epic operatic theater for ordinary people. The woman artist has evolved from anonymity through egotism and female identity back to anonymity. She wrote to Ethel Smyth in 1933,

> I didn't write "A Room" without considerable feeling even you will admit; I'm not cool on the subject. And I forced myself to keep my own figure fictitious, legendary. If I had said, "Look here, I am uneducated because my brothers used all the family funds"—which is the fact—"Well," they'd have said, "she has an axe to grind"; and no one would have taken me seriously,

though I agree I should have had many more of the wrong kind
of reader, who will read you + go away + rejoice in the personalities, not because they are lively and easy reading; but
because they prove once more how vain, how personal, so they
will say, rubbing their hands with glee, women always are; I
can hear them as I write.[14]

While she herself was pushing the literary she-condition further
and further towards the objective universal condition, she nevertheless
valued very highly women writers who told the truth about their
feelings. In February 1940, Woolf wrote to Ethel Smyth:

> I was thinking the other night that there's never been a woman's
> autobiography. Nothing to compare with Rousseau. Chastity and
> modesty I suppose has been the reason. Now why shouldn't you
> be not only the first woman to write an opera, but equally the
> first to tell the truth about herself? But the great artist is the
> only person to tell the truth. I should like an analysis of your
> sex life as Rousseau did his. More introspection. More intimacy.

Ethel Smyth had written in her diary that after meeting Virginia Woolf
in 1930 she thought of little else for eighteen months. "I think this
proves what I have always held—that for many women, anyhow for
me, passion is independent of the sex machine."

I have written elsewhere of the important influence in Virginia
Woolf's life of two contemporary "mothers," Margaret Llewelyn Davies
and Ethel Smyth.[15] Here let me suggest that the social worker and
the musician embodied the dual characteristics which fascinated her
in her own mother. One might see Margaret Llewelyn Davies as the
Mrs. Ramsay who goes off to visit the sick and worries about how
sanitary the milk is and Ethel Smyth as the Mrs. Ramsay who gives
a glorious dinner and draws people together. Woolf once told her friend
that she had given a party as classical as Jane Austen's Box Hill party
and tried to describe its effect (July 1930). She had mastered "the
difficulty of keeping one's atmosphere unbroken . . . rolling and war-
bling from melody to melody like some divine quartet, no, octet. I
say, Ethel, what a party! What a triumph."

Remembering her mother in "A Sketch of the Past" she uses the same musical imagery. Julia Stephen brought people together, made life musical and whole. Leslie Stephen was deaf to music, interrupted and destroyed the family harmony.

The first raiders on the patriarchy have untied the mother tongue and come back with words. Then we must have music, and that too is marked "female" and associated with the harmony and rhythm of daily life with her mother, before the interruptions of the aggressive male ego of her father. She wrote to Ethel Smyth, "Writing is nothing but putting words on the backs of rhythm. If they fall off the rhythm, one's done." Earlier she had written to Vita Sackville-West, "Style is a very simple matter; it is all rhythm. Once you get that, you can't use the wrong words," In "Professions for Women" words are fish caught by letting down one's line in the collective unconscious of mother water. The rhythm then rides the back of that dolphin of *The Waves,* whose fin shows above the waste of waters. All this activity of the artist is "dangerous"; "one slip" means death for Jane Austen, "instant dismemberment by wild horses" for herself. It is as if the generations of women artists are marching single file across the "narrow bridge of art," crossing the "abyss" or "chasm," as she called the male mind, "to find a sentence that could hold its own against the male flood." The path has been cleared by "some mute inglorious Ethel Smyth," for men have always obstructed the way. (Woolf wrote that a history of male opposition to women's emancipation might be more interesting than the story of women's struggle.) Of the fact that it was a battlefield, she had no doubt.

With all the violence of her pacifist conviction she described Ethel Smyth's work for women artists:

> She is of the race of the pioneers: She is among the ice-breakers, the window-smashers, the indomitable and irresistible armoured tanks who climbed the rough ground; went first; drew the enemy's fire; and left a pathway for those who came after her. I never knew whether to be angry that such heroic pertinacity was called for, or glad that it had the chance of showing itself.[16]

Ethel Smyth, who only wanted to write symphonies, was forced into being "a blaster of rocks and the maker of bridges," and in literature "I owe a great deal to some mute and inglorious Ethel Smyth." "All that we have ought to be expressed—mind and body—a process of incredible difficulty and danger." It is indeed "dangerous" to say, as she said, "I detest the masculine point of view," but it is worse to compromise one's moral feminism, as in her fight with Bruce Richmond of the *Times Literary Supplement.* She wanted to describe Henry James's fiction as "lewd"; it was not allowed to criticize "poor, dear Henry James."

But the full force of Woolf's violence in this speech/essay is reserved for her description of the murder of the "Angel in the House," who is throttled and bombarded by inkpots. This creature is the ladylike self, the pride of Victorian parents, that prevents the artist from telling the truth. Despite the romantic tone of her memories of her mother, Woolf dared in *To the Lighthouse* to express her ambivalence as well as her love. That indeed is one source of the novel's greatness. For Mrs. Ramsay demands that all women be angels, and as readers we lay at her door the deaths of a son in battle and of a daughter in childbirth, for she has demanded that men and women play their Victorian roles. Not only is Lily freed for art at her death, but Mr. Ramsay has an identity crisis in old age and grows up. Thus James can identify with him and come to manhood, and Cam can vaguely fish in imaginative streams. While Julia Stephen is not the angel in any neat equation, the psychic difficulties of coming to terms with one's own mother in personal as well as historical ways is given dramatic form by Virginia Woolf.

Are we then to murder in our minds our own mothers (and all the messages they gave us about how to live in the patriarchal world) in order to think back through the mothers of literature and history? Is mental matricide necessary for the woman artist? No, Woolf tells us. Abandoned, motherless daughters must find new mothers, real and historical, a linked chain of sisterhood over past time in present space, and rescue and redeem their own mothers' lives from their compromises with the patriarchy. She set us a good example, Persephone who rescues herself from the underworld, forgiving and understanding why Demeter died.

The Irresistible Armored Tank

In her 1931 speech to professional women, Virginia Woolf followed Ethel Smyth onto the platform, publicly giving her praise in Dame Ethel's presence. (She had also praised Margaret Llewelyn Davies at a Working Women's Cooperative Guild meeting.) After attending her concerts Woolf had always wanted to meet Ethel Smyth, and had praised her memoirs in print as well as arguing with "Affable Hawk" in *The Nation* that there were few such women composers not because of "intellectual inferiority," but because men refused to train women except to sing and play for men's amusement. Their meeting and their intense relationship was very important for Virginia Woolf as an artist, for she had worked all her life to give her fiction musical form and operatic structure. To be loved by the great composer of English opera was a trying but thrilling experience. *The Waves* owes some of its beauty to the intensity of its author's relationship with the composer, and Ethel Smyth's memoir, *As Time Went On,* is dedicated to Virginia Woolf. Finishing *The Waves* while writing "Professions for Women," Woolf wrote that "the mind bobs like a cork on the sea" and imagines Ethel (who had tried conducting) "waving your hand over that chaos." *The Prison,* which Ethel was composing at the same time as *The Waves,* is set to a poem by Henry Brewster on Plotinus' lines about individual death as merging with the universal sublime—surely a source for Bernard's brave and beautiful challenge.

Virginia told Ethel that her own speech was "clotted up and clogged," that she would not print it as it stood, but it might make "a small book, about the size of A Room." "Your speech, meanwhile, was divine and entirely expressive," she praised Ethel. "Leonard says about the best of its kind he ever heard, and done, he says, with supreme skill, which I interpret to mean that you liquidated your whole personality in speaking and threw in something never yet written by being yourself there in the flesh—anyhow we must print your speech, by itself entire."

Hogarth Press did not publish Dame Ethel's speech, but she published several amusing lectures on women and music in *Female Pipings in Eden.*[17] Chapter 4, "The Difficulties of Women Musicians," must have been at least part of her speech because it contains a funny story about the Working Golf Course which Vera Brittain reported in her column in *The Nation* (January 31, 1931, p. 571).

Dame Ethel begins with the legend of Eve "picking out a tune" in a hollow reed in which she has bored holes. Adam tells her to stop that horrible noise and, "if anyone's going to make it, it's not you but me." She is tired of being asked the same question for the millionth time, and her answer is "There are no great women composers for the same reason there are no female Nelsons . . . it is absolutely impossible in this country for a woman composer to get and to keep her head above water; to go on from strength to strength, and develop such powers as she may possess." Nowadays Adam silences the hollow reed with cotton wool and the music dies down. Dame Ethel explains the determination with which men have kept women out of orchestras and confined them to singing in choruses and teaching children their scales. "I burned with curiosity as to whither woman's wings will carry her once she is free to soar. . . . Few deny that the Brontës and Jane Austen brought a new note into our literature. Why then should not our musical contribution be equally individual and pregnant?" She describes her slow process of infiltration into the second violins only to find the taboos against women enforced again after the war—"a metamorphosis such as we read of in V. Sackville-West's *Orlando* took place [Woolf pointed out the error, but Ethel let it stand] only the other way around. By degrees these female back-benchers turned into men and as in the "Orlando" business it seemed impossible to learn how and when and why the change had come about." Men's "vicarious sense of modesty" has kept women from playing the cello but allowed her to play the "unlucrative" harp, cherishing her "white-armed presence in their midst, much as the men in the Welch regiment cherish the regimental goat." Not a single woman alive has had the musical training necessary to compose, so it is no surprise that "no advancing army of eminent women composers is to be described on the horizon."

Ethel Smyth then contrasts literary and musical careers, agreeing with Virginia Woolf that since Jane Austen's time women have been allowed to write "on the sly." It is not expensive, there is only a publisher between a writer and her public, and she stands in no one else's way. But musical engraving is very costly; conductors add little to the standard repertory and less that is controversial because of the composer's sex or difficulty. In an Appendix Dame Ethel lists sixteen performances of her important choral works in England in forty years, despite rave reviews from isolated critics, such as Shaw's for her Mass in 1892, when he prophesied the conquest of musical composition by women. As did Virginia Woolf in her speech, Ethel Smyth cautions against "natural bitterness" and for patience. She tells the story of the fourteenth hole at Cromer Golf Course falling into the North Sea. Several generations of committees had seen the erosion but wanted it to remain a purely seaside links, and so they waited a century to lay out new holes. A man disapproved of Amy Johnson's flight over Africa.

> "Well," I said, "speaking for myself, at any age [she was in her seventies] I would willingly risk all that happened to that lady, and worse, rather than have men settling for me what I might and might not do! If one came to grief among these savages it would be a bit of bad luck, but to be deprived of one's freedom would be a bit of bad luck that would go on all the time!"

She tells how disappointed she was to read that Albert Einstein was opposed to women in science. "Are then even the greatest men half-witted?" she asked herself, on the subject of women. She wrote to inquire, and he replied denying that he had said such things and insisting on women's right to participate in "all branches of intellectual endeavour." She says, "Surely there are enough rocks, papyri, flowers, insects, stars and corpses to go round?"

Man will not "*see* a woman's work until the psychological moment has arrived" and "the male eye has been broken in"; "that is, as eventually happened in literature, prejudice has been broken down, twig after twig." Like Virginia Woolf, Ethel Smyth believed that the development of genius takes generations of moderate exercise:

> you cannot get giants like Mont Blanc and Mt. Everest without the mass of moderate-sized mountains on whose shoulders they

stand. It is the upbuilding of this platform that is impossible so long as full musical life is denied to women, and I suppose it is unnecessary to say that conductors and Committees are generally of one mind about keeping us out of Parnassus. . . . We know what "Candide" said about the duty of cultivating your garden; but what if the authorities keep all the agricultural instruments under lock and key?

Like Woolf, she could go on composing because of a small independent income and the money she earned by writing memoirs. This was the only way to eternal fame for a composer whose operas were not staged, as it has been for women painters whose pictures were not hung, and for actresses before film and tape could record their gestures and voices. Their memoirs sometimes save them from total oblivion.

"So far," Ethel Smyth wrote in the 1930s, "admission to the house of music on equal terms with men is unthinkable for a composer of my sex." But taboos can be broken "though a future chain of great women composers may seem as improbable even today as the arrival in the channel of a battleship full of incipient female Nelsons." She complained that it was nonsense to insist on all-male orchestras in the interests of "unity of style"; "Art is bi-sexual." Keeping women out is like Nazi propaganda about racial superiority "bullying the Jews," she argues here (though her private letters contain anti-Semitic remarks about Leonard Woolf).

The situation for women in music has been so bad for so long that some women have accepted male values in order to survive. All good voice teachers are women, she asserts, but to get ahead the woman student may ask for a singing master: "I hope she gets a bad one and that he ruins her voice!" Once women have "slipped the slave's collar" they will show "mental independence" and "directness." The directness she illustrates with a story of the substitution in Spain of cows for bulls in the ring, unsuccessful because the cows paid no attention to the red flags but went straight for the toreadors and killed them all. She urges her audience to form local branches of the *SPCWM*, the Society for the Prevention of Cruelty to Women Musicians. "That men have been on top of the wave since time was, whereas we are still fighting our way upwards from the bottom of the sea, is a fact that will surely set an eternal stamp on our destiny as does the difference of sex."

She wants women to be original and say with James Fitzjames Stephen exactly what they think and feel:

> perhaps it lies at the bottom of the sea, where we are at home; and perhaps our fate, not an ignoble one, is to bring it up to the surface . . . non-creative women, listening to the song of their sisters, be it literature, painting, or music, will say: "O what is this that knows the way I came?" . . . then would my girl student pause a moment, contemplate her half-finished serenade for eight harps, eight trumpets, ten trombones, twelve percussion instruments, and two dozen explosive bombs, and murmur: "But this is imitative rubbish," tear up her MS. and throw it into the wastepaper basket.

The peroration of the speech Virginia and Leonard Woolf admired so much is worth quoting in full, for, despite its unfortunate title, *Female Pipings in Eden* does for women in music what Virginia Woolf did for women in literature; it gives women artists a myth of their own creative origins and urges them to struggle for possession of the past in order to forge the future. Ethel Smyth's Eve is the mother of music:

> Let her once more take up her hollow reed and start afresh. And if Adam should again awake and bid her stop that horrible noise, Eve need not be rude. Let her merely say *dolce senza expressione:* "My dear Adam, if you don't admire my tunes I don't always admire yours. But don't threaten as you once did to make this particular horrible noise yourself, for it's my own composition and I hold the copyright. Besides which you couldn't make it yourself it you tried. Some other tune, yes. But not this." . . .

> Ah me! if Act I Scene I of the human drama had only been more carefully thought out, what happy days might have been spent in Eden! No hunting poor Eve into the marsh; no ramming

cotton wool up the little reed she had fashioned for her own
fingers! She and Adam would each have constructed a sound-
proof hut in different corners of the garden (as far apart as
possible), and towards evening they would have been heard
piping peaceful pastorals in two parts, later on taking it in turns
to conduct the family orchestra . . . if from the very first Eve
had been granted a chance of self-development, there would
have been no furtive hanging about the Tree of Knowledge, no
illicit truce with serpents and apples, and of course—this would
have been rather sad—no Militant Suffragettes.

There were thirty years between Dame Ethel and Virginia Woolf,
great differences in temperament and political ideas. Ethel Smyth (who
appears as Rose in *The Years* and contributes to Miss Latrobe in
Between the Acts) was as thoroughly British as Virginia Woolf was
internationalist. She was as fiercely militant, patriotic, and egotistical
as Woolf was pacifist, socialist, and "anonymous." Yet on the question
of women and art their answers and actions formed a united feminist
front. Ethel Smyth drove a tank across the narrow bridge of art; danger
and struggle were her element, and her music reaches sublime heights
after ferocious skirmishes in the field. Virginia Woolf was a sniper in
the ranks of women writers, leading the unknown female foot soldiers
across less difficult territory.

While the composer was in the position of Jane Austen with a gap
unfilled by those necessary "second rankers" between her and the
Greeks, the novelist claimed many good mothers. Conscious of being
women warriors, they were struggling toward a "woman's republic"
in art in which their daughters would be free. The word, the sentence,
the appropriate female form would be found; the serenade for explosive
bombs would go off, and all the flutes, cleared of cotton wool, could
play any tune they wished. But the battles are not all won; some
daughters are still skirmishing on the bridge, and some men still need
education in tolerating free speech in women. It is still "dangerous"
for a woman to say what she really thinks and feels, but we are
almost over the abyss and we can see the other side. Because of
women like Virginia Woolf and Ethel Smyth, we know our own voices

when we hear them; they sing in Ethel Smyth's and Virginia Woolf's choruses, and the "we" expands to include others whose tongues have been tied, whose flutes have been silenced. The "heart of the woman's republic" will be reached by thinking back through our mothers. As Woolf wrote to Ethel Smyth in 1930 while writing *The Waves,* "though the rhythmical is more natural to me than the narrative, it is completely opposed to the tradition of fiction and I am casting about all the time for some rope to throw the reader." Catch.

5

"No More Horses"
Virginia Woolf on Art and Propaganda

"If we use art to propagate political opinions," wrote Virginia Woolf in *Three Guineas,* "we must force the artist to clip and cabin his gift to do us a cheap and passing service. Literature will suffer the same mutilation that the mule has suffered; and there will be no more horses."[1]

If art is a splendid and noble horse and propaganda a baser beast of burden, a donkey, their coupling is implied in sexual terms but also in class terms. The mule which is produced is a stubborn creature, and sterile to boot, with the dash and daring of one parent and the patience and persistence of the other. When propaganda propagates with art as its partner, Woolf warned in 1938 (after England had seen almost a decade of political poetry, painting, and prose), then artists may degenerate into mute, brute mules. The gentle brays of the donkeys, the high whinnies of the horses will be lost to history.

The argument is, I think, historical. Woolf means that if the artist sacrifices his freedom for the momentary historical cause, he will be doing a disservice to the past and future history of art. Once "indifference," "disinterestedness," "impersonality," those qualities she valued so highly, are given up, then art loses its fertility.

Worried as she was over the health of poetry and its younger practitioners in the thirties, one wonders how she would have felt about Auden's later change of heart, his praise of Yeats, his assertion that "poetry makes nothing happen." And what do we think now of the poetry of Auden and his fellows in the anti-fascist thirties? Was their collective voice mulish? Woolf objected to the "enterprising book-fed brains" of the young poets, and to their "uni-sexual bodies," and she captures the 1930s poet's egotism brilliantly in his appearance at the last party in *The Years.*

But Virginia Woolf was no more certain of what the proper relations between art and propaganda should be than she was ready to dictate what exact proportions of "truth of fact" and "truth of fiction" would make a good biography. A case in point occurs in the note I have just quoted. *Three Guineas* is itself an extremely polemical work, and the point in the note comes as an afterthought about a rather interesting propagandistic act. Woolf has been comparing Mrs. Pankhurst, leader of the English suffragette movement, to Antigone. She goes on to apply the comparison to Frau Pommer, the wife of a Prussian mines official at Essen who was to be tried (it was 1938) for the act of slandering the state and the Nazi movement by saying, "The thorn of hatred has been driven deep enough into the people by the religious conflicts, and it is high time that the men of today disappeared" (*TG*, p. 169). Virginia Woolf argues here that *Antigone* could be made "into anti-Fascist propaganda," that Creon, tyrant and patriarch, resembles Hitler and Mussolini—even though Sophocles in the end is such a great artist that he makes us sympathize "even with Creon himself." The plot and the "buried alive" theme of *Antigone* form the mythology and structure of *The Years,* and as a *novelist* Woolf makes her reader sympathize with her English Creons. It is only as a "pamphleteer" that she chooses between good and evil.

Why does she then describe the coupling of art and propaganda as "mutilation," having just done rather a good job of coupling them in her own note and in *Three Guineas* as a whole? Perhaps there are good mules and bad mules, some less mutilated than others? We know that Woolf believed that women and the working class would produce great works of art when their historical identity and continuity were once accomplished, and that several generations of women and workers had laid claims to their own history and their own literature. She also believed that each individual work of art was the product of collective historical consciousness, that the writing of women and workers would improve through the ages. "For masterpieces are not single and solitary births," she wrote in *A Room of One's Own* (68–69), "they are the outcome of many years of thinking in common, of thinking by the body of the people, so that the experience of the mass is behind the single voice." She was by no means uncritical of the individual artist, nonetheless, and felt that any woman writer would have difficulty "flying" free, with the "shoddy fetters of class on her feet" as well as the socially determined limitations on any open discussion of sexuality. Working-class writers, she felt, had an unfortunate habit of imitating the mincing speech of the middle class rather than celebrating the traditional rich vitality of their own culture.

The mule who stops the fertile flow of literary history is suspiciously like the "middlebrow," neither upper class nor working class, who writes and teaches for money and fame. The mule is suspiciously like the "uni-sexual" and egoistical young poets who take up "the masses" as a cause in poems which their subjects cannot read, ignoring what Woolf felt was their real mission, to persuade men of their *own* class to give up their privileges.

That Virginia Woolf used her own art for propagandistic purposes is a fact. *Three Guineas* is a socialist, pacifist, and feminist polemic. Perhaps she felt that, because her cause was just and her point of view unheard in the daily press, the book did not fall into her own category. Or perhaps that Fascism had already had such a pernicious effect on art and artists that she was justified in producing another mule for her side (since she did very vociferously take sides), hoping that a few well-placed kicks from its sterile body would serve the cause of political justice and intellectual freedom.

In "Middlebrow"[2] Woolf defined the highbrow as "the man or woman of thoroughbred intelligence who rides his mind at a gallop across country in pursuit of an idea," and a lowbrow as "a man or woman of thoroughbred vitality who rides his body in pursuit of a living at a gallop across life." As for middlebrows, they are not capable of riding at all, and the sight of them on horseback is ridiculous. Horses represent both art and sexuality, but the middlebrow is a prostitute in both areas: "How can you let the middlebrows teach *you* how to write?" she asks the lowbrows, "you, who write so beautifully when you write naturally, that I would give both my hands to write as you do—for which reason I never attempt it, but do my best to learn the art of writing as a highbrow should." "What will become of us," Woolf asked, her mind mating class conflicts with artistic conflicts, "men and women, if Middlebrow has his way with us, and there is only a middle sex but no husbands or wives?" The androgyny she approves is in the artist's mind, not his body. High and lowbrow horses obviously can stomp out the middlebrow, for in the last line of the essay, he is reduced to a "half-crushed worm."

The figure of the horse and the mule continued to work in Virginia Woolf's mind as she wrote *Three Guineas,* her great book on woman as the scapegoat of history. She described in her diary two kinds of writing, "donkey-work" and "galloping," as earlier she had described "stonebreaking" and "flying"; writing was to her always divided into two categories, one of hard work and one of speed and release. "After a most dismal hacking got into a little canter," she wrote in February 1937, and later, "Once I get into the canter over *Three Guineas* I think I shall see only the flash of the white rails and pound along to the goal."[3] "I've been having a good gallop at *Three Guineas*" (267). "So now I'm straining to draw that cart across the rough ground . . . one always harnesses oneself by instinct" (268). "Oh how violently I have been galloping through these mornings! It [the book] has pressed and spurted out of me" (276).

It is interesting that Virginia Woolf imaginatively divides herself into artist and pamphleteer, horse and donkey (in a new metaphor for the androgynous mind of the artist), yet at the same time criticizes the union of art and propaganda, even in *Three Guineas* itself, for sterile progeny. In the course of composition she noted that we really need two separate languages, one for fact and one for fiction, for words, like artists, need privacy. "Why?" she asked, and answered herself in sexual terms: "For their embraces, to continue the race" (*AWD,* p. 268). But in *Three Guineas* she urges not the fertility of language but the purging of obsolete words like "feminism," which is dramatically burned in her book. And she wishes for the day when words like "tyrant" and "dictator" may also be purged from the language.

"Feminism," by the way, is obsolete because the only freedom and equality that matter, the economic, have been achieved. (This was rather premature and optimistic.) Quentin Bell asserts that Virginia

Woolf was "amazed" at his "socialist" analysis of the world crisis as economic. Now it is true that Virginia Woolf was not in the habit of using the rhetoric of vulgar Marxists. But any reader of her political essays and pamphlets knows full well that the weight of the argument always rests on economics. Women's oppression is economic, she argues in A Room of One's Own, and art is determined by the class origins of the artist, she argues in "The Niece of an Earl." Art is part of the superstructure, she maintains in "The Artist and Politics"; its flourishing and failure depend most certainly on the economic and political conditions of the state. All through her own writings she identified herself as artist and worker, and defined the necessity of the artist's involvement in politics (not to write at the dictates of the politician but to be politically active to ensure personal survival and that of art). "Art is the first luxury to be discarded in times of stress; the artist is the first of the workers to suffer."[4] "The rose and the apple have no political views," she states in the same essay. But the artist who contemplates them must be both economically and politically free to work. She does not call for political bias in the work of art but in the artist. This essay was written for the *Daily Worker* in order to explain why artists in the thirties were forming political organizations. Just as Leonard Woolf (in an impulse of whitewash?) forgot to tell the reader the essay's source when he compiled the *Collected Essays,* the editors of the *Daily Worker* had been anxious to tell their readers that they did not agree with her views.

Virginia Woolf was truly an outsider, for this is a complex position she expounds, although her lack of rhetoric makes her sound uncommitted. She took her leftist politics very seriously. She was very upset by the criticism of her politics by Wyndham Lewis, a serious rightist, but not in the least upset by the scurrilous personal attack of Queenie Leavis on *Three Guineas* in *Scrutiny.* For she realized that the "scrutineers," as she called them, had no serious political ideas at all and did not understand hers.

Modern readers have been led to believe that Virginia Woolf's acute sex and class consciousness derived from a Victorian virginal and "ladylike" misunderstanding of politics (Leavis, Forster, Bell) or, more recently, were part of her "madness." But Woolf's socialism and feminism were very much a response to nineteenth- and twentieth-century experience. It was the *timing* of her publication of polemical views that disturbed the critics. What was the use of being a feminist after women had the vote, they asked in 1929? What was the point of being a pacifist in the face of Hitler and Mussolini, they asked in 1939? Woolf had a particularly acute sense of history and an internationalist distrust of local patriotism; these large ideological attitudes produced her self-definition as "outsider." She had seen the suffragettes under Emmeline Pankhurst and her daughter Christabel turned into warmongers overnight. She knew that one could be female and fascist, despite the contradictions. She knew that the vote had not been "won" by women after more than fifty years of agitation but had been granted, along with full manhood suffrage, when the government could no longer deny the claims of returning soldiers and sailors. Ever since the 1832 Reform Bill had first deprived women of what citizens' rights they had, women had fought bits and pieces of battles with patchwork ideologies to fit local and particular fights. Virginia Woolf, like her heroine Mary Datchet, flew her feminist and pacifist colors under the banner of international socialism. Only Wollstonecraft, Olive Schreiner, and Sylvia Pankhurst, as her literary feminist forebears, held such clear and consistent convictions.

The timing of the publication of *A Room of One's Own* is a case in point. In 1928 women could vote, and feminism was unfashionable. In that essay Virginia Woolf braced herself against what Rebecca West called "an invisible literary wind."[5] West called the book "an uncompromising piece of feminist propaganda," "the ablest yet written," and remarked on the courage which "defied a prevalent fashion among the intelligentsia, which is particularly marked in the case of her admirers." The argument is inflexible and "all the more courageous because antifeminism is so strikingly the fashion of the day among intellectuals," she explained. "Before the war conditions were different. The man in the street was antifeminist, but the writers of quality were pro-suffrage." She explained the change as "due to the rising tide of effeminacy which has been so noticeable since the war. The men who despised us for our specifically female organs chastised us with whips; but those to whom they are a matter for envy chastise us with scorpions." West saw Woolf's honesty to be as remarkable as her sensibility, because she was willing to risk losing by expressing her politics to those who most admired her art.

"It is a fact," Woolf explained, "that the practice of art, far from making the artist out of touch with his kind, rather increases his sensibility. It breeds in him a feeling for the passions and needs of mankind in the mass which the citizen whose duty it is to work for a particular country or a particular party has no time and perhaps no need to cultivate" (*Essays*, 3:231–32). The artist is a worker; as such he must defend his position economically and politically. But his product, which is limited enough by his class and determined by his origins, must be consciously free from the desire to preach and teach. As she told the young poets, "then you become a biting and scratching little animal whose work is not of the slightest value or importance to anybody" (*Essays*, 3:184).

I think the complexity of this carefully worked out theory about art and politics was a little difficult for some her critics to follow. Much to the annoyance of Quentin Bell, and, one thinks, Leonard Woolf, she defended her pacifist position in 1936, allying herself with Aldous Huxley, even though her husband—and most active socialists—were forming a united front against fascism.

"But were we then to scuttle," protested Bell, "like frightened spinsters before the Fascist thugs?" He tried to account for her advocacy of peace, when for him the only thinkable stand was for war, by arguing that she was out of touch. "She belonged, inescapably, to the Victorian world of Empire, Class and Privilege. Her gift was for the pursuit of shadows, for the ghostly whispers of the mind and for Pythian incomprehensibility, when what was needed was the swift and lucid phrase that could reach the ears of unemployed working men or Trades Union Officials."[6]

Quentin Bell seems to have felt that while he was trying to do something "urgent, vital and important," his aunt was only interested in gossip. She happened in truth to have spent some of her formative years teaching working men at Morley College; she knew them well enough to be aware that they could write their own manifestos—furthermore that they despised meddling missionaries. She had led meetings of her local branch of the Women's Co-operative Guild for years and was, at the time Mr. Bell wanted to pass his "United Front" resolution, secretary of the Rodmell Labour Party—scarcely a shadowy voice of Empire and Privilege. Did he quite fail to realize that her "gossip" was something hardly to be dismissed as feminine silliness—that it might have been a conscious political maneuver by a committed pacifist?

The pacifism of *Three Guineas* is probably the most difficult position for modern readers to accept, even for those who appreciate the socialism, feminism, and antifascism of the essay. The origins of her abhorrence of violence, I suspect, can be found in the ethics of her ancestors, in the Clapham Sect and her Quaker aunt. Christopher Caudwell saw pacifism as the strongest of the liberal bourgeois illusions because it pretends that violence is an ethical rather than a political problem and thus allows the pacifist to avoid the idea of the revolutionary attack on private property.[7] Woolf knew that wars were fought essentially over property, but she could not quite bring herself to urge women and workers to any violence stronger than that of "trespassing" on the property of patriarchal culture.

Were Bell's allusions to sex and class intentionally diversionary? "Spinster" and "Victorian" make her not only older than she was and more upper class, but frigid. When Quentin Bell disapproves of his aunt's politics, he attacks her womanhood and her birth. Virginia Woolf may have been more sexually serious and active, more politically serious and active, than any nephew can ever conceive in his aunt.

Bell could not accept the connection between feminism and antifascism in *Three Guineas*. He wanted a simple description of what should be done: "True criticism of *Three Guineas* came from events; for the events of 1938 did not turn upon the Rights of Women but upon the Rights of Nations" (Bell, *Biography*, 2:205). Quentin Bell, I think, disliked the antipatriotic tone of *Three Guineas*, its international outsider's stance. Virginia Woolf did, of course, offer a course of action: fight English tyranny and chauvinism at home.

But it was to "daughters of educated men," women of her own
class and profession that she addressed the pamphlet. Hence its title.
Only luxuries are sold in guineas; the words and the coin have a ring
of obsolescence and gentility whose effect is carefully calculated; the
reader thinks the writer can afford the "luxury" of antipatriotic views.
(Who would read a book entitled *Three Pounds*?) Her "Outsiders'
Society" would "consist of educated men's daughters working in their
own class—how indeed can they work in any other?—and by their
own methods for liberty, equality and peace" (*TG*, p. 106), because
"as a woman, I have no country. As a woman I want no country. As
a woman my country is the whole world" (109). These women are
to reform themselves first:

> The glamour of the working class and the emotional relief af-
> forded by adopting its cause, are today as irresistible to the
> middle class as the glamour of the aristocracy was twenty years
> ago (see *A La Recherche du Temps Perdu*). Meanwhile it would
> be interesting to know what the trueborn working man or woman
> thinks of the playboys and playgirls of the educated class who
> adopt the working-class cause without sacrificing middle-class
> capital, or sharing working-class experience. [177]

Woolf directs her reader to Margaret Llewelyn Davies' *Life As We
Have Known It* and to *The Life of Joseph Wright* for firsthand accounts
of working-class life not seen through "pro-proletarian spectacles."
Readers objected then and still object to the exclusiveness of her
audience, but Woolf's logic is inescapable. "Our ideology is so inveter-
ately anthropocentric," she asserted, "that it has been necessary to
coin this clumsy term—educated man's daughter. . . . Obviously, if
the term 'bourgeois' fits her brother, it is grossly incorrect to use it of
one who differs so profoundly in the two prime characteristics of the
bourgeoisie—capital and environment" (146).

The revolutionary artist is revolutionary in form, wrote Christopher
Caudwell. We are by now well aware of Virginia Woolf's formal rebel-
lions in the shape and design of her novels. Her political works can

be considered even more revolutionary by these same standards because they are radical in both form and content.

"Oh it pleased me," she wrote in her diary after *Three Guineas* was published, "that the *Lit. Sup.* says I'm the most brilliant pamphleteer in England" (*AWD,* p. 284). It may well be argued that *A Room of One's Own* and *Three Guineas* are in the first rank of English literature in their mode. The Milton of *Areopagitica* and the Swift of *A Modest Proposal* were her models, and her essays rank with theirs as passionate polemic enhanced by innovative technical genius. *A Room of One's Own* argues that women artists need time, money, and privacy, as well as an establishment of alternate female institutions of power, in order to produce great works of art. The analysis combines Marxist economics with Freudian psychological insights and Wollstonecraft's revolutionary feminism. What marks the essay as a work of genius, aside from the avoidance of the rhetoric of her distinguished forebears, is a fictional narrative technique which demands open sisterhood as the stance of the reader. This technique not only puts the male reader on guard and makes him feel "other," alien; it reminds him quite forcibly how "other," how alien, women must feel while reading most of literature. The female reader, while she delights in being so directly addressed, realizes how often she has been excluded and alienated. The conversational intimacy of the tone, the invented narrator and fictional characters, the sharing of specific insults and pleasures, and the sharpness of the intellectual assault on patriarchal institutions, are audacious in their breaking of the formal conditions of the essay.

Although we read *Three Guineas* for what it says, its extraordinary use of form assures its place on the shelf of English literature in the satiric mode. The stance of "daughter of an educated man" responding by letter to requests for donations to Good Causes is itself a radical reflection of women's powerlessness. The writing of letters had been, after all, the approved and often the only means of expression for middle-class women. That Woolf should choose the epistolary mode almost two centuries after *Clarissa* was a matter of deliberate strategy. Her anger and hostility at the exclusiveness of male institutions are all the more effective because "cabin'd and cribb'd" in limited and limiting letters. Like prison journals and letters read while we know the author is in jail, they serve their cause not only by what they say but by their very form.

In its original edition *Three Guineas* included several photographs of men in patriarchal garb. Beribboned, bemedaled, begowned, and bewigged, they exhibit the author's sharp eye for how the powerful assert their power. The message is very clear, as clear as the photograph of white men leering at the hanging bodies of blacks with which the South African feminist Olive Schreiner introduced her brilliant anti–Boer War pamphlet, *Trooper Peter Halkett*. Women, as Woolf noted, have a good eye for the obvious.

"I strike the eye," she wrote in 1920, after the publication of *Night and Day,* "and elderly gentlemen in particular get annoyed" *(AWD,* p. 25). *Three Guineas'* antifascist theme is derived from photographs of dead children and ruined houses in Spain. What is the connection she was trying to make? She refers several times to these photographs of fascist atrocities, but the photographs before us as readers are of men in their garb of power. We are meant to put the patriarchal horse before the fascist cart. It is a very clever device.

Although Woolf's nearest literary ancestor is Swift, given the difference in political attitudes she might prefer to be compared to Swift's spiritual heir on the opposing side, the witty Sydney Smith. In April 1940, she wrote to the composer Dame Ethel Smyth, "I'm reading Sydney Smith—his life—with only one wish in the world: that I'd married him. Isn't it odd when the rumble tumble of time turns up some entirely loveable man?"[8] Sydney Smith's causes were the emancipation of slaves and of Catholics, but he preached them with humor, wit, and style and with a lack of that egotistic patronizing tone, the smug holier-than-thou Puritanism, which Virginia Woolf felt characterized reformers of her own and Victorian times. Smith's gay, elegant eighteenth-century detachment, so effective in propaganda, did not prevent him from being the kind of man who put antlers on his donkeys' heads to please a lady visitor who complained that he had no deer. Virginia Woolf, "brilliant pamphleteer," was not above renting a donkey's head to take her bows for her play *Freshwater,* to show that she considered it to be "donkey-work."

After hearing Annie Besant lecture at the 1917 Club, Virginia Woolf wrote: "The only honest people are the artists . . . these social reformers and philanthropists get so out of hand and harbour so many discreditable desires under the disguise of loving their kind. . . . But if I were one of them?" (*AWD,* p. 17). Of course the men of her circle did think she was one of them. One makes worse enemies out of one's colleagues who share *some* of one's views than out of those on the opposite side.

"Art is being rid of all preaching," she wrote later (*AWD,* p. 183). The preacher's tone was wrong, she felt, not only for fiction but for pamphlets. *Three Guineas* gestated for six years as *On Being Despised,* a draft inspired by personal insults—salt in her wounds—from Yeats, Huxley, E. M. Forster, and others. But all of the personal lamentation and the preaching were removed to make the essay grow into *Three Guineas* as we have it, from what she called in her diary "this little piece of rant" (*AWD,* p. 236). "Truth is only to be spoken by those women whose fathers were pork butchers and left them a share of the pig factory" (an example of the rant that did not survive her final test [*AWD,* p. 236]). (This may refer both to Arabella's familiarity with the "pig's pizzle" in *Jude the Obscure* and to Jane Austen's letter about pork while the battle of Waterloo was being fought.)

In commenting on the chips on Ethel Smyth's shoulders in her published memoirs, Virginia Woolf wrote in 1933: "I hate personal snippets more and more. And the mention of 'I' is so potent—such a drug, such a deep violet stain—that one in a page is enough to colour a chapter" (St. John, *Ethel Smyth,* p. 228). Woolf explained that she was often tempted to do the same thing but was restrained by the large, ugly "I":

> I didn't write "A Room" without considerable feeling even you will admit; I'm not cool in the subject. And I forced myself to keep my own figure fictitious, legendary. If I had said, "Look here, I am uneducated because my brothers used all the family funds"—which is the fact—"Well," they'd have said, "she has

an axe to grind"; and no one would have taken me seriously, though I agree I should have had more of the wrong kind of reader, who will read you and go away and rejoice in the personalities, not because they are lively and easy reading; but because they prove once more how vain, how personal, so they will say, rubbing their hands with glee, women always are; I can hear them as I write. [229, 230]

Virginia Woolf did of course grind her own axe in *Three Guineas,* so much that she feared criticism of its autobiographical stance. Her mental life was so much a part of her identity that she did nor realize that the exposure of her intellectual self was not considered "autobiographical" by others. She need not have feared exposure. What is interesting is that while Woolf chastised Ethel Smyth for complaining as a feminist at actual injustices and prejudices against her as a woman composer, she wanted a fuller and more honest account of Dame Ethel's bisexuality:

I was thinking the other night that there's never been a woman's autobiography. Nothing to compare with Rousseau. Chastity and modesty I suppose has been the reason. Now why shouldn't you be not only the first woman to write an opera, but equally the first to tell the truth about herself? But the great artist is the only person to tell the truth. I should like an analysis of your sex life as Rousseau did his. More introspection. More intimacy. [St. John, *Ethel Smyth,* pp. 232–33]

Both the great artist and the pork-butcher's daughter tell the truth; perhaps Virginia Woolf felt she was neither. But she tried. The simultaneous "truth of fiction" and "truth of fact" about women of her own generation and her own class in *The Years* and *Three Guineas* ("one book," she called them) made her feel that she had spoken as plainly as possible on all the subjects which concerned her most—feminism (and sexual relations), pacifism (and antifascism), and socialism (the importance of recognition of the class struggle, the role of the female intellectual in the class struggle). "One can't propagate at the same time as write fiction," Virginia Woolf admonished herself in the *Diary,* "and as this fiction is dangerously near propaganda, I must keep my hands clear." As *The Years* and *Three Guineas* show us, she could and did, but only at the expense of a terrific struggle. The *Diary* records that Leonard felt that art and politics should not be mixed, but it also provides evidence that Woolf was uncertain about this. The early manuscript of *The Years* shows us that she had alternated each chapter, at the beginning, with an historical essay; had she dared to publish these we might have had one of the first modern documentary novels. Ironically, *The Years* has seemed to be the least experimental in form of her novels and consequently is not beloved by modern critics. It was a bold plan; one wishes that Leonard Woolf had had the taste and lack of timidity to encourage its boldness.[9]

But *Three Guineas* is not the same kind of propaganda as *A Room of One's Own*. In fact, I think one might make a distinction here between the propaganda of hope and the propaganda of despair. *Three Guineas* is not in the least amusing. Her friends who did not share her views could not single out passages of wit and fine writing while ignoring or deprecating her arguments, as E. M. Forster had done with *A Room of One's Own*. She herself felt that *Three Guineas* was better written because it had less of the "egotistic flaunting" of *A Room of One's Own* (*AWD,* p. 279). "The more complex a vision the less it lends itself to satire," Woolf told herself; "the more it understands the less it is able to sum up and make linear" (236). *Three Guineas* documents this more complex vision; the feminism-and-art problem of *A Room of One's Own* is only part of the serious intellectual grasp of the political problems of the twentieth century. *Three Guineas* was her last work, as civilization destroyed itself; it was "a moth over a bonfire" (*AWD,* p. 282). "For having spat it out, my mind is made up. I need never recur or repeat, I am an outsider" (282).

Three Guineas is for modern readers neither as indigestible as the second figure suggests nor as frail as the first. Aptly named, it is about the relation between money and property and conflicts between the sexes, the classes, and the nations. The essay "tunnels" back, as Woolf's novels do, to first causes. Fascism is derived from patriarchy; patriarchy is defined as power chasing itself in vicious circles around "the mulberry tree of property." Woolf demanded that women crush shoots of incipient fascism in all the men around them, the "caterpillars of the commonwealth." She met with a reply even angrier than she expected, led by Queenie Leavis,[10] who called for the uniting of those very caterpillars in the name of *real* wife and motherhood.

How many professional women, writers, and teachers—for it is to us that Virginia Woolf speaks here—have been able to meet her rigorous demands? We are the guardians of culture and its future promise, *if* we do not join the professions on the same terms as men, but remain in poverty, intellectual chastity, and "freedom from unreal loyalties."[11] The terms are hard: do not teach literature to middle-class students; do not lecture, write, or speak for money on any subject you do not believe in; do not allow any publicity which capitalizes on your personal charm; do not have anything to do with "the pimps and panders of the brain-selling trade." Woolf insists: "Do all in your power to break the ring, the vicious circle, the dance round and round the mulberry tree, the poison tree of intellectual harlotry." What would happen if women followed her advice?

> Slaves who are now kept hard at work piling words into books, piling words into articles, as the old slaves piled stones into pyramids, would shake the manacles from their wrists and give up their loathsome labour. And "culture," that amorphous bundle, swaddled up as she now is in insincerity, emitting half truths from her timid lips, sweetening and diluting her message with whatever sugar or water serves to swell the writer's fame or his master's purse, would regain her shape and become . . . muscular, adventurous, free. [*TG,* p. 99]

Three Guineas is a final declaration of independence from patriarchal values pushed to the extreme, which Woolf believed had produced fascism. It is a long, agonized, rational argument, unemotional and impersonal, defining the role of the outsider—with Coleridge, "to find a form of society according to which each one uniting with the whole shall yet obey himself only and remain as free as before"—and with Walt Whitman, "of Equality—as if it harm'd me, giving others the same chances and rights as myself—as if it were not indispensable to my own rights that others possess the same." These are not the words of an elitist or a snob or a "fragile middle-aged poetess, a sexless Sappho—a distressed gentlewoman caught in a tempest and making little effort either to fight against it or to sail before it," as Quentin Bell judges. He continues: "She made far less of an attempt than did Forster to contribute something to the debates of the time, or rather, when she did, it was so idiosyncratic a contribution that it could serve no useful purpose" (*Biography*, 2:185).

E. M. Forster asserted that Virginia Woolf was not a great writer because she had "no great cause at heart." He meant that he did not share her cause, the brilliant and sustained attack on private property as the foundation of corrupt capitalist England that she makes in *Three Guineas;* the devastating rationality of the argument that fascism is simply a natural result of an extremely patriarchal value system; the impassioned cry to women to remain indifferent to war and war-makers and the capitalist greed which would begin to corrupt them as they entered the professions on equal terms with men.

Forster obviously felt that feminism was a social disease. "There are spots of it all over her work," he says, hardly concealing his distaste. But distaste is different from dishonesty, in a critic and a friend. Class was a touchier subject than sex, and here Forster declares to posterity that Virginia Woolf was a snob, a lady, and was detached from "the working class and Labour." He must have known better. He dedicated the Rede Lecture to Leonard Woolf, which suggests that Leonard approved of his estimate. Leonard Woolf *certainly* knew better.

Snobbery, elitism, hatred or distrust of the working class—not true. What her enemies have in common is that they are liberals, that they mistake Woolf's honesty about the working class for snobbery. Because they dislike the rationality, the inescapable logic of *Three Guineas,* they declare it frivolous. The liberal imagination is infuriated with her logic; in the person of Queenie Leavis they call her "silly," "ill-informed," "emotional," and "dangerous." They accuse her of lacking "mind," when it is her rational argument which so disturbs them. The liberal likes to be first in the cause of freedom; often enemies to the left can be put down by attacking their class or sex or by declaring that they are not really democratic socialists at all.[12]

Unfortunately this has been the fate of Virginia Woolf's political ideas. And Leonard Woolf has contributed to this vision of her. In 1927 Leonard Woolf wrote:

> In classes the mentality at the top—i.e. in Royalty & the uppermost aristocracy—is exactly what it is at the bottom—i.e. in the basement. . . . My theory is that the minds of a Duke and butler, of a Countess & a kitchen maid, have a natural affinity, and at certain periods of the world's history become indistinguishable. Whether the Duke becomes more like the butler, or the butler more like the Duke, is a nice question; probably the influence is reciprocal. But whenever in history the moment comes at which the mentality of the Duke and Countess is absolutely indistinguishable from that of the butler and the kitchen maid, there is an elementary catastrophe—not indeed a conflagration of the earth, but a revolution. [*Essays on Literature, History, and Politics,* p. 229]

Now Leonard Woolf's words do not betray a particularly socialist sympathy for the working class, and this is certainly not a serious Marxist's view of the making of a revolution. Some critics of Virginia Woolf have felt that while they do not share Forster's view of her complete lack of political sense, they will allow the influence of Leonard's politics. Frankly, it seems to be the other way round. She was often considerably to the left of Leonard, and remained a pacifist despite his arguments that art and politics should never be mixed.[13] Clearly her views upset him enough to cause him to leave out, for example, the fact that she had written some of her essays for the *Daily Worker* and, in his selection of texts for the *Collected Essays,* to remove some of her views altogether.

The most pronounced editorial bias appears in his choice of the text of her essay on the Women's Co-operative Guild. It concerns a meeting held in June 1913, but it was heavily revised for publication in 1931 as the introduction to Margaret Llewelyn Davies' *Life As We Have Known It, By Cooperative Working Women,* a book the Woolfs printed at the Hogarth Press.[14] Most of Virginia Woolf's revisions were of a political nature and were meant to clarify her opinions about the relation of class to art. She printed the original in the *Yale Review* in 1930 but revised it with the help of Margaret Llewelyn Davies and the working women writers themselves for publication in England; in choosing the unrevised first draft for the *Collected Essays* Leonard Woolf was acting politically.

In the revised essay Virginia Woolf changed the meeting place from Manchester to Newcastle and included a photograph of the cooperative women's conference in session. She brought her original fictional characters, Miss Wick and Miss Erskine, out of the parsonage and down to earth, giving them back their real names, Miss Kidd and Miss Harris. Lilian Harris is brought to life with an actual photograph, next to one of Margaret Llewelyn Davies herself.

Originally Virginia Woolf had written of the agitation at the conference that their reforms "would not matter to me a single jot." In the book she changed this to read, "If every reform they demand was granted this instant it would not touch one hair of my capitalistic head." The earlier essay contains a passage which describes what seems to be rather frivolous and pointless housekeeping on the part of the women. She revised it to show both their collective consciousness and their politics: "The world was to be reformed, from top to bottom, in a variety of ways . . . after seeing Cooperative jams bottled and Cooperative biscuits made." The added "Cooperative" transubstantiates the biscuits and the jam.

Woolf had at first created a rather sinister and bored figure in Miss Erskine, who smoked a pipe and read detective stories. The revision shows the sure hand of the novelist and more sympathy than cynicism. Here Miss Harris, "whether it was due to her dress which was coffee coloured or to her smile which was severe or to the ashtray in which many cigarettes had come amiably to an end, seemed the image of detachment and equanimity." The first essay said it was "bad manners" for working women to imitate the mincing speech of ladies; the revision called it "foolish." The first essay had described all working people as servants, "those who touch their foreheads with their fingers." Her revision recognized the proletariat as well: "And they remain equally deprived," she wrote. "For we have as much to give them as they to give us—wit and detachment, learning and poetry, and all the good gifts which those who have never answered bells or minded machines enjoy by right." Most important, she removed the offending sentence, "It is not from the ranks of working-class women that the next great poet or novelist will be drawn." Her revision reads:

> The writing, a literary critic might say, lacks detachment and imaginative breadth, even as the women themselves lacked variety and play of feature. Here are no reflections, he might object, no view of life as a whole, and no attempt to enter into the lives of other people. . . . And yet, since writing is a complex art, much infected by life, these pages have some qualities even as literature that the literate and instructed might envy.

These qualifications are important ones for those still troubled about the relations between class, sex, and art.

The most significant change Woolf made was in tone. The *Yale Review* essay is narrated in the voice of an "irritable" middle-class visitor. She is annoyed by what seems to be a waste of all that working-class energy, suspicious of full-time organizers of the cooperative women, and confident that the scraps of writing are not literature. While Woolf remains as scrupulous as ever in the new essay, the cynicism is gone. She has become both more politically committed to the cooperative cause and more artistically Woolfian. She names names in the new essay, recording the reality of the "lives of the obscure." And her storyteller's art rejects the earlier cynical adjective "squat" for "sombre," as in the end she describes her character's reason for dedication to the cause. Woolf respectfully records the secretary's dry and reserved tale of her rape by "a gentlemen," "At eighteen, I was a mother." What Virginia Woolf did in her revised essay was to make another contribution to the propaganda of hope.[15]

Virginia Woolf's editor[16] and her biographer have, it seems to me, for whatever reasons of their own, wished her to appear as a thoroughbred horse. They have attempted to remove for posterity the donkey of hard work and of fun from her own image of herself. They were also, it seems, quite seriously troubled by Virginia Woolf's confirmed pacifism during the last years of her life, as many of her readers are. The image of someone silly and apolitical is less threatening than the image of someone as sure of her intellectual position as the Virginia Woolf who wrote *Three Guineas.* It is easy to see why *Three Guineas* makes people uncomfortable. One can hardly argue with its logic or its morality. Pacifism is to me an ethical luxury, a self-indulgence at some historical moments, but in Woolf it is understandable. Her pacifism and feminism are more moral than political and are directly inherited from the Clapham Sect reformers in her family and, more important, from the Quaker pacifism of her aunt, Caroline Emelia Stephen.

The declaration that "There will be no more horses" was not so much a criticism of the coupling of art and propaganda in the age of fascism as a facing of the facts. Her novels were as thoroughbred a stable as any noble Englishwoman could wish. But Woolf could see the necessity for donkeys and "donkey work" as well. In *Three Guineas* she produced her own mule. Perhaps it was sterile, but it did kick and it did bite.

She repeated, in August 1940, her advice to women in "Thoughts on Peace in an Air Raid." A "mind-hornet," this advice is called, meant to sting her sisters into consciousness: "We must create more honorable activities for those who try to conquer in themselves their fighting instinct, their subconscious Hitlerism. We must compensate the man for the loss of his gun" (*The Death of the Moth,* p. 247). But it would not be much use for women and workers, outsiders all, to beat the dead horse of society as the poets of the thirties had done. If "commoners and outsiders like ourselves," she said to the Workers' Educational Association in May 1940, are to be the artists of the future, they must take advantage of the war to prepare themselves for the task. "Let us trespass at once," she demanded, on the grounds of English Literature as patriarchal private property. "Literature is no one's private ground;

literature is common ground. It is not cut up into nations; there are no wars there. Let us trespass freely and fearlessly and find our own way for ourselves."[17]

Virginia Woolf declared herself an "outsider" in *Three Guineas.* The official guardians of her image, it seems, preferred a view of Virginia Woolf as another kind of outsider, a class snob and an artist alienated from ordinary people. Any bourgeois husband, one feels, would be disturbed if he felt he had treated his wife as a sensitive, blueblooded, elegant racehorse only to find that she saw part of herself as a hard-working donkey. Woolf, on the other hand, saw part of herself as Miss LaTrobe, the lonely artist, preserver of culture, allied with the people who keep history and art alive while the upper classes ignore or destroy civilization. In *Between the Acts,* Miss LaTrobe leaves her bits of property at the big house, where they care about such things, but she takes her lonely, misunderstood, awkward, visionary self down to the local pub. This view of the alienated artist allied with ordinary people to educate the middle and upper classes is consistent with Woolf's view of herself as an "outsider," a feminist, socialist, artist, and worker.

6

Art and Anger: Elizabeth Robins and Virginia Woolf

Fie on the falsehood of men, whose
minds go oft a madding, and whose
tongues can not so soon be wagging,
but straight they fall a railing. . . .
Oh Paul's steeple and Charing Cross!
A halter hold all such persons! Let the
streams of the channels in London
streets run so swiftly as they may be
able alone to carry them from that
sanctuary! Let the stones be as ice,
the soles of their shoes as glass, the
ways steep like Etna and every blast
a whirlwind puffed out of Boreas his
long throat, that these may hasten
their passage to the Devil's haven!
. . . and shall not Anger stretch the
veins of her brains, the strings of her
fingers, and the lists of her modesty to
answer their surfeitings?
—Jane Anger, 1589[1]

Anger and righteous indignation are the two emotions that provoke the most hostility from the powerful when expressed by the powerless. When men are angry and indignant, they are godlike, imitating Jehovah. The Bible tells us that it is better to dwell in the wilderness than with an angry woman. The scold's chair, bridle, and gag remind us of our ancestors' remedies for outspoken women. Art is even more judgmental. An angry artist is a polemicist. Her writing is judged in a special category, as if writing inspired by anger were not worthy of the name of art. I want to explore the techniques through which

122

women have disguised their anger and expressed it. We will examine Elizabeth Robins' bitter anonymous last book, *Ancilla's Share,* along with Virginia Woolf's growth into an angry old woman, from *A Room of One's Own* to *Three Guineas.*[2]

Jane Anger's curse is remarkable for its directness. There are few enough examples of the female's wrath surviving British patriarchal culture. One thinks of Mary Wollstonecraft, the Brontës, Olive Schreiner, Sylvia Pankhurst. Most women writers have learned to disguise their anger. But their protest never died. Whining and nagging, those peculiar forms of protest which we are taught to associate with the powerless— women, slaves, children, and servants—are testimony to the danger of the powerless and its survival in the form of indirect discourse.

Anger and righteous indignation are the least likely of expressive forms to be learned by the oppressed, for survival has often been dependent on the appearance of humility. Christianity and Western culture have insisted that the meek shall inherit the earth, while history tells us the opposite. And pacifism itself as a cause and as a political weapon has been popularly associated with Gandhi in India, with women and blacks, with those excluded from the ranks of empire and privilege.

Anger and righteous indignation are the emotions of patriarchs in the state and in the family. These emotions are justified as imitations of Jehovah, god of retribution and justice. Hell is the source of woman's wrath, we are told; the anger of the victim comes from the devil, while the fury of a general or a prime minister is heroic and godlike. Women are not supposed to raise their voices, shake their fists, or point their fingers in accusation. That so many women actually have seems miraculous.

Photographs of suffragettes lying bloody, hair disheveled, hats askew, roused public anger toward the women, not their assailants. They were unladylike; they provoked the authorities. Demonstrations by students and blacks arouse similar responses. The justice of a cause is enhanced by the nonviolence of its adherents. But the response of the powerful when pressed for action has been such that only anger and violence have won change in the law or in government policy. Similar contradictions and a double standard have characterized attitudes toward anger itself. While for the people, anger has been denounced as one of the seven deadly sins, divines and churchmen have always defended it as a necessary attribute of the leader. "Anger is one of the sinews of the soul" wrote Thomas Fuller. "He that wants it hath a maimed mind." "Anger has its proper use," declared Cardinal Manning. "Anger is the executive power of justice." Anger signifies strength in the strong, weakness in the weak. An angry mother is out of control; an angry father is exercising his authority. Our culture's ambivalence about anger reflects its defense of the status quo; the terrible swift sword is for fathers and kings, not daughters and subjects. The story of Judith and the story of Antigone have not been part of the education of daughters, as both Elizabeth Robins and Virginia Woolf point out, unless men have revised and rewritten them. It is hardly possible to read the poetry of Sappho, they both assure us, separate from centuries of scholarly calumny.

One of the particular ways men have dealt with defiance or insolence in women (aside from treating it as mental illness deserving treatment in an asylum, sin deserving excommunication or penance, or political crime deserving ostracism or prison) is to assert that female anger is the result of sexual frustration or sexual jealousy—a tactic of ridicule to obscure the justice of women's claims. "Vengeance is mine," saith the Lord. "And mine," say the prime ministers, patriarchs, fathers, assuming divine right. "And mine," says the woman who demands education, recognition, equal pay. Yet her demand is regarded as treasonable, blasphemous, unladylike or, at present, unreasonable.

But Freud has argued that anger is not associated with libido and is not a result of sexual frustration. Anger is a form of primary narcissism, a result of the ego's first struggle to maintain itself, to find an identity separate from the mother. Self-preservation is the source of anger. Love and hate are not opposites; hate and anger come first as the ego learns to defend itself. The narcissism of the artist has often seemed a frail and fragile vessel for carrying the weight of society's anger and rebellion, our dreams and wishes for both freedom and peace. Yet we have generally regarded the artist's narcissism as healthy. Even in exaggerated form it has seemed necessary for the deepest forms of self-expression.

But the narcissistic female artist is a rarity. It still takes our breath away to read in *The Diary of Marie Bashkirtseff,* "I am my own heroine!" Even the admiring Shaw felt it necessary to declare that "woman artist" was a contradiction in terms and would require inventing a "third or Bashkirtseff sex" to accommodate her ego. Such ego strength as it takes to be a great artist, such fearlessness and ferocity he felt to be unnatural and unwomanly. We accept women's narcissism as a fact, but we note its deflection over centuries to a vanity of body and dress. When not deflected, as in the case of Mme. de Staël or George Sand, for example, the artist can express herself both in anger and joy.

Both Elizabeth Robins and Virginia Woolf, as artists, analyzed their own anger, tried to capture its energy for their art, and yet were in certain ways victims of the need to sublimate some of that anger in order to survive. Elizabeth Robins (1862–1952) was an American who spent most of her life in England. She came to London in the nineties having worked with Booth and O'Neill in America, and is best known for producing, directing, and playing the leading roles in the first English productions of Ibsen's plays. She appears to have been an actress of extraordinary talent, England's first "intellectual" actress, and she won much acclaim. But her struggle to get Ibsen's plays staged, at first simply a hungry actress's response to meaty roles for women, became a larger struggle against the actor-manager system and a working woman's struggle as a feminist, socialist, and pacifist for social justice. She left the stage to become a novelist and playwright; she helped to organize the Women Writers' Suffrage League and the Actresses' Franchise League and became a well-known speaker and writer for the feminist cause, a champion of the Pankhursts' militancy. She wrote the most successful propaganda play for women's suffrage, *Votes for Women!* (1907) and a novel on the same subject, *The Convert* (1907), with a barely fictionalized Christabel Pankhurst as its heroine. Her fiction, while fascinating and full of intellectual and dramatic power, is not as great as Virginia Woolf's primarily because of its use of traditional Victorian forms. If a revolutionary artist is revolutionary in form—as Christopher Caudwell tells us—then

Woolf was doubly revolutionary, in form and in content. Robins' real genius was in her voice and power as an actress, a power she used on platforms all over Edwardian England to convert women to the cause of feminism.[3]

Elizabeth Robins was one of those "mothers" of fiction we think back through. She and hundreds of other unknown women writers prepared the literary soil for the eventual creation of the woman of genius, the Shakespeare's sister. "For masterpieces are not single and solitary births; they are the outcome of many years of thinking in common, of thinking by the body of the people, so that the experience of the mass is behind the single voice."[4]

Elizabeth Robins lived to be ninety; she and Virginia Woolf were friends and neighbors in Sussex. Leonard and Virginia Woolf published Robins' *Ibsen and the Actress* and her autobiographical *Raymond and I*. Robins left Backsettown Farm, her home, as a rest home for professional women. In her later years she supported many women medical students. One of them, Dr. Octavia Wilberforce, became her close friend and companion. Dr. Wilberforce was also Virginia Woolf's last doctor. Woolf considered writing Wilberforce's biography, fascinated by a family tradition close to the Stephens in Clapham Sect social reform. Dr. Wilberforce wanted to write Elizabeth Robins' biography, but died before she could do so.[5] Leonard Woolf tells us in his autobiography that Elizabeth Robins' energy wore him out, but he did his best to sort out her papers and execute her will. Octavia Wilberforce's letters to Elizabeth Robins describing the last illness and death of Virginia Woolf survive. When they are published, I think they will tell us a great deal about Woolf's supposed madness from a source we can trust.[6]

Elizabeth Robins published *Ancilla's Share: An Indictment of Sex Antagonism* anonymously in 1924. She need hardly have bothered with anonymity, for the world had ceased to remember her. The sisterhood for whom she had written and worked hard had disappeared. She had even less of an audience than Virginia Woolf had four years later when she published *A Room of One's Own*. The anger in *Ancilla's Share* alternates with bitter disappointment, and the "indictment" of male sex antagonism loses some of its force as she counts women's losses and licks her veteran feminist's wounds. Bitterly she surveys the wreckage around her, realizing that women's suffrage was granted not as a reward for war work but because "the services women had rendered in the Great War constituted a ground which the men in the street could understand."[7] With the gain of the vote came the loss of the power to work. She devastatingly counts and quotes Labour's fierce fight to exclude female workers in factories, the closing of the great teaching hospitals to female medical students, the exclusion of married female professionals and workers from all the jobs they had done during the war. Class hatred between women was being stirred up, and the new generation would have to fight all the old battles over again.

As an artist she was appalled at the depth of oblivion that overshadowed the reputation of the women of her generation. She and Mrs. Humphry Ward had been archenemies over the suffrage question. Mrs. Ward, as the leader of the Anti-Suffrage movement, had made her home a conservative salon, and she had stood for the patriarchal values of the politicians, intellectuals, and writers whom she had encouraged. Dead, she was not mourned by any of them, least of all by Elizabeth Robins' old friend, Henry James, who had taken Mary Ward's favors and laughed at her literary efforts behind her back. The same is true of Edith Wharton; Robins saw that a lifetime of friendship had only inspired in James "a certain worried desire to do this duty." And Shaw had just written a play about Catherine the Great, leaving out her politics, which Robins thought should have been called "Kitten of the Adelphi" or "Puss in Boots" for "in cheapening Catherine he cheapens his own talent." James and Shaw had been Elizabeth Robins' champions when she was the champion of Ibsen. When she herself began to write they were silent. But James and Shaw were unconscious sexists; the conscious woman-haters H. G. Wells, Wyndham Lewis, and Aldous Huxley she called "this brace of Minotaurs." Calmly, Robins went on to explain the source of active woman-hating in modern writers as "a need to protect something which has been assailed or is believed to be threatened."

You do not protect yourself from the helpless. You may deliberately insult your peer and get what is called satisfaction by giving him the privilege of shooting at you. You do not insult a slave. You merely revile and ill-treat him. As to his "answering back," whether with tongue or bullet or blade, that is for his superiors. When the slave comes to a place where it is possible deliberately to insult him, he is no longer the helpless thing he was. Woman, having ceased in some measure to be helpless, had become, in the polite phrase of Mr. Henry James, "impeachable." Stated bluntly, men despised her at their ease for her helplessness. From no manifestation of hers do the majority of the opposite sex recoil so sharply as from signs of her ceasing to be helpless.[8]

Elizabeth Robins had been brought up with an ideal of service to art and to social progress. Even in the heyday of her success as Hedda Gabler, she justified her personal desire for glory by her belief that her talent served to bring to the public Ibsen's poetic and political genius. Her genius was to play the role of ancilla well. The source of this role was not religious, for her father was as firmly antireligious as Virginia Woolf's. She would not be handmaiden to the Lord, but handmaiden to history, ancilla to an age that, in her view, would see women free and socialism in power. At sixty-two she saw that ancilla's share in the patriarchal pie was nonexistent, that "ancillary" meant secondary, and that servants and women held no honorable places in history books except when they were sexually related to famous men. "Where is woman's inventiveness, her humour, her intellectual passion, her vision, her poetry?" she asked. "Dorothy Wordsworth's is in her brother William's. Mary Lamb's is in her brother's. Henrietta Renan's is in her brother's. Mary Shelley's is in her husband's. Louise Colet's in *Madame Bovary.*"[9]

It was too late in 1924 for Robins to develop the narcissism necessary to write a great novel. She had seen writing as a way to earn her living; social ideas and moral power animate her prose, but art for art's sake or even the artist's sake were notions utterly foreign to her. Virginia Woolf had class, tradition, and money to free her for the struggle between art, moral and political ideas, and her own ego. *A Writer's Diary* is testimony that the political and moral concerns died hard. She concentrated her energies on breaking old forms and forging new ones. But first she had to kill the "angel in the house," the desire bred in women to play the role of ancilla. Elizabeth Robins, like many Victorian women novelists, did not kill the angel but directed the angel's energies into service to a cause. It was often easier to see oneself as a vessel of historical consciousness than to deal with the guilt aroused by declaring oneself an artist. Self-expression was a social sin. As the voice of the oppressed, she was not a sinner but a saint. Robins preaches and teaches; Woolf condemned self-appointed missionaries to the masses, and she feared those feelings in herself. Robins chose writing to keep her self-respect. She had no time for formal experimentation. In the theater as director and actress she could have forged her own art form. The only way she could have secured a theater of her own and plays as appealing to women as Ibsen's was to sell her body, as generations of actresses had done before her. When she refused a villa in St. John's Wood, she gave up not only her future as an actress of genius, but her achievements, invisible now to the world. To Shaw goes praise for distilling the quintessence of Ibsenism, although Elizabeth Robins' acting was the cup he drank it from.

While the *Times Literary Supplement* could eventually label Virginia Woolf "the most brilliant pamphleteer in England," a reviewer in its back pages attacked *Ancilla's Share* as a "long series of illusions and special pleadings," and lambasted Robins for a "clumsy and confused style," for her "captious suspicion of everything man does," and asserted that women went back to their "natural" functions after the war. The review granted praise only to Robins' remark that women leaders had failed to cooperate with one another. The reviewer complained of women's antagonism to men, of which "the book itself is indeed a conspicuous manifestation."[10]

I'm sure Robins' one-sentence paragraphs made the reviewer nervous and jumpy. They were meant to. For *Ancilla's Share* is an "indictment." It is written in the form of a legal brief, as if the brilliant forensic powers of that lawyer who was never allowed to practice, Christabel Pankhurst, were reading it aloud in court. The indictment proceeds in little spurts as if the author is squeezing out bits of long-repressed anger. She has packed the court. "These pages are not addressed to the masculine mind," she begins. And many younger feminine minds are excluded as well, for they have been made to "feel" inferior to men; the judge, of course, is History, since Robins doesn't believe in God and will bow her head to no man. She pleads with a jury of her peers for a kind of justice seldom received by women. The plea is eloquent. As Virginia Woolf said when reviewing *The Mills of the Gods,* "she writes like a man," meaning that the text is a "fine hard fabric" and the style has "bare brevity" and the mind is "robust." But she is misled "largely by her strong dramatic sense" says Woolf.[11] The oratorical prose of *Ancilla's Share* was meant to be spoken, declaimed in defense of a prisoner in the dock. There the pauses would be dramatically effective. A lawyer's brief may be electrifying in court, yet boring on the printed page. *Ancilla's Share* is charged with anger; but much of it turns against herself and her generation for accepting "ancilla's share." Certainly it is a literary triumph to demand justice for women in the form of a legal brief from the very system which perpetuated injustice to women.

I am not certain that *Ancilla's Share* was among the books of Elizabeth Robins which Virginia Woolf read and admired.[12] But there seems to be ample evidence that she did. In my view, the germ of the idea for *Three Guineas* could have come from Robins' remark: "We would like to think we might receive a pound for the fund needed by the Women's Colleges . . . from everyone who, as a girl, had a taste of that rapture of the high places, if not a taste of chastisement for seeking to climb there."[13] Robins argued for women's independence of political parties; we must first remove abuses "older than capitalism, older than imperialism," a view Woolf pushed even further in her vision of women as "outsiders." Both writers speak essentially to women, a technique that has infuriated male readers and has reminded women of the psychic displacement necessary for them to read most literature.

"Much as passages of doubtful propriety pass the juvenile reader unnoticed," Elizabeth Robins asserted, "women of all ages seldom consciously register the judgments slighting or condemnatory meted out wholesale to her sex. Little short of amazement is in store for women who reread their poets and historians with a view to collecting evidence of man's account of her character and of her place in the scheme of things."[14] A "separable spite" must be attained by women, an awareness of insult and a refusal to take it. Her evidence was all around her, in the daily papers, in the books on her shelves. She, like Virginia Woolf after her, steeled herself to collect it, to publish it, and to make us take note of it as well. This is obviously the source for the scrapbooks of news clippings and notes Woolf kept all during the thirties, only a fraction of which were used for *Three Guineas.* A useful experiment for students in women's studies would be to record every instance of sexism encountered in a day.

One of the most moving passages in *Ancilla's Share* concerns Robins' visit to the British Museum, where she is fascinated by the Egyptian frescoes of "the daughters of the college of Amen-Ra." Her delight is dashed, her zest for discovery destroyed by the contempt of the Keeper, who fears she will encourage women from the colleges of Newnham and Girton to investigate their ancestresses. Temple prostitutes he says they were, and "college" a little joke on the part of the museum staff. Virginia Woolf has taken a similar scenario in *A Room of One's Own* and made it immortal.

While Woolf felt that one must be a pork butcher's daughter and have inherited a share in a pig factory to have access to the vulgar power of language, she often felt it was necessary to carry the weight of her own rage. She habitually recorded that rage in her diary, to use its energy in the melting-down-of-the-mind process she called "incandescence" so that the anger, when expressed, would have more fire than smoke. Being patronized by patriarchal institutions was more than she could bear with equanimity, however, and she attacked them vigorously—St. Paul's, Westminster Abbey, Oxford and Cambridge, the Houses of Parliament—in both pamphlet and fiction. Some feminist critics have felt that *A Room of One's Own* criticizes Charlotte Brontë too severely for her anger. But Woolf's argument is more complex; Woolf's anger is directed at Haworth parsonage, not at Brontë. She felt that Brontë was a writer of genius and that she might have been a Shakespeare if she had had some money, travel, and experience. Far more space in that book is filled with analysis of her own anger and men's anger at women. She is sympathetic to Brontë. Her own anger, demonstrated with an uncanny ability to see the economic source of social, personal, and artistic problems, was cooled by a generous amount of money to buy time, privacy, and freedom.

The British Museum is the scene for the dramatization of her anger at the mythical Professor von X, author of the scores of misogynist books that overwhelm her attempt at research:

> His expression suggested that he was labouring under some emotion that made him jab his pen on the paper as if he were killing some noxious insect as he wrote, but even when he had killed it that did not satisfy him; he must go on killing it; and even so, some cause for anger and irritation remained . . . the professor was made to look very angry and very ugly in my sketch, as he wrote his great book upon the mental, moral and physical inferiority of women . . . it is in our idleness, in our dreams, that the submerged truth sometimes comes to the top. A very elementary exercise in psychology, not to be dignified by the name of psycho-analysis, showed me, on looking at my notebook, that the sketch of the angry professor had been made in anger. Anger had snatched my pencil while I dreamt. But what was anger doing there? Interest, confusion, amusement, boredom—all these emotions I could trace and name as they succeeded each other throughout the morning. Had anger, the black snake, been lurking among them? Yes, said the sketch, anger had. It referred me unmistakably to the one book, to the one phrase, which had roused the demon; it was the professor's statement about the mental, moral and physical inferiority of women. My heart had leapt. My cheeks had burnt. I had flushed with anger. There was nothing specially remarkable, however foolish, in that. One does not like to be told that one is naturally

the inferior of a little man—I looked at the student next me—who breathes hard, wears a ready-made tie, and has not shaved this fortnight. One has certain foolish vanities. It is only human nature, I reflected and began drawing cartwheels and circles over the angry professor's face till he looked like a burning bush or a flaming comet—anyhow, an apparition without human semblance or significance. The professor was nothing now but a faggot burning on the top of Hampstead Heath. Soon, my own anger was explained and done with; but curiosity remained. How explain the anger of the professors? Why were they angry? For when it came to analysing the impression left by these books there was always an element of heat. This heat took many forms; it showed itself in satire, in sentiment, in curiosity, in reprobation. But there was another element which was often present and could not immediately be identified. Anger, I called it. But it was anger that had gone underground and mixed itself with all kinds of other emotions. To judge from its odd effects, it was anger disguised and complex, not anger simple and open.[15]

As an analysis of the feeling of anger, Virginia Woolf's paragraph is hardly "elementary"; we might even call it "rationalization," except that the act of writing it down is social and feminist. "Do not blame yourself; I have felt it too, that 'black snake' lurking," she tells us, and she shows us that we deflect anger heaped on us from above to those below. She does not tell us that she felt superior to the ill-kempt student because she is proud of her class distinction or is a snob. It is a lesson about how the "foolish vanities" or prejudices are passed on from top to bottom. Note that she encircles and defaces her drawing of the professor; he is blotted out by the humble cartwheel. Her essays join women and the working class as natural allies against the patriarchs and professors, although aware that they are constantly being divided by pressure from above. She makes the professor into a "burning bush." She makes his hatred a "faggot" in the bonfire to provide a torch for the light of her own imagination. By analyzing the source of her own anger, and its deflection not directly back at the enemy but "down" onto the "little man" sitting next to her, Virginia Woolf articulates the "scapegoat" theory of prejudice in a few words. "The pathetic devices of the human imagination" for feeling superior to others include, Woolf says, "a straight nose, or the portrait of a grand-father by Romney." When she tells us that the great professor, who said that the minds of the best female students were not equal to the worst of the men, went home to bed with a pimply-faced working-class boy, she is expressing neither classism nor hatred of homosexuality nor arousing us to such prejudice, but demonstrating again the process of scapegoating. She can understand anger in the powerless but asks why the powerful were angry:

> With the exception of the fog, he seemed to control everything. Yet he was angry. I knew he was angry by this token. When I read what he wrote about women I thought, not of what he was saying, but of himself. When an arguer argues dispassion-ately he thinks only of the argument; and the reader cannot help thinking of the argument too. If he had written dispassion-ately about women, had used indisputable proofs to establish his argument and had shown no trace of wishing that the result should be one thing rather than another, one would not have been angry either. . . . But I had been angry because he was angry. Yet it seemed absurd, I thought, turning over the evening paper, that a man with all this power should be angry. Or is anger, I wondered, somehow, the familiar, the attendant sprite on power? Rich people, for example, are often angry because they suspect that the poor want to seize their wealth. The pro-fessors, or patriarchs, as it might be more accurate to call them, might be angry for that reason partly, but partly for one that lies a little less obviously on the surface. Possibly they were not "angry" at all; often, indeed, they were admiring, devoted, exemplary in the relations of private life. Possibly when the professor insisted a little too emphatically upon the inferiority of women, he was concerned not with their inferiority, but with his own superiority.[16]

If women ceased to act as enlarging mirrors of male vanity, Woolf muses, we might cease to produce Napoleons and Mussolinis. She talks about the power of money to modify her own anger—"What a change of temper a fixed income will bring about." In a few years her own fear and bitterness were replaced by pity and toleration, she tells us. But that was in fact wishful thinking, for ten years later she was in a towering rage, as the distance between herself and the pork butcher's daughter shrank, and she came to write *Three Guineas.*

While Woolf's anger in *Three Guineas* is held in harness by the epistolary form and by as formidable a set of footnotes as ever Professor von X produced for the opposite side, Woolf disobeyed her earlier injunction: "If you stop to curse, you are lost." She did stop to curse, and part of the power of *Three Guineas* is in the incantatory spell of its repetitions of the evils of capitalism, fascism, and imperialism and her declaration that men and only men have produced these systems of oppression. She was so choked with rage, she says, she "spat it out." For someone with so little practice, one must say her aim was good. *Three Guineas* spits in the eye of Professor von X, the patriarchs, generals, and bishops who are to blame for the destruction of civilization. Earlier she had said, "I strike the eye, and elderly gentlemen in particular get annoyed." She strikes again in *Three Guineas,* with its photographs of the patriarchs in their pompous robes and wigs, their decorated uniforms. As Gerald Brenan said, "Wherever Virginia Woolf goes she undoes a knot like a Lapland witch and lets out a war." I like the image of Woolf as a Lapland witch, making war, not love, untying the knots of social convention, encouraging the open expression of hostilities. She killed her own "angel in the house" and out of her ashes came an angel of vengeance, recalling Jane Anger:

> Our good counsel is termed nipping injury, in that it accords not with their foolish fancies; our boldness rash, for giving noddies nipping answers, our dispositions naughty, for not agreeing with their vile minds, and our fury dangerous, because it will not bear with their knavish behaviors. If our frowns be so terrible and our anger so deadly, men are too foolish in offering occasions of hatred, which shunned, a terrible death is prevented. There is a continual deadly hatred between the wild boar and tame

hounds. I would there were the like between women and men.[17]

Woman as wild boar is not exactly a common simile in our literature, but perhaps it is the ancestress of Woolf's pork butcher's daughter. I suspect, however, that her source was Arabella in *Jude the Obscure* and that character's easy familiarity with the "pig's pizzle." Woolf must have envied the vulgarity and vitality of Arabella's language. Leslie Stephen's daughter could not be so free with male organs. Nor, did she imagine, would female writers be so free for a long time to come; they would "still be encumbered with that self-consciousness in the presence of 'sin' which is the legacy of our sexual barbarity. She will still wear the shoddy old fetters of class on her feet."[18] Sexuality and the class struggle—those subjects which most critics have felt Virginia Woolf did not deal with—hence their dismissal of her from the ranks of the great modern novelists. But these were indeed her major concerns in the novels, the essays, the literary criticism.[19] But the expression of her concern is limited by "highbrow" (to use her own term) language. Those moments in *The Years*—the pervert exposing himself to Rose, Sara's "Wasteland" speech to North about the hair of the Jew in the bath, Peggy shocking Eleanor by remarking that the statue of Nurse Cavell reminds her of an advertisement for sanitary napkins—are remarkable not only because they are unexpected, but because the sexuality of each situation is political and charged with anger. The scenes strike the eye, visual versions of the sexual battlefield of *The Years* just as surely as the photographs in *Three Guineas* refer us to the faces of incipient fascism among us, not to the victims of rampant Spanish fascism abroad.[20]

There is great violence underneath the polished surface of Woolf's writing. Indeed, the composer Ethel Smyth felt it was this violence which was the major characteristic of her prose style. In his autobiography Leonard Woolf raises the question again in a psychological explanation of their personalities as political pacifists—a great deal of violence and anger was constantly being suppressed. In " 'No More Horses' " I discuss Leonard Woolf's editorial suppression of his wife's anger. In the interest, I'm sure, of protecting her reputation, Leonard Woolf suppressed some of his wife's feminist and socialist writings.

In *Collected Essays* he tells us when an essay originally appeared in the *Times Literary Supplement,* but not when one appeared originally in *The Daily Worker.* He reprinted an early draft of Woolf's introduction to Margaret Llewelyn Davies' *Life As We Have Known It* rather than a later version which she reworked with the help of the working women themselves.[21]

The latest instance of such editorial "protection" which has come to my attention is the essay "Professions for Women." It does not seem to be an accident that this essay exists in the Berg Collection in a version three times as long and as strong as the one Leonard Woolf printed in *The Death of the Moth* and *Collected Essays.*[22] Vera Brittain attended the meeting at which Woolf presented this lecture, following Dame Ethel Smyth, the great composer, militant suffragette, and fighter for female musicians. Dame Ethel had once conducted her own "Women's Marseillaise" from her jail cell with a toothbrush. Vera Brittain had just come from celebrating Beatrice Webb's seventy-third birthday, and she called Webb, Smyth, and Woolf the three greatest women of their generation. Having written passionately herself about the extreme poverty of the women's colleges, Vera Brittain was interested "to hear both Dame Ethel and Mrs. Woolf attribute their success largely to a private income, which enabled the one to take up a nonlucrative career, and the other to flout the displeasure of authors and editors by writing honest reviews."[23] After the speeches, Virginia Woolf wrote to Dame Ethel praising her speech and asking to print it at the Hogarth Press. Leonard said it was the best of its kind he had ever heard, that it was done "with supreme skill." Her own speech she called "clotted up and clogged, partly owing to the rush I was in—no time to comb out."[24] It is that old bugbear anger which does the clotting and the clogging and makes the speech unkempt. It is worth quoting Virginia Woolf at her unkempt best and asking ourselves why she was able to express anger in a speech before the National Society for Women's Service, a speech whose subject is the courage one needs to kill "the angel in the house." It is about women's violence, and its images are angry, military, and murderous. On one issue, and one issue alone, Virginia Woolf was not a pacifist—

the forging of female professional identity. The speech was positively ferocious; the palimpsest of her reading draft with her own corrections reveals she was angrier still in her original expression of her ideas.

We know from *A Writer's Diary* how often anger was the primary impulse of Woolf's art, but here is proof that she was among that sisterhood of great women writers whose pens were driven by anger— Mary Wollstonecraft, George Sand, Olive Schreiner. She then edited out a good deal of it, combed out a good many furious snarls, but that anger was often the primary source of her power as a writer there is no doubt. Anger transformed into art is what she saw in all the great writers she admired from the Greeks to Jane Austen. That Jane Austen inspired fear in people is a quality she pounces on in her essay. Woolf argued the importance of letting anger out, but she was worried about women's becoming consumed by bitterness at real oppression. When she urges us to fight tooth and nail for power in our professions she also urges us to keep a sense of humor and offers fantasies to make us laugh. Imagine yourself in man's place, she tells us. What a predicament he is in. Like Elizabeth Robins' demands, Woolf's idea of healthy anger is "a separable spite," separable from the attempt to live a joyful life. Perhaps it is not possible. Woolf did inspire fear in people, and her work still does. We have yet to examine as critics just how full of social criticism her work was; preoccupation with its beauty has obscured its terror. But we must finally acknowledge that it was anger that impelled her art, and intellect that combed out the snarls, dissolved the blood clots, and unclogged the drains of that great sewer of the imagination, anger.

The draft of "Professions for Women" begins with Woolf comparing herself to Ethel Smyth as "an idle and frivolous pleasure boat lolloping along in the wake of an ironclad."[25]

> She is of the race of pioneers, of pathmakers. She has gone before and felled trees and blasted rocks and built bridges and thus made a way for those who come after her . . . when I read her books I always feel inclined to burn my own pen and take to music—for if she can toss off a masterpiece in my art without any training why should not I toss off a symphony or two

without knowing a crochet from a quaver?—we honour her not only as a musician and a writer, but also as a blaster of rocks and the maker of bridges. It seems sometimes a pity that a woman who only wished to write music should have been forced also to make bridges, but that was part of her job and she did it.

This a remarkable enough omission from the printed essay, but the cancelled passage it replaces is more remarkable still, calling Ethel Smyth "one of the icebreakers, the gun runners, the window smashers. The armoured tanks, who climbed the rough ground, drew the enemies [sic] fire." Ethel Smyth should be honored, Woolf says, not only for being a musician "but also for being an armoured tank. I never know whether to be angry that such heroism was needed, or glad that such heroism was shown."

The way for women in literature was cut long ago, Woolf points out, owing to "the cheapness of writing materials" by "some mute inglorious Ethel Smyth" who "smashed and broke and toiled" through "hostility and ridicule" to write. This relative ease is economic: "Pianos, models, studios, north lights, masters and mistresses (Berlin, Paris, Vienna and all the rest of it) are not needed." Then comes the brilliant description of "the Angel in the House" as "she was the woman men wished women to be," and the exemption of herself from the category of the "real" angels because she had £500 a year, "and angels never have a penny." It was the ideal angel who plagued her: she had been created for reasons "that have to do with the British Empire, our colonies, Queen Victoria, Lord Tennyson, the growth of the middle class . . . a real relationship between men and women was then un-attainable." Woolf then quotes Tennyson, Rossetti, and Lowell on woman being made for man's delight. "And so they went on paying each other compliments," she writes, "in a style which to me is really disgusting." The word "disgusting" is uncharacteristic, to say the least. The murder of the angel is described as self-defense, for she has more blood on her hands than all the murderers.

Writer after writer, painter after painter and musicians I dare say too she had strangled and killed. One is always meeting their corpses laid out in biographies. But she has a special hatred for writers and with good reason. Her province, you see, is the House. Painters and musicians—it is one of their chief assets— have very little to do with the house. When Vanessa Bell paints a picture it is as often as not a picture of red apples on a plate. It may be a pity to waste your time painting; but if you must paint paint apples (there is no harm in apples).

Similarly, music has "no nasty meaning" either, so the angel leaves the Ethel Smyths alone. She does get upset when "I did have to say for example that I thought that Mr. Carlyle ought to have had a child and that Mrs. Carlyle ought to have written a novel." She kills the angel in a severe struggle by flinging her inkpot at her.

To illustrate her point that a female critic's point of view is entirely different from a man's, Woolf quotes from a Keynes review in that week's *Nation,* remarking: "The members of Clare College have spent six thousand pounds upon a history of their college. And that made me angry." The incident and the anger occur in *The Years,* where Kitty's father is engaged on just such a project at Oxford, and her cousin Edward inherits it from her father. The point is very well made that women's education is neglected even when their families are part of the university. "Had the Editor of the *Nation* sent it to me," she wrote,

> I should have been compelled by that different sense of values to write in a very different strain. Oh you old humbugs, I should have begun. O you have enjoyed for all these centuries comfort and prosperity—O you who profess devotion to the lady of Clare and love for the Sentiment of colleges, would it not be better to spend your £6,000 not upon a book, clothed in the finest dress of paper and buckram, but upon a girl, whose dress allowance is very meagre, and who tries to do her work, as you will read if you turn the very next page in the *Nation,* in one cold gloomy ground floor bedroom which faces due North and is overrun with mice. (Somerville it seems is very hard up.)

Woolf is referring here to Vera Brittain's remarks on the poverty of women's colleges. Her review would not have been printed, she assumes, "for I am a woman."

She warns her audience that they too will be brought to loggerheads with the chiefs of their professions when they work to bring these professions "more in touch with human needs." Writing fiction creates different problems. She describes the writer as a "fisherwoman" letting her imagination roam the subconscious on a "thin . . . thread of reason."

> . . . Then suddenly this fisherwoman gave a cry of dismay. What had happened? The line had suddenly slackened; her imagination had floated limply and dully and lifelessly upon the surface. The reason hauled the imagination on shore and said What on earth is the matter with you? And the imagination began pulling on its stockings and replied, rather tartly and disagreeably; it's all your fault. You should have given me more experience to go on. I can't do the whole work for myself.

Then the novelist-fisherwoman has a worse experience when the imagination escapes.

> The reason has to cry Stop! . . . The novelist has to pull on the line and haul the imagination to the surface. The imagination comes to the top in a state of fury. Good heavens she cries—how dare you interfere with me . . . with your wretched little fishing line? . . . And I—that is the reason—have to reply, My dear you were going altogether too far. Men would be shocked. . . . Calm yourself, I say, as she sits panting on the bank—panting with rage and disappointment. We have only got to wait fifty years or so. In fifty years I shall be able to use all this very queer knowledge that you are ready to bring me. But not now.

Here we are now, fifty years later. Have we come as far as Woolf expected, or do we still chastise our imaginations so as not to upset men?

"You see I go on, trying to calm her," Woolf continues. "I cannot make use of what you tell me—about women's bodies for instance—

their passions—and so on, because the conventions are still very strong. If I were to overcome the conventions I should need the courage of a hero; and I am not a hero. I doubt that a writer can be a hero." Then there are several crossed-out trials of a passage in which Woolf explains that when she becomes heroic her imagination shrivels and hardens, and she becomes a preacher. Even Lawrence, she says, "injures his imagination terribly" although it is easier for men to go against convention. "Very well says the imagination, dressing herself up again in her petticoat and skirts, we will wait. We will wait another fifty years. . . . I will wait until men have become so civilized that they are not shocked when a woman speaks the truth about her body. *The future of fiction depends very much upon what extent men can be educated to stand free speech in women*" (emphasis added).

She tells her audience that they will have more difficulty than she did; they must be the Sapphos and Jane Austens of their professions, meeting much ridicule, derision, and opposition. They should not add to their burdens "the burden of bitterness," and she asks them to put themselves in men's shoes. It is very much her friend Elizabeth Robins' argument for a "separable spite." Then follows a feminist fantasy kindled by the light of laughter and the fire of anger. She asks us to imagine a man returning from a hard day in the city to find that his women servants have taken over the house.

> He goes into the library—an august apartment which he is accustomed to have all to himself—and finds the kitchen maid curled up in the arm chair reading Plato. He goes into the kitchen and there is the cook engaged in writing a Mass in B flat. He goes into the billiard room and finds the parlourmaid knocking up a fine break at the table. He goes into the bedroom and there is the housemaid working out a mathematical problem. What is he to do? He has been accustomed for centuries to have that sumptuous mansion all to himself, to be master in his own house. Well of course his first instinct is to dismiss the whole crew. But he reflects that he would have to do the work of the house himself—He can make the most cutting and disagreeable remarks about housemaids playing the piano and scullerymaids

reading Plato; he can turn them out of the library, lock the billiard room door, and put the key of the cellar in his pocket. . . . But there is a spirit in the house (not by any means an angel) —a very queer spirit—I don't know how to define it—it is the sort of spirit that is in Dame Ethel Smyth—you have only got to look at her and you will feel it for yourselves—and this spirit . . . is impossible to lock up or lock out. . . . Suddenly he discovers . . . (that nature—but he did not call it nature—he called it sin—had made them also) doctors, civil servants, meteorologists, dental surgeons, librarians, solicitors' clerks, agricultural workers, analytical chemists, investigators of industrial psychology, barristers at law, makers of scientific models, accountants, hospital dieticians, political organizers, storekeepers, artists, horticultural instructors, publicity managers, architects, insurance representatives, dealers in antiques, bankers, actuaries, managers of house property, court dress makers, aero engineers, history instructors, company directors, organizers of peace crusades, newspaper representatives, technical officers in the royal airships works,—and so on.

The list, often a powerful weapon in the hands of the propagandist, is used here with great skill. By the time she has finished the outraged man in his private house seems to belong to the Dark Ages.

"Naturally he swore they are mutinous, base, ungrateful hussies. They are taking the bread out of my mouth and making it quite unnecessary that I should support them. I am the breadwinner; how am I going to support a wife and family, if my wife and family can support themselves?"

After this fantasy she urges her audience not to be angry but to be patient and amused with men who have had such a "lop-sided education"; there are, she asserts, *some* men capable of a wider humanity. One is then to direct one's anger at the enemy without letting bitterness spoil the possibility for personal happiness. This speech is an important document, for it shows us Virginia Woolf not in her own room, but in a meeting room with other women, in her element as a public woman, where the sisterhood of her peers makes possible the expression of both feminist anger and feminist humor. And we should cherish her statement—"The future of fiction depends very much upon what extent men can be educated to stand free speech in women."

The source for Woolf's provocative but correct portraits of the powerful in *Three Guineas* may be derived from Robins' *Ancilla's Share,* where she writes of man's "intensity of self-importance, his love of the sceptre and the big stick, of dressing up and playacting hero, priest or king."[26] Robins sees the social function of ribbons and rosettes, stripes and hoods and wigs as allaying doubts of one's personal value. The "rag or ribbon or hieroglyph" is not just snobbery but a symbol of aspiration, an incentive to achievement for the next generation of patriarchs. Robins jokingly comments on "a sober respectable British gentleman content to be officially known as a Rouge Dragon, another as Blue Mantle, or most blessedly nonsensical of all, a Unicorn Pursuivant—."[27] She laughs, but realizes the social function of the rags and ribbons; "the British government issued four million Great War medals and bedecked the reputed-worthy with eighteen miles of ribbon."

We know Virginia Woolf's amused disdain of the public schoolboy view of life as a war of perpetual competition for the prize of a "highly ornamental pot" from the headmaster. Robins before her had been a little less certain whether women should enter this competition themselves, giving prizes to female achievement to encourage the daughters as well as the sons. Fiercely pacifist as Woolf always was, she thought that man would continue to see women's achievement in sexual terms, and she imagined women wearing a tuft of horsehair on the left shoulder as a symbol of motherhood. Competition, she felt, like the foolish vanity of medals and ribbons, belonged to the childhood of social life in the patriarchy. On this issue Woolf had no doubts at all. From Italy, where she was observing Mussolini's fascism firsthand, she refused the order of Dame of the British Empire with a simple and defiant "No." Few, even self-defined "outsiders," would refuse the honors and awards of the "insiders," if they would not indeed openly scramble for them. But Woolf, as she says in *Three Guineas* with painful logic, was not about to accept favors from her enemies. She would then be forced to swallow her anger and stop criticizing the state. Like Antigone, revived as the heroine of *The Years* and *Three Guineas,* she obeyed a higher law and was willing to be buried alive for it, cursing, as the chorus in Sophocles does, "the old men who use big words."

When Woolf rejects the labels "bourgeois" and "capitalist," it is as an independent working middle-class woman. She owns no property and by international law must even accept her husband's country as her own. When she wrote "as a woman I have no country," she lost most of her audience. For if *Three Guineas* is a serious attempt at a tripartite philosophical and political statement of socialism, feminism, and pacifism, she was not, in Britain in 1939, surrounded by a band of likeminded triple thinkers. Her socialist friends were male and like E. M. Forster, openly antifeminist; her one pacifist compatriot, Aldous Huxley, was antifeminist; her feminist friend Ethel Smyth was as pro-British a patriot as most of her fellow suffragettes had been in World War I. If people shared her antifascism, they went to war zealously to prevent its spread. Her insistence that it was more important to kill fascism in the very structure of the British patriarchy annoyed her friends and still seems to many a ridiculous position when even the most internationalist of socialists joined the united front. She believed in the natural alliance between women and workers and urged them both to let the patriarchs and capitalists fight a war which was essentially based on the desire to annex or protect private property. In the meantime women and workers should trespass on all the private property of patriarchal culture at home and build their own new and better state. *Three Guineas* is the work of a moral revolutionary, and it advocates the position that during the war outsiders (women and the working class) should seize the means of the reproduction of culture. But she did not rouse her readers to violence. *Three Guineas* roused a great deal of anger, best seen in Queenie Leavis' review of it in *Scrutiny,* where Mrs. Leavis took up the battle cry of the patriarchal state, "Caterpillars of the Commonwealth, Unite!" Like Mrs. Humphry Ward before her, Queenie Leavis angrily denounced feminism as dangerous and silly, attacked Woolf personally as not being a real woman because she was not a mother and as incapable of being a true socialist because she was not a member of the working class. Most vigorously she defended Oxford and Cambridge for excluding women, insisting that most women were not bright enough to deserve an education. Patriarchal institutions are adept at finding "exceptional" women like Mrs. Humphry Ward and Queenie Leavis to denounce other members of their sex.

Angry as *Three Guineas* is at male dominance, it remains a primer for protest and an encouragement for women to struggle. She names a litany of female saints and heroines, as she did in *A Room of One's Own;* the female reader who studies the footnotes and the intricate web of reference can educate and arm herself as a feminist. The funny and eccentric Woolf of the beginning of *A Room of One's Own,* the well-fed guest of the men's college, amusingly characterized women as strange outsiders, like the Manx cat, tolerated on the Isle of Man. "What a difference a tail makes," she mused. By the time she had "spat out" *Three Guineas,* the wry, ironic tone is gone, and she warns, a prophetic Cassandra, that when there is no freedom in the private house, there is no freedom in the public world. Creon took Antigone and shut her "not in Holloway or in a concentration camp, but in a tomb. And Creon, we read, brought ruin on his house, and scattered the land with the bodies of the dead . . . things repeat themselves it seems."[28]

Elizabeth Robins wrote that "the most immediately urgent study of womankind is woman,"[29] and Woolf later made the same assertion. They both commented on man's fascination with women's chastity, and both, as socialist feminists, wanted to know what it was like to be a working woman in the past; they urged future historians to write "the lives of the obscure." "And there is the girl behind the counter too . . . I would as soon have her true history as the hundred and fiftieth life of Napoleon or seventieth study of Keats and his use of Miltonic inversion which old Professor Z and his like are now inditing."[30] Robins complains that she wants to "hear of Sappho from some Aspasia of an earlier day!"[31] and mourns the loss of the memory of fighting heroines, for man "tended to suppress not only the women who departed from his rules, but the very record of these departures."[32] While Woolf in *A Room of One's Own* uses the images of woman as enlarging mirror to make her points, Robins refers to the scold's chair, bridle, and gag as "less a badge of woman's humiliation than of man's fear."[33]

The scold's voice was the voice of all women, to Robins.

> It rang with the old courage that so perilously insisted on giving discontent a tongue. The phantom sat there, grotesque, half-throttled, dishevelled, wild, being wrenched and choked into submission. Then the release in a rabble of triumphant men and boys, not voiceless they, nor voiceless those of her own sex needing to win immunity from man's reprisals by joining in the hue and cry. . . . "Did he ever once" she asks the suffering scold "invite you to cleanse your bosom of perilous stuff by so much as blowing a blast on his blessed horn?"[34]

Both Robins and Woolf recognize that the source of women's oppression is economic, and lest they be accused of genteel anticapitalism, I would argue that they wrote for and about their own class out of intellectual commitment, fearing more than anything else the smug satisfactions of missionaries to the masses. In arguing with unenlightened middle-class women, both were doing feminism a great service. Woolf said that men were often very "nice" on a personal level. Robins had said "While they are the blessing of the individual woman's life, 'good' men may be the enemies of progress."

> We catch ourselves saying with a happy superiority: "Men have always been very nice to me." As if that touched on the outermost fringe of the question! No one has said men are not human. Naturally there are those who are "nice" to some women. It is sometimes their business to be nice to certain women. It is often their pleasure to be nice. That men are commonly more generous in their private dealings than just in their public acts is undoubtedly a snare to women who have only private dealings with men. Women who sit in the sun of private benevolence have

been soothed to a mean complicity in the misery of the mass. In the eyes of many a woman to whom men have been "very nice" there seems an ungraciousness too raw in pointing out that man's private attempt to right the public balance by compensatory kindness to individuals, by conferring special immunities and privileges, by all that he has thought of as chivalry, is to offer a dole of bright farthings in lieu of the gold of equal inheritance.[35]

Elizabeth Robins had the wisdom of experience and years of pent-up anger to spark these statements. Well-meant aid that comes too late she compared to the Oriental visionary who put dead fish back into the sea. She felt, I suspect, very like some panting fish exhausted after a lifetime of struggle for the woman's cause. Men's politeness seemed futile to a woman who had been an ardent champion of suffragist militancy. Woolf had not been a militant suffragist, but had espoused the cause of adult suffrage, the Independent Labour Party's policy, which stressed the solidarity of women and workers. She had supported Margaret Llewelyn Davies' Working Women's Co-operative Guild in its nonviolent struggle. In the thick of things Robins had abandoned pacifism and defended symbolic violence against the Liberal government as a healthy expression of women's justified anger with the state. In contrast, Virginia Woolf wrote:

> No age can ever have been as stridently sex-conscious as our own; those innumerable books by men about women in the British Museum are a proof of it. The Suffrage campaign was no doubt to blame. It must have roused in men an extraordinary desire for self-assertion; it must have made them lay an emphasis upon their own sex and its characteristics which they would not have troubled to think about had they not been challenged. And when one is challenged, even by a few women in black bonnets, one retaliates, if one has never been challenged before, rather excessively.[36]

But later, in *Three Guineas,* she saw Mrs. Pankhurst as Antigone, defiantly obedient to a higher law than that of the patriarchal state, a fit historical mother to her own impassioned statement. Elizabeth Robins had been one of those black-bonnetted challengers, and in *Ancilla's Share* she urged women to "cease to think even of the inimical man as powerful and wicked":

> He is bewildered and helpless. . . . He shows it by his anger, his galled wincing when the sure way is taken to scotch his sex contempt. Clearest of all, when he takes refuge in cruelty, does he show woman his heart of fear. . . :
>
> He is afraid he will lose his home if he cannot compel a slave class to keep it for him.
>
> He is afraid he will lose his food supply if he cannot find low-paid, low-living labour to cultivate his fields.
>
> He is afraid he will lose his country if he cannot compel conscripted men to . . . fight conscripted men . . . we see the closest analogy between the struggle inspired by man's fear of the moral power of woman and the struggle inspired by man's fear of the material power of his brother man. . . .
>
> It would seem as though man had long known that when he could no longer successfully obstruct the power of woman, she would take war from him. And if he were deprived of his power to inspire fear, what refuge, then, from that fear in his own soul?[37]

Robins argued for "a separable spite" on the part of women, for "the beginnings of civilisation depended on her endurance of man's yoke. The continuance of civilisation depends on her refusal."[38]

"Separable spite" is exactly what Woolf calls for in *Three Guineas*. But in *A Room of One's Own* ten years earlier she had written: "The history of men's opposition to women's emancipation is more interesting perhaps than the story of that emancipation itself. An amusing book might be made of it if some young student at Girton or Newnham would collect examples and deduce a theory—but she would need thick gloves on her hands, and bars to protect her of solid gold."[39] Defining herself as an uneducated woman, she took on the task herself, gloveless and without the economic advantage of a gilded cage. *Three*

Guineas was not an amusing book. Thus vulnerable to the anger of friends and enemies alike, Woolf, I feel, removed herself from the scene. She claimed madness as an ethical justification for the act.

But here I see another connection with Elizabeth Robins. Woolf published Robins' *Ibsen and the Actress* at the Hogarth Press. It contains a curious and fascinating reading of Hedda Gabler's suicide as angry and rebellious as well as a work of art. Robins argues that those who are oppressed psychologically or economically have "one sort of power over their own lives, the power to end them." Ibsen shared a peculiar kind of Social Darwinism with the actress who brought his works to England, a view of suicide as an ethical and political act. Woolf's half-brother, Gerald Duckworth, had been a close friend of Elizabeth Robins in the 1890s. He was the treasurer of the subscription series of Ibsen productions which was the only way she could get Ibsen's radical plays staged in a West End dominated by actor-managers and their Victorian melodramas. Quentin Bell has given us details of Virginia Woolf's guilt and anger late in life over her half-brother's sexual assaults. That he introduced her to Ibsen and a method of dramatizing incest guilt is not surprising. Ibsen also dealt with hereditary madness, a subject which would have interested brother and sister because of the incurable madness of their sister and Virginia's own mental instability.

When Robins published her novel *The Open Question* in 1898, she worked out similar nineteenth-century themes. The incestuous hero and heroine, before their own "ethical" suicide because they fear the birth of an "unhealthy" child, have organized in Paris a group who suggest to the oppressed, the prostitutes and destitute workers, that they might find personal dignity in suicide. The youthful Woolf was strongly influenced by Ibsen and Wagner, both of them in some senses Social Darwinists who made suicide into an ethical imperative. In fact, this is why Shaw regarded *Tristan und Isolde* as much more dangerous and revolutionary than Marx. I would here simply like to suggest that Woolf's suicide may have been the result of an ethical imperative rather than the result of "madness" or despair. Gerald Duckworth wrote to Elizabeth Robins praising *The Open Question* as one of the greatest books ever written.[40] He was not alone in his opinion, as the reviews testify. Woolf says in a letter of 1905 that she had been arguing the ethics of suicide with her sister all morning.[41] Her letters in the thirties to Dame Ethel Smyth beg for an ethical defense of suicide. She was not "mad" when she wrote those letters exonerating Leonard Woolf from any guilt about her death. She was angry: at Leonard, at the Germans bombing England, and at men for making war. Yet she was helplessly hampered from expressing that anger by a pacifism as deep-seated as other people's religions. *Between the Acts,* the book she wrote before she died, shows us how fully she saw the source of the violence of war in the violence of human sexuality.[42] Woolf did not die violently by her own hand, nor was she a masochist. In a dignified and deliberate way she filled her pockets with stones and returned to "mother water."

The "influence" of Robins on Woolf as here demonstrated is both an instance of "thinking back through our mothers" and a demonstration of Woolf's own proposition that art improves with the generations. When they can lean on the accumulated history of their own accomplishments, women and the working class will produce "great" literature. Even Woolf's idea of the collective historical effort behind each individual work of art can be found in *Ancilla's Share,* where Robins declares that works of art are collaborations with the ghosts of dead women. Both women felt that they voiced woman's collective historical anger.

The burden of their effort is continually being carried forward by feminist artists. In "The Phenomenology of Anger," Adrienne Rich writes:

> *The only real love I have ever felt*
> *was for children and other women.*
> *Everything else was lust, pity,*
> *self-hatred, pity, lust.*
> This is a woman's confession.[43]

The central image of Rich's poem is fire; the burning rage produces a kind of angry truth-telling, fulfilling, one feels, Woolf's demand that women *tell the truth.* That "the truth" is synonymous with anger is testimony to its power and the history of its suppression. Few women poets have dared Rich's angry confession. The twentieth-century disguise is not pseudonymity nor anonymity but another form of indirect discourse which Hortense Calisher calls "mental hysterectomy," the kind of nonthreatening female art which is "beautifully mandarin or minor." She sees for herself "the feminism that comes straight from the belly, from the bed and from the childbed," but rejects anger as a source of female artistic energy. "Humor is a better answer to that. And anger should be directed against the rules."[44]

Elizabeth Robins was almost eighty when E. M. Forster gave the Rede Lecture on Virginia Woolf after her death. She made a typescript of her notes and wrote furiously about his sexist remarks. Robins quotes an introductory remark of his which does not appear in the reprint of the lecture: "She'd probably mock . . . and why if you want to discuss my books must you first disguise yourself in a cap and gown?"[45] Robins underlines Forster's remark: "Improving the world she would not consider, on the ground that the world is man made, and that she, a woman, had no responsibility for the mess. This last argument is a curious one." Here Robins put three exclamation marks and wrote "scalpel-like 'curious' cuts F(eminism) open wide." Three more exclamation points mark Forster's remark about Woolf's "peculiar" feminism, which he found "responsible for the worst of her books—the cantankerous *Three Guineas,* and for the less successful streaks in *Orlando.*" Forster always sees feminism as a kind of social disease in "spots" or "streaks" in her work. Here Robins writes, "Feminism not responsible for *Orlando.* I must look at O. again and see if my old first impression that an effort toward Antifeminism wasn't the true motive-power. That effort expended itself; it had by her geography no Continuing City. She was too aware of the world's need." Did Elizabeth Robins sit in the audience while Virginia Woolf's "friend" E. M. Forster explained that Woolf was not a great writer because she "had no great cause at heart," that she despised the working class, and that she was "a lady?" Robins asked herself in the margin whether being an American, despite slaveholding grandparents on both sides, had saved her from seeing "the lady" as a problem.

She underlined his remark on Woolf that "women must not condone the tragic male-made mess or accept the crumbs of power which men throw occasionally from their hideous feast. Like Lysistrata she withdrew. Now there is to me something old-fashioned in this feminism. . . . In the 1940's I think she had not much to complain of and kept on grumbling from habit." Across this Robins has written "Oh God!" Imagine her emotions as he went on in his public-schoolboy way to award Woolf "a row of little silver cups" for her novels, as if fiction were a competition. Woolf had mocked this view of life in *A Room of One's Own* as part of the childhood of patriarchal civilization. But it still prevailed in 1941, and its defenders had their revenge. It may be a long time before men are educated to tolerate free speech in women; Woolf herself was not deceived about Forster. She confessed to Ethel Smyth that she had once been influenced by him, but now found him the "most inflexible of men" and his books "shrivelled and immature."[46]

Virginia Woolf and Elizabeth Robins ended their lives as angry old women, as cursing Antigones, as Lapland witches. But both hoped for a new generation of angry young women who would tell the truth about themselves and about men. Think, Virginia Woolf says, not altogether ironically, of all we have learned from the Strindbergs and Tolstoys, and what men may hope to learn from the Lapland witches and Jane Angers. Up with spite—separable, yes, from the pursuit of personal happiness, but also as a collective historical act so that every generation of female artists need not fight the same battles but may begin where their mothers left off, inheriting as long as necessary the gloves and golden bars of self-defense.

Anger is *not* anathema in art; it is a primary source of creative energy. Rage and savage indignation sear the hearts of female poets and female critics. Why not spit it out, as Woolf said, blow the blessed horn, as Robins said? Why wait until old age, as they did, waiting long to let out their full quota of anger? Out with it. No more burying our wrath, turning it against ourselves. No more ethical suicides, no more literary pacifism. We must make the literary profession safe for women as well as ladies. It is our historical responsibility. When the fires of our rage have burnt out, think how clear the air will be for our daughters. They will write in joy and freedom only after we have written in anger. It is up to us to see that the academy gives its little silver cups to those who deserve them. We must ourselves forge a great big golden bowl in honor of Virginia Woolf, inscribing on it her words: "The future of fiction depends very much upon what extent men can be educated to stand free speech in women."

WRITING PRACTICE

††††

The Lupine Critic
Writes a (Biased) History
of Virginia Woolf Scholarship

7

Tintinnabulations

Virginia Woolf used to complain of Christians' ringing their church bells on Sunday mornings, disturbing good people at their work. The irony of this remark stems from her self-identification as an outsider in British society—not only as a non-Christian, the wife of a Jew, a pamphleteering left-wing pacifist, the uneducated "daughter of an educated man," a woman writer in an intellectual world of male homosexuals, but also as the creator and upholder of severe and radical moral and aesthetic standards in a society that valued and to some extent still values far more the patriarchal mythmaking of Joyce, Lawrence, and Eliot.

The Bells, Quentin and Olivier, and Nigel Nicolson have been ringing so loud a paean to "their" Virginia Woolf that her own voice has been drowned in the process, not to mention the voices of critics who have captured a Woolf other than the one the Bells have cornered and tamed behind bars in the Bloomsbury zoo. She haunted other streets besides those, as their own publication of the letters and diaries abundantly proves. Exhibited as she is among the Bloomsbury painters, literary lions and tigers, and exotic birds, she serves the same function as the monkeys and apes do in any zoo. We go to see them and manage a peek at the adjoining cages on our way in and out.

Quentin Bell is not only the biographer of Virginia Woolf. He is an art critic and a son. He has wished to promote the reputation of the painters Vanessa Bell and Duncan Grant and of the critic Clive Bell. He is clearly not the nephew Woolf imagined playing North to Eleanor Pargiter in *The Years,* who saw the family as the enemy of art and freedom. He naturally prefers his mother to his aunt. It is difficult having a genius in the family, and Vanessa Bell emerges as the heroine of his biography of Virginia Woolf, excelling in the womanly arts that always escaped her more angular sister.[1] Woolf certainly admired these qualities, needing mothering more than anything else from friends, relatives, and husband. While Quentin Bell seems to have found her satisfactory as an aunt, he resented her meddling in politics and says so vigorously, describing her as an antiquated spinster among her male juniors in the 1930s, when she produced her strongest antifascist work. Yet, thanks largely to him, his wife, and the editors of the letters, we now can see her with eyes other than those of an art critic or a nephew.

Visually, her novels have little in common with the painters of her circle, though critics have given much attention to this subject. One of Woolf's essays first appeared in an issue of *The Dial* that contained a painting of an army barracks by Georgia O'Keeffe, with a flagpole curved and bent in the center. The two odd innovative "outsider" women artists have a great deal more in common than the wit of their antipatriotic, antipatriarchal protests. Another avenue not explored is her non-English, non-Bloomsbury love of music. When a fine critic like Allen McLaurin in *The Echoes Enslaved*[2] takes it, the view one sees of the novels commands considerably more interest.

Since we are all attached to our families, Bell is not to be blamed for being as a biographer less a good nephew than a good son. He should hardly be surprised, however, if, following his lead, critics regard a great novelist and major intellectual figure as merely the object of a cult or as the scapegoat establishment figure on whom to hang guilt for criticizing the poets of the 1930s. In two recent general books both Elaine Showalter and Samuel Hynes have taken their cues on Woolf from Quentin Bell's biography. In *A Literature of Their Own*,[3] Showalter finds the "adoption of a female aesthetic" for Woolf a "betrayal of her literary genius," and her suicide "one of Blooms-bury's representative art forms." Bell has given her all the materials for an ugly discussion of anorexia, menstrual shame, obsession with the father, the poor Duckworth brothers as monsters, and female versions of madness. Showalter has made Virginia Woolf into a case study of female failure, and her books "the sphere of the exile and the eunuch"; she follows Bell's lead in seeing Woolf's vision as "deadly" and "disembodied." Hynes has managed to write a book on "Literature and Politics in the Thirties"[4]—the decade of *The Waves, The Years, The Common Reader,* and *Three Guineas,* all of which contributed to the moral and political debate—and yet to present her only as the embodiment of Auden's scolding mother figure.

By stressing how alien to him was Virginia Woolf's kind of femaleness and by de-emphasizing or disapproving of a lifetime of political engagement, Bell has provided two different sets of symptoms from which the literary doctors may make their diagnoses. One leads to the production of a female cult and its subsequent denunciation by a new generation of Queenie Leavises. The other leads to her exclusion from the literary/historical canon on the grounds of "aloofness" or "having no great cause at heart," as Forster claimed. In fact, her political and moral beliefs, antiauthoritarian and antiheroic as they were, compared to those of Yeats or Pound or Lawrence or even Auden, are among the very few that bear close scrutiny. A consistent socialist, pacifist, and feminist, she presented ideas that survive unscathed and undated—which is more than one can say for most of her contemporaries.

It is time for a new biography. Bell's has been widely read and highly praised. With a few notable exceptions: Ellen Hawkes's "The Virgin in the Bell Biography"[5] speaking for feminists; Michael Holroyd, speaking as a professional biographer who sees a missed opportunity for the subject to write in collaboration with the biographer, rendering the book mere external history, so "protective" of a certain view of Virginia Woolf that she has "slipped through his fingers";[6] and Rebecca West, speaking as a friend and contemporary female artist. Dame Rebecca sees Bell as responsible for "the conversion of biography from a form of literature to a blood sport. Virginia Woolf's official biography is to me a scene of carnage."[7]

The new biographer ought to be neither bloodthirsty nor bloody-minded. But she should be perhaps an artist in her own right, considering the problems of female artists on their own ground. And it ought to be a critical biography, so that life and work are one. She might concentrate on that Victorian household in which men were so emphatically men and women women, in which Leslie Stephen's alpenstocks lay about, and maps of the Alps, marked with the peaks he had conquered, hung on the walls, in which Julia Stephen reigned as "half madonna, half woman of the world," demanding of her daughters that they be beautiful as a duty to the family. What was it like, this new biographer might ask, only to feel attracted to manly, unsuitable men, to have to "gallop" away at the first sexual stirrings, to try to find a mate among the Cambridge intellectuals and "apostolic buggers"? In a literary world populated by the kind of male homosexuals who disliked the female body as well as the female mind, and said so, no wonder Woolf turned for solace and strength to a community of women writers and reformers living and dead, for whom she wrote and worked and studied, to whom she sent her articles and stories. The new biographer ought to take another look at the Duckworth brothers, the villains of the official biography, and see how they brought Ibsen into the house when Virginia was in her teens, his radical ideas and dramatic form becoming a permanent influence on her style as well as her ideology.

The biographer might look again at the sustaining and ambivalent relations with other women writers and artists, from Violet Dickinson to Dame Ethel Smyth, and find there a structure that shapes the whole life around the search for a mother. "Thinking back through our mothers" as a literary philosophy then coheres with everything from the maternal role of Leonard Woolf to the love letters to Vita Sackville-West. This imaginary biographer would examine more carefully the political and moral ideas of the fiction and essays and would try to net the "frozen falcon" as she listened to music and tried to imitate its structures in words. Why, she would ask, did words always seem erotic to Woolf? Why did she fuss so about chastity? Was she haunted by her name throughout her life? Once married did she see herself as simultaneously savage and pure—a Diana out of Meredith's imagination, living the Persephone/Demeter myth in the twentieth century?

The new biographer will have to look at more than the hypotenuse of the Clive/Vanessa/Virginia triangle by reading their letters to her. What awful guilt led her to please her sister by acting as go-between to that unpleasant man, his mistress, and his wife? Woolf seems to have slipped once, and volume 3 of the *Letters* suggests that she was made to pay for it for the rest of her life. She was a trial to her sister, no doubt, but could she get attention and affection only by cultivating Clive and then tattling? And then, there is the suicide and the sanity of the notes on approaching insanity, and the repetition in her letters to Leonard of the exact words that her mother had used to describe her first marriage to Herbert Duckworth and that the relieved hero uses at the death of Rachel Vinrace in *The Voyage Out*. The suicide notes are the work of a great artist and a good generous woman, following the advice of her doctor to "reassure Leonard" and absolve him of any guilt. This brave new biographer is going to have to deal with all the theories from madness to menopause, with the family, the official version, with Woolf's attitude toward war and fascism and anti-Semitism, with the requests for ethical arguments against suicide in the letters to Ethel Smyth, with the reports of her doctor, Octavia Wilberforce, and, finally, with her radical mysticism. It will not be easy.

The publication of the *Diary*[8] provides a major tool, and one is grateful to Anne Olivier Bell for the patience and effort of providing it. But here the Bloomsbury view again prevails, and we never get a naked Virginia Woolf; she is always dressed in a jacket designed in the Omega Workshop. With the *Diary* the problem grows more serious, with Bells ringing all over the page to drown out the voice of Virginia Woolf. They disapprove, they want to set the record straight. They scold and scold and ring and ring. The diarist's voice is muffled, wrapped in footnotes of cotton wool: One can hardly hear the voice, often so shrill and high-pitched, so critical or intimate, which she saved for her diary. The only way to read volume 1 of the *Diary* is to cover up the footnotes. They creep up and up and threaten to devour the whole page; like the Sunday church bells, they distract the ordinary reader and the scholar alike from reading; and they betray an uncommon case of editorial antagonism. The editor's apologia for the method explains the length, not the hostility. Quentin Bell's introduction may be seen as a brief Revised Authorized Version of the life. Although he is now willing to venture a critical judgment that the diary is "a masterpiece," the profoundly patriarchal point of view remains. One would never know from this description that Woolf had a mind at all, let alone one of the greatest artistic minds of the twentieth century.

Bell has given her an extended family setting that branches out a bit beyond Bloomsbury. But where is that solitary, strange, antisocial woman who valued privacy so highly that she made it the first principle of her aesthetic? One sees all her nests, their furniture in detail with learned labels on every stick and straw. But where is the Virginia Woolf who wrote novels—that great blue heron of a writer, in flight, alone? She once complained that biography, like sculpture, was all head and shoulders, that one would never know from the biographies of great men "that they had a body between them." The Bell view of Virginia Woolf is from the opposite angle and shows her only from the neck down and in the bosom of her family. This is often the trouble with biographies of great women; one never knows what kind of heads graced their feminine shoulders, and sometimes one can hardly see them at all in the family album. Much of Woolf's best writing attacked private property and the family, and she considered herself an outsider to it all.

The notes lean heavily on the "plunge into madness," "suicidal mania," "fearful tempests of lunacy," which pander to the taste of certain kinds of readers. There is a characteristic entry in the *Diary* about Pippa Strachey that includes a discussion of women's suffrage and a disagreement between the conservative feminist and the radical over Virginia's support of cooperative housekeeping. "The talk was hampered by the suspicion that she was a jingo" is Woolf's most telling sentence. It brings alive all those issues which tore apart the British feminist movement, the left-wing pacifists opposing the conservative patriots.[9] But the equally characteristic footnote ignores Woolf's concern over Phillipa Strachey's jingoism and defends her as a "force at the centre of the constitutional woman's movement." Virginia Woolf's opposition to this kind of bourgeois feminism is left unnoted, though it would contribute at the very least to an understanding of the differences between Sally Seal and Mary Datchet in *Night and Day*.

Another thing one learns from the *Diary* is how distinctly Covent Garden and the concert halls of London were her Cambridge.[10] While the men had debated philosophy or the Greek view of life with G. E. Moore, she continued, in her alert way, to listen to Mozart and Wagner. The failure of the editors to discuss Woolf's politics creates the impression that she had none and raises another curtain of darkness before a British audience already trained by the Leavises to think of her as a snob. No wonder J. I. M. Stewart says, "She was not an intellectual woman" and "Those lower classes continue to appear through mists of prejudice and dislike."[11] Here was a woman tormented by her desire to preach and teach, forcing herself to write without lecturing, controlling a desire to follow a nature akin to the Leavises themselves—"all that is highest and driest in Cambridge." Fascinated by reformers of all types, she saw their smug superiority toward the poor, the easy satisfactions of meddling missionaries. Her criticism of reformers and politicians, suffragettes and Thirties poets, derives not from snobbery but from an intimate knowledge of her own reforming heart's desire to dominate. She was an insider to labor and left politics, not a "lady" who looked on them with disdain. She called the Labour Party "that timid old sheep" because its policies were not radical enough for her. To ignore the evidence of meetings, discussions, 1917 Club teas, Co-operative Working Women's politics, when it is on the page, is equivalent to assuming that Shaw was not a socialist because he spent as much energy attacking his fellow Fabians as promoting their policies. There is nothing so romantic or radical as oneself when young, and Quentin Bell's fury is aroused because *Three Guineas* did not endorse his own brand of "united front" politics. How can an old aunt compare with a brave young man?

But Virginia Woolf spent most of her adult life alone, working, thinking, writing. Hence she was able to write so many novels, essays, letters, diaries. This simple fact seems never to occur to people who cannot root out from their minds that old turnip that women only care about personal relationships. Insisting on seeing her in society where she was out of her element, they miss the genius altogether and see only an eccentric woman. One would have to work very hard to find in *Ulysses* the broad scope of social criticism and moral and historical vision that fills the pages of *Mrs. Dalloway* or *The Years.* "Patriotism" and "family feeling," always the object of her wit and anger, take their revenge as the Bells tie her tightly to the family tree with a label that says "British Victorian Female Spinster."

Samuel Hynes had to make her into a matriarch to fit his myth, Quentin Bell a spinster. The facts are not enough for the male myth-mongering mind; someone of such stature must be either a virgin or a mother. That she was an ordinary married woman who produced books instead of babies is too prosaic an existence except to those who live it. Some readers of the *Diary* have found Virginia Woolf malicious. But the kind of malice one finds here is that of Hedda Gabler's deliberately mistaking Tesman's aunt's hat for the maid's. Bored and angry at the conventions of dishonesty in bourgeois family life, the high-strung intelligent artist lashes out in rather predictable ways. Most of the harm she really does is to herself. The *Diary* is buttressed by a prodigious amount of research, but there are a few lapses. Woolf wrote that she must one day write an essay on "The Eccentrics." The footnote traces essays on the individuals mentioned but fails to note one of this title.[12] Woolf wrote, "Surely the world has been right in conferring biographies where biographies are due? Surely the shower of titles and honours has not always descended on the wrong heads? That the world's estimate has been perverse from the start, and half her great men geese, are themes too vast to be disposed of in one short article." But then one might be better off reading the *Diary* as she did herself when writing of Pepys: "Not a confessional, still less a mere record of things useful to remember, but the storehouse of his most private self, the echo of life's sweetest sounds. . . . . When he went upstairs to his chamber it was to perform no mechanical exercise, but to hold intercourse with the secret companion who lives in everybody."[13] While some readers may feel that she kept a diary for the same reason Gwendolyn did in *The Importance of Being Earnest*—"to have something sensational to read in the train"—and Freudian critics may find intercourse with her secret companion to have been a substitute for intercourse with a real husband, others will find a great writer talking to herself as frankly and fearlessly as she could talk to no one else.

Nigel Nicolson and Joanne Trautmann, as editors of the *Letters,* have been far more modest and discreet in their footnotes, though the introductions express similar views on Woolf's madness and lack of interest in politics. Some readers may be a little surprised at Nicolson's censure of Virginia Woolf's flirtation with the "lecherous" (her word) Clive Bell, since Nicolson's own moral judgment allows him to call the marriage of his parents, Vita and Harold, "perfect." He does not find the letters interesting until Virginia Stephen begins to write "seriously" to men. But volume 1 has a rarely preserved portrait of a female artist in the making, love and work intensely intertwined in her relations with women who encouraged her to write, read, and think and gave her the nourishment of womanly love and literary criticism, which she was to seek and find in female friendship all her life. Bloomsbury fades into insignificance as an "influence" next to the radiance of Woolf's relationships with Margaret Llewelyn Davies, head of the Co-operative Working Women's Guild, Janet Case, her Greek teacher, Violet Dickinson, Madge Vaughan, and her aunt Caroline Stephen, the Quaker whom she called "Nun." It was this aunt who encouraged her to discipline her mind, to make herself into a historian, and provided her with the £500 a year for a room of her own. Much as she mocked the purity of her aunt's life, her own resembles it far more than it resembles Lytton Strachey's. Her future biographer will find more in Caroline Stephen's *The Light Arising: Thoughts on the Central Radiance* than in *Eminent Victorians* to explain the mystical vision of Woolf's greatest works.

In volume 1 of the *Letters,* Woolf writes to Violet Dickinson, "I saw Miss Ll. Davies at a lighted window in Barton St. with all the conspirators round her and cursed under my breath." What she cursed was her own exclusion from their visionary political work for women's suffrage and cooperative socialism. Margaret Llewelyn Davies become a lifelong friend, and her socialism and feminism as an ideal is enshrined in Mary Datchet's lighted window in *Night and Day* and Eleanor Pargiter's sunflower in *The Years.* When Woolf left off cursing and began to bless, and when a central radiance began to permeate her own prose, twentieth-century British literature took a great leap out of the patriarchal fog, for the myths and images that rise in all her work tell us the opposite of what our culture tells us—that light and rationality are female, darkness and chaos male. When Nigel Nicolson writes, "She needed the harness of a disciplined political brain, like Leonard's," he misses a point that Leonard himself probably did not miss. She did indeed see herself as a spirited racehorse, but she also saw herself as a donkey. What she needed was a good warm stall and regular feeding, so that fine self-disciplined political and artistic brain could race free in the wind over the downs. What harnesses she needed she had already learned to fashion for herself, being the daughter of a man who deprived her of the discipline of a formal education among her peers. Many critics have waxed lyrical about the pleasures of having the freedom of Leslie Stephen's library. They do not mention the pains of Leslie Stephen's temperament. Female relatives served only one purpose to Leslie Stephen: they were supposed to sympathize. And his enormous appetite for sympathy left little time for the education of daughters. One of Woolf's own trusty harnesses was reading Greek with Janet Case. The discipline of writing and rewriting, which she taught herself, will astonish those who study her manuscripts. We can see that her own standards are higher than those university training might have given her. But she was never sure. With the anxieties of any self-made, self-educated artist, the hurdles she erected for herself to jump were higher than mere examinations, and her fiction is the better for it.

In 1920 Woolf called Stevenson a bad writer because his letters were so boring: "A writer's letters should be as literary as his printed works." By volume 2 of the *Letters* (1912–22) her letters promise not only to be "literary," sparkling with wit and alive with imagery, but to interest the social historian as well. All her life she encouraged her women friends to keep and read and edit and publish the letters and diaries of their mothers and their aunts so that another view of history might be kept alive—just in case biographies were not conferred where biographies were due.

Nicolson, in his introduction to volume 2 of the *Letters,* makes clear that he thinks Virginia Woolf was an "elitiste," not a snob. He assumes that if one hates poverty one hates the poor, and he misinterprets, as many others do, the socialist intellectual's desire to bring the poor up to her level rather than show her solidarity by sinking to theirs. Failing to understand *Night and Day* or *Jacob's Room* as novels of social protest—as the socialist feminist artist's reply to the patriarchy's Great War—he assumes she was more interested in personal relationships than in the politics of war. But antipatriotism, anticapitalism, and antinationalism as she expressed them are just as political as their positives. Volume 2 takes us into her marriage, madness, the founding of the Hogarth Press, and the publication of her first three novels. She expands her talent for friendship beyond the feminine and the family but still begs for Vanessa's love; and the reader knows that Leonard and the doctors will decide that the cradle her beloved Violet Dickinson sends for a wedding gift will never rock a baby of her own. (In 1927 she wrote to Ethel Sands, "I'm always angry with myself for not having forced Leonard to take the risk in spite of the doctors.")

In 1913 she wrote to Ka Cox while on a political tour, "Nothing—except perhaps novel writing—can compare with the excitement of controlling the masses. . . . I see now why Margaret and even Mary MacArthur get their Imperial tread." Some of her mongoose-mandrill letters to Leonard are here, but what is remarkable in them and also in her later letters to him is that she is not the beloved responding to an active lover; she is the active partner. One discovers interesting things: how much she liked Hardy and disliked Dickens; how she asked Lytton Strachey if there really was any sense in Henry James, finding his novels "faintly tinged rose water, urbane and sleek, but vulgar and pale as Walter Lamb." She finds that the war fills her compatriots with "violent and filthy passions" and wants to know if the French are any better; she calls Rupert Brooke "a fully grown person among mummies and starvelings"; she reads *The Times* during the war—"this preposterous masculine fiction"; she grows steadily more feminist. Beatrice Webb turns up "rather like a moulting eagle," and Shaw as a pathetic egoist.

Woolf's flamboyant wit sets off her puritanism well, and her talk moves easily from toilets and sanitary napkins to Clytemnestra and Conrad. She is proud that her hairpins fall in the soup at elegant dinner parties and concerned that the women at her branch of the Co-operative Working Women's Guild are upset at the discussion of syphilis. She writes to Ottoline Morrell about Joyce, "The poor young man has only got the dregs of a mind compared even with George Meredith. I mean if you could weigh the meaning on Joyce's pages it would be about 10 times as light as on Henry James'." Even though Eliot has prepared her for "heavy" intellectual content, she finds "the bucket is almost empty," and expects to be "struck down by the wrath of God" for such dissent from the universal acclaim. One does get, as in this paragraph from a letter to Janet Case in 1922, a sense of what their lives were like:

> We've been sitting in the dark and listening to the Band and having a terrific argument about Shaw. I say he only influenced the outer fringes of morality. Leonard says that the shop girls wouldn't be listening to the Band with their young men if it weren't for Shaw. I say the human heart is touched only by the poets. Leonard say *rot,* I say damn. Then we go home. Leonard says I'm narrow. I say he's stunted. . . . There's not a single living writer (English) I respect. . . . How does one come by one's morality? Surely by reading the poets. And we've got no poets.

The British edition of volume 3 (1923–28) is called *A Change of Perspective* and runs from *Mrs. Dalloway* to *A Room of One's Own,* through *Orlando* and the love affair with Vita Sackville-West. It contains fascinating letters to the dying Jacques Raverat, as good as earlier ones to Gerald Brenan. The female friendships continue and deepen: Vanessa Bell, Margaret Llewelyn Davies, Janet Case, Violet Dickinson. Vita Sackville-West is in and out; Jane Harrison, the great classical scholar whose work had a profound influence on Woolf's symbolism, is mentioned a good deal. Ottoline, Dorothy Brett, "Todd," the editor of *Vogue,* the painters Ethel Sands and Nan Hudson, form new female circles. The memory of Katherine Mansfield is revived, and Edith Sitwell and Rebecca West make striking impressions. More and more, Virginia Woolf concentrates on loving her own sex. It seems perfectly natural that she should fall in love with Vita, and just as natural that she should fall out again. Exciting as the adventure was, Vita lacked both the mind and the maternal selflessness as a lover that Virginia sought in female friends. Having satisfied her curiosity in the satin sheets, Virginia soon returned to her customary austerity—Vita's values, traditional and conservative in luxurious style, being very much at odds with her own radical ascetic commitment to the future.

The letters to Jacques Raverat are superb, as one artist to another she respects, and full of extraordinary feeling. Her own romantic memory of the Raverats as the ideal young lovers—Does he appear as Renny in *The Years?*—is revealed, as well as an explanation of her unwillingness to write about her husband. She had assumed they were anti-Semitic and so never mentioned him. A whole ocean of feeling pours out in this brief remark, making the reader pause to wonder what social sacrifices life with Leonard required her to make, how she bore them, and how she protected him. She early outgrew the prejudice of her class. But it is not clear which word in her description of him as a "penniless Jew" to her friends when she was about to marry held more weight in her rebellious pride. It is not race or class prejudice but her own wicked eye and ear that capture for his sister Vanessa a visit from her Jewish mother-in-law. She had had years of experience as an unsatisfactory daughter-in-law and had been made to feel how inadequate books were as a substitute for babies. Since it was Leonard who insisted she was too "insane" to have children and who sought out other opinions when Savage, the family doctor, claimed it would "do her a world of good," there are some painful ironies here. The monologue she records rings true. Mrs. Woolf tells "Len" he should have gone to the bar and then says Radclyffe Hall's book is corrupt, but she likes it. (Virginia disliked the book but defended Radclyffe Hall's right to write a lesbian novel.) *Mrs. Woolf:* "We did not do such things at my boarding school. *Leonard:* We did at my boarding school. It was the most corrupt place

I have ever been in. And you let me go there when I was twelve without knowing a thing. *Mrs. W:* But I had given you good principles, Len. *Len:* You had given me no principles at all." Mrs. W. then changes tactics, reminding him that she used to bring his socks to bed with her so she could start darning them the minute she woke up. This is the same ear that records a quarrel with Clive Bell or a scene with Ottoline Morrell. Her own victories over anti-Semitism are explained in letters to Ethel Smyth and should appear in the next volume.

"An elderly bugger is always something of a priest," she writes of E. M. Forster reading Dante. (But she was reading Dante, too. Maybe an aging lesbian is something of a priestess.) Her description of Edith Sitwell as "like a clean hare's bone that one finds on a moor with emeralds stuck about it" is perfect, and again more like Georgia O'Keeffe than Duncan Grant. She writes to Vita about her own "shingled head" as "like the hind view of a frightened hen partridge" and wants to know what Vita is going to do about menstruating on her twelve-day walking tour in the Persian mountains. She begs information about face powder. A box promptly arrives, and Virginia thinks she can rise to powder but not to rouge. Women's worries, when expressed with Woolf's wit, drop all the veils of taboo as trivia. She thought during the late 1930s that perhaps in fifty years' time men could be educated to tolerate free speech in women novelists. Her letters have some lessons of their own, and, painful though men may find them, women will burst out laughing.

In 1927 she praises Vanessa's paintings: Virginia and Vanessa are now both "mistress of our medium" and must "buttress up this lyricism with solidity." She answers Saxon Sydney-Turner's criticism of her use of "vapid" and "insipid" by explaining that her sense of words derives from the number of syllables. "One writes, I suppose, by ear, not dictionary." Steeled in trusting her own critical responses, she reads *Udolpho,* cannot understand why Mrs. Radcliffe is considered a laughingstock, and declares she will "lead a Radcliffe relief party." To Vita she writes, "Style is a very simple matter; it is all rhythm. Once you get that, you can't use the wrong words"—which is a little more profound than calling Edmund Gosse a "little grocer" when he criticized Vita's writing. She writes to Roger Fry of her genuine difficulties over Gertrude Stein, whose *Composition as Explanation* she was publishing: "For my own part I wish we could skip a generation—skip Edith and Gertrude and Tom and Joyce and Virginia and come out in the open again, when everything has been restarted and runs full tilt, instead of trickling and teasing in this irritating way. I think it's bad for the character too, to live in a bye stream, and have to consort with eccentricities," by which she means that T. S. Eliot is behaving like "an old maid who has been kissed by the butler." The only patronymic is Joyce.

This mixture of the profound and the hilarious is to be found in all her letters. If it were only by her brain she could give pleasure to others, then she shared the language of her thoughts. She was remarkably clearheaded about moral principles, and one of the funniest and most serious episodes is her debate with Logan Pearsall Smith about writing for *Vogue.* "He says it demeans one. He says one must write only for the Lit. Supplement and the Nation and Robert Bridges and prestige and posterity and to set a high example. I say Bunkum. Ladies clothes and aristocrats playing golf don't affect my style; and they would do his a world of good. Oh these Americans! How they always muddle everything up! What he wants is prestige: what I want, money." She sent him an article written for the *Nation* but printed in *Vogue* to see if he could tell the difference. But she pointed out that having one's articles cut by the editor of the *Times Literary Supplement* was much worse for a writer than being printed in a fashion magazine, "perhaps worse than the vulgarity, which is open and shameless, of *Vogue.* . . . Todd lets you write what you like, and its your own fault if you conform to the stays and the petticoats." Thinking of *Vogue* as an organ of free speech is a little startling, but Woolf had been constrained by the maidenly stays of the *Times Literary Supplement* for years. (It is a shame that her letters to Bruce Richmond do not survive.) That *Vogue* should have given a great writer money as well as freedom merely proves Woolf's instinct that women can be trusted in important things.

Virginia Woolf's *Letters* are among the finest of the twentieth century, for light and speed and beauty of language and image, for a moral strength and intellectual vigor unmatched by her contemporaries. These qualities would make them singular enough in modern letters, but their enduring value lies in their lack of ego. They were written to please the recipient and do not, like most letters of great men, nag, whine, or complain. She really did manage to stamp out the hated "I, I, I," a small miracle in the age of ego.

Moments of Being, some of Woolf's unpublished autobiographical writings edited by Jeanne Schulkind, is doubtless the most exciting of recent publications, for the Bells are silent, and Woolf's voice rings true, on her childhood, her parents.[14] Here one finds in a couple of sentences the most extraordinary expression of a "Marxist" aesthetic imaginable. (It is there in all her essays, but the Leavis-trained reader has been taught to ignore it; and it would put any Thirties poet to shame.)

> We—I mean all human beings—are connected with this: that the whole world is a work of art; that we are parts of the work of art. *Hamlet* or a Beethoven quartet is the truth about this vast mass that we call the world. But there is no Shakespeare, there is no Beethoven; certainly and emphatically there is no God: we are the words; we are the music; we are the thing itself.

No highbrow or snob could express such a radical democratic concept of art. It matches Marx's definition of history. The political implications of her thought, buried by her critics, ought now to come to light. We know now that Leonard Woolf, while claiming to publish the last best version of each article in *Collected Essays,* printed a flippant early *Yale Review* version of the essay on the cooperative working women. The final version, edited with the help of the working women themselves, differs considerably as printed in *Life As We Have Known It.* The capacity to contain the most brilliant economic and historical analysis in plain language ought to be studied by all who are concerned with the relation of propaganda to art.

The publication of *The Pargiters,* the novel-essay portion of *The Years,* is a major event. Earlier, a large selection from the novel, removed at the last moment in galley form, was published in the *Bulletin of the New York Public Library*'s special issue on *The Years* (Winter 1977)—a distinguished journal that died and rose again as *Bulletin of Research in the Humanities.* As it stands, *The Years* was Woolf's most popular novel, her strongest antipatriarchal political work, a testament to her vision of the artist as charwoman to the world. Leonard's lack of faith caused her to abandon the documentary form, or she would have produced a contribution to the modern genre of antifascist art, the best example of which is Rebecca West's *Black Lamb, Grey Falcon.* One rarely has the opportunity to see the artist as her own critic in such detail. She is a historical critic and "patiently explains" with facts and dates all the details of the oppression of Victorian women and, significantly, the formation through "self-mastery" of the character of the British male with his idealization of and contempt for women. The documents, in their psychological and aesthetic aspects, show us how class-conscious her feminism was. Her hero is Joseph Wright, the working-class editor of the *English Dialect Dictionary.* She took scenes from his biography and found him refreshingly respectful to women.

Few recent critical books are up to the mark when weighed against the excitement of Woolf's own words. There are two novenas to the nine novels—which will please devout students—an English one by Hermione Lee and an American one by Avrom Fleishman.[15] Allen McLaurin's *The Echoes Enslaved* remains the most original and suggestive. The Woolf issue of *Women's Studies* (1977) contains some fascinating new work from the Santa Cruz Woolf Conference and the continuing MLA Seminar. Thomas S. W. Lewis has collected a volume of recent essays, all except one previously published. John Lehmann has published a book of photographs interspersed with gossip called *Virginia Woolf and Her World,* and Lucio Ruotolo has modestly and faithfully edited Woolf's comedy *Freshwater,* a funny spoof of the Victorians in which the characters are Tennyson, Watts, the Camerons, and Ellen Terry; it ought to have been illustrated by Mrs. Cameron's photographs.[16] A further selection of Woolf's critical essays and two unsuccessful sketches have been edited by Mary Lyon as *Books and*

Portraits.[17] Very few essays remain uncollected, and there ought to be a complete, scholarly edition, including a check of Leonard Woolf's edition against the manuscripts, where they exist. There are some fine essays in this collection. In one on Coleridge as a critic she says, "The same desire to justify and protect one's type led him no doubt to perceive the truth that 'a great mind must be androgynous.' " Was she justifying and protecting her own type when she defined the great artist's mind as androgynous in *A Room of One's Own*? She was, at any rate, identifying consciously with Coleridge and perhaps not intending to have the statement hardened into doctrine.

For their edition of *Virginia Woolf: The Critical Heritage,*[18] Robin Majumdar and Allen McLaurin ought, perhaps, to have waited for the publication of the diaries and letters, for often one does not find the particular review that enraged or delighted her. More of Rebecca West's should have been included, in particular the brilliant review of *A Room of One's Own.* Where is G. M. Young's fulminating in the Sunday *Times* over *Three Guineas,* and *Time and Tide*'s reply? One wishes the unsigned *Times Literary Supplement* reviews had been identified. Queenie Leavis and the "scrutineers" are represented in full force. The review of *Three Guineas* is a sad example of the "token woman" attacking her own sex and defending the institutions of the patriarchy from Woolf's attacks. Mrs. Leavis calls *Three Guineas* "Nazi dialectic without Nazi conviction." In "Profession for Women" Woolf warned that women must become the Sapphos and Jane Austens of their new professions, the cardinal rule being that they open the doors for women to come after them. Mrs. Leavis' defense of the closed doors from safe inside is embarrassing and instructive, for the battles Woolf fought have still not been won.

Common readers are convinced of the political relevance of Virginia Woolf's fiction. There remains the task of a new critical biography, not only to confer biography where biography is due, but to do Virginia Woolf justice—to collaborate with her in the writing as she collaborated with history and demanded collaboration of her readers. It will have to be someone who can say as a critic, "There is no Leavis; there is no Bell; we are the words and music."

Aarhus, Denmark, January 1978

The above appears to have been written many years ago and from another country. In less than a year a Danish perspective from which English social and literary attitudes appeared antiquated has been altered to an American perspective in which the quaintness of Quentin Bell looks virtuous in comparison to his successors. One is in the position of the child whose three wishes were granted, leaving her worse off than before. Wishes are not horses. They are not even donkeys, and, despite the new books, we have ridden no closer to the heart of Woolf country. In fact, the Bloomsbury zoo has a lot more appeal than the Sussex barnyard view of Ian Parsons' and George Spater's pet Woolves in *A Marriage of True Minds*.[19] This is a silly book, and the authors have "admitted" so many "impediments" that they ought to have found another title. Chief among the impediments is the observation that Leonard Woolf used his wife's proofs and manuscripts as toilet paper. This is worth mentioning, since the new biographers are ingenious in their explanations for Virginia's supposed phobias about eating and excretion.

The whole business could be settled with common sense and a historical imagination. Leslie Stephen died of cancer of the bowel. He was very thin, ate very little, tortured the successive women who ran his household about money spent on food, and berated his wife about inadequate toilet facilities.

His suffering was genuine, and he tried to minimize it by eating little; wanting company in his misery, he saw to it that his necessities became his family's virtues. Abstemiousness was next to godliness in Hyde Park Gate. Virginia nursed him as he died, and the competent discharge of these duties was a matter of pride. But it is no accident that she later described patriarchal culture in *Jacob's Room* as "that whole bag of ordure" threatening to spill out on the pavement. While she tried to disengage herself from her family, the suffragettes' militancy was being punished by the forcible feeding of women in prison.

The horrors of the situation and its similarity to rape were not lost on Virginia Stephen. At the time, her contribution was limited to meetings and licking envelopes for the Adult Suffragists, but *A Room of One's Own* and *Three Guineas* were more permanent gifts to the feminist cause. When she worried about water closets and rebelled against the forced feeding prescribed by Leonard's doctors, it must have seemed to her that she was as much a political prisoner as the suffragettes, punished for having expressed anger at the patriarchs.

The new biographers do not recognize the political nature of Woolf's plight, nor do they see that the universal appeal of her novels rests in her ability to transform private suffering into a public appeal for a redeeming socialist-feminist ethic. It is all very well to see Septimus Smith as Virginia Woolf, as Roger Poole does in *The Unknown Virginia Woolf*,[20] and *Mrs. Dalloway* as a personal vendetta against Leonard Woolf's conspiracy with the psychiatric establishment. But the novel's enduring value, however personal the experience that prompted it, is its objective relating of the psychiatric establishment to the political establishment, its indictment of the class system, patriarchy, and imperialism, and its uncanny ability to condemn capitalism for destroying the lives of two unlikely figures at opposite ends of the scale, consumed by guilt at their repressed homosexuality. Many writers have been able to create themselves in fiction. Virginia Woolf's genius was not in making Septimus Smith out of herself but making him, as Florence Howe always says, out of a boy she taught at Morley College for working men. This alliance between all women and working men against the common enemy as a recurrent theme in Woolf's work is stubbornly resisted by the critics. Poole's Laingian view sees her as a private prisoner of one particular patriarch, Leonard Woolf. However fashionable Poole's method, the result is the same: Woolf and her work are diminished, reduced to the personal. She is a victim, not a survivor.

The woman lived for almost sixty years and produced an extraordinary amount of work. She is not to be pitied, but admired. Mr. Poole ought to remember that neither Septimus nor Clarissa demands our pity in the novel. Both are heroic in their refusal to bend to the beastly goddess of the bourgeoisie, Proportion, Divine Proportion. It is Mrs. Dempster, the recurring charwoman/Greek chorus figure, who asks "pity for the loss of roses." The suppressed sexuality of the suffering protagonists is never seen as a more serious source of alienation than is the backbreaking physical labor of the working classes.

There is a lot of nonsense about the novels in Poole's book, a naive reading of Mrs. Ramsay as Julia Stephen, assuming both were perfection. Jane Lilienfeld and others have shown that the poignant power of the mother figure lies in the ambivalence of her presentation and the ambivalence of the reader's perception of her as both the Good Mother and the Terrible Mother.[21] James is not Virginia; Cam, the abandoned fisherwoman, may be. (And, since Camilla is the name of Leonard Woolf's heroine in *The Wise Virgins,* one is on safer ground there in the girl who felt rejected, solacing herself with imaginary stories.)

Poole pounces on a point long discussed by American feminist critics: that Virginia Woolf (and Septimus) heard the birds speaking in Greek when under stress. To Roger Poole, since Leonard and his friends among the Apostles were Greek scholars, we have evidence that the voices reminded her of her inadequacy and show emotional suffering at exclusion. If he had somewhat more respect for Woolf's intelligence, he would see an intellectual problem at the root, prompted by memories of George Duckworth's fondling her over her Greek lessons. Virginia Woolf studied Greek with Janet Case for many years, and she felt the way a slave or an immigrant feels at conquering the language of his master. Music, mathematics, and Greek were all-male disciplines, closely guarded proofs of the genius of Western patriarchal culture. Virginia Woolf mastered two of them and made the heroine of *Night and Day* into a "secret geometrix." She did not wallow in self-pity but reacted with rage at the exclusion of women and workers from culture as private property. "Trespass," she advised. And her example in shaping her novels as Greek plays and the attempt at creating a collective narrative voice in choruses was a political and intellectual problem, not an emotional one, and in those terms she solved it. The interesting point about the birds' speaking Greek is that it was not "Greek" to her. She understood the masculine obscenities and their direct connection to King Edward. There was a method in her madness, and we might call it Marxist-feminist.

Virginia Woolf was no fool, and Poole is wrong to blame Leonard for faults she would have blamed on the system that produced him and made him insecure. American feminist critics long ago gave up blaming Leonard for Virginia's sufferings. One can wish that he were a splendid lover, generous enough to overcome her guilts, able to give her the child she longed for, sensitive enough to respect her distaste for too much food and milk, her fear of "rest homes." But, realistically, he was the only heterosexual male in her circle who was her equal in mind and morals, and these were the things that really mattered to her. Poole's dichotomy between the rational man and the intuitive woman is false and reductive, for she was blessed with both reason and intuition in abundance.

There is an American domestication and diminishing of Virginia Woolf's life that is even less palatable than Poole's—*Woman of Letters* by Phyllis Rose.[22] The form is British, and it used to be called "potted biography." But Woolf stewed in these juices has none of the succulence of Mrs. Ramsay's *boeuf en daube*. If the sauce is feminist, as author and editor assert, I must give up my claim to literary taste. For it is sauce for ganders, not for geese. The recipe seems concocted in the kitchen of a *Ladies' Home Journal* and written in appropriate style. Rose's Virginia Woolf is a mad housewife with a gift for writing stories. There is an interesting chapter on Lytton Strachey and an original reading of "forcing the soul" in *Mrs. Dalloway*. The dismissal of *Night and Day* and *The Years* is a clue to dependence on standard criticism. Ideas and readings from recent feminist critics have been absorbed, yet carefully avoided in the footnotes. If the aim was to reach more common readers, the method surely should have included a study of Woolf's ideas and the development of her mind.

Virginia Woolf: Sources of Madness and Art by Jean O. Love[23] domesticates and diminishes the Woolf in a more "scientific" style. It is a sly and subtle book, sure to please the Bells, for the author continues their method of questioning Virginia's veracity. The story of the Duckworths is repeated several times, and each time the author asks again, "Is she telling the truth?" Common sense again comes to the rescue. What the Duckworths did was far worse than she could ever have written down and read before the mostly male Memoir Club. In self-analysis she was surely only able to touch the surface of her sufferings. By suggesting that Woolf was a liar, Love betrays a condescending attitude toward her subject that will allow one to dismiss the work as well as the woman. Love regards Woolf's retreat into memories of the past as a symptom of her "madness." But memory makes us moral. And memory as the mother of the muses was Woolf's most reliable imaginative source of power as an artist.

The reader is hampered by the author's paraphrase and interpretation of unpublished material. The footnotes often supply no quoted evidence for this version of character and events. Perhaps she was prevented from extensive quotation by the family. But the reader is asked to take a great deal on trust from an author who does not trust her subject. Leslie Stephen is presented as a tyrannical monster of self-pity, bellowing with rage to cover up quivering insecurity about his masculinity. But he comes off rather well in the end, for Love blames his mother for all his faults. Julia Stephen is painted as an "absent mother" off on her nursing expeditions and neglecting her family, rather like the current popular psychologists' explanations of the breakdown of the family caused by working mothers who neglect their latchkey children. There is a crude Freudian interpretation of the Stephen family's animal names and games. Do not all families do this, or do I blush for myself alone? Worse is the discussion of Virginia Woolf's youthful desire to create a utopia and her literary experiments in imagining a new world. This Love describes as her "naive cosmography." The underlying assumption is that the writing is merely personal self-expression and has no public moral or political motive. It was a dangerous game she was playing, Love assumes, keeping her out of touch with reality. Apply this method to Blake or Shelley, and what are the results?

Surprisingly enough, the most interesting new book is Mitchell Leaska's *The Novels of Virginia Woolf from Beginning to End,*[24] despite a "new Bloomsbury" afterword by John Lehmann, which asserts yet again that "his" Virginia Woolf was not political. This book was singled out for special savagery by a reviewer in the *Times Literary Supplement*. Since Virginia Woolf is consistently presented in that publication as "the queen of gossips," this represents hostility to the seriousness with which Leaska treats the texts of a novelist he clearly regards as one of the finest modern minds. He respects her intelligence, is thoroughly steeped in her essays, and has studied the development of the manuscripts. Leaska is wise, original, and imaginative as a critic. And I say this despite my own reservations about the psychological method, which is based on Leon Edel's study of Henry James. There is not one reading that the historical critic will take as gospel, but each essay is rich with original insight into the spiritual, social, and literary complexity of Woolf's thought. Further, he is far more sensitive than either Love or Rose to the presence of sexuality and violence in the novels. His ingenuity in research is based on sympathy and respect. While their books diminish writer and woman, Leaska's enlarges her. Hence the reader is led to feel awe for the writer of genius, quite the opposite effect from the Poole, Rose, and Love conspiracies of author and reader to feel superior to her.

The second volume of the *Diary*[25] is mercifully less obtrusive in its editing and is worth buying immediately for the reprinting of "The Intellectual Status of Women" from the *New Statesman* in 1920, written for the general reader. It is disingenuous of the editor to claim that this has been "overlooked," since it has been standard fare in the feminist classroom and often quoted by feminist critics: "It seems to me indisputable that the conditions which make it possible for a Shakespeare to exist are that he shall have had predecessors in his art, shall make one of a group where art is freely discussed and practised, and shall himself have the utmost freedom of action and experience. Perhaps in Lesbos, but never since, have these conditions been the lot of women."

The two most interesting subjects here are first, the death of Katherine Mansfield and the immediate canonization in Woolf's memory of the woman she despised for her sexuality and deplored as a shallow writer into a saint and a virgin with a white wreath, a woman she had loved, and a writer who would have been Woolf's only prose competitor. Second, is the writing of *Mrs. Dalloway,* essentially Woolf's thoughts during revision. Here one finds the source for Peter Walsh's knife, and the answer to the question, "When did she read *Clarissa*?" It would have been wise, I think, for the editor to have included the notes for *Mrs. Dalloway* from the Berg Collection, notes scribbled in reading notebooks, as well as those on Greek and the use of choruses and dramatic form. One of them contains the question, "Can one admit rhapsodies?"

We are, in the end, grateful for the work of Quentin and Olivier Bell for providing these documents and remain hopeful that a new biographer with some of Woolf's literary taste, historical imagination, and moral vision will make full use of them. The misreadings of the critics and the muddled condescensions of the biographies are, alas, due to her sex. One may echo her challenge to Arnold Bennett:

> I have often been told that Sappho was a woman, and that Plato and Aristotle placed her with Homer and Archilocus among the greatest of their poets. That Mr. Bennett can name fifty of the male sex who are indisputably her superiors is therefore a welcome surprise, and if he will publish their names I will promise, as an act of that submission which is so dear to my sex, not only to buy their works but, so far as my faculties allow, to learn them by heart.[26]

8

Storming the Toolshed

[More than most essays in this collection, this one bears the marks of its origin and its author's anger. What it records most significantly is a moment of male resistance to feminist theory in 1982, as well as my own suspicion of academic cooptation of the feminist movement.]

Feminist Scholars and Literary Theory

Sections 2 and 3 of this article reflect their occasions. "Lupine Criticism" was given as a talk at the MLA meeting in San Francisco in 1979. Florence Howe chaired the session with panelists Mary Helen Washington, Sidney Janet Kaplan, Suzanne Juhasz, and Tillie Olsen.[1] There was a large and enthusiastic audience, and the session was remarkable historically for discussion of race, class, and sexual identity, particularly lesbianism, and for vocal criticism and participation from the audience. The sparse audience for feminist sessions the following year in Houston, the current debate in the National Women's Studies Association over the primacy of the issues of racism and lesbian identity,[2] and the concurrent minimization of differences in feminist literary criticism itself by Annette Kolodny and others in recent issues of *Feminist Studies,*[3] make it imperative that we reexamine our history. It was, after all, a playful but serious prediction made in "Lupine Criticism" that aggressive, historical feminist scholarship on Virginia Woolf might cease if the practitioners became absorbed into the academy and stopped combining political activism and the position of "outsidership" with their scholarly work.

In "Dancing through the Minefield," Kolodny's liberal relaxation of the tensions among us and the tensions between feminists and the academy reflects a similar relaxation on the part of historians and political activists. What this does is to isolate Marxist feminists, lesbians, and blacks on the barricades while "good girl" feminists fold their tents and slip quietly into the establishment. There is a battlefield (race, class, and sexual identity) within each one of us, another battlefield where we wage these wars with our own feminist colleagues (as in *Signs*), and a third battlefield where we defend ourselves from male onslaughts both on our work and on the laws that govern our lives as women in society. It is far too early to tear down the barricades. Dancing shoes will not do. We still need our heavy boots and mine detectors.

The most serious issue facing feminist critics today is that which divides the profession as a whole, the division between theory and practice. Leaning on the Greeks, our culture still posits philosophy, music, and mathematics as the highest forms of intellectual endeavor. They have been the fields most zealously guarded against female incursion, the fields where it has been most difficult for women to gain training. The English composer Dame Ethel Smyth defended herself from criticism of her battles for status and position among women musicians: she could not withdraw from the world to compose, to act the artist who simply cultivates her own garden, she said, when someone had locked up all the tools.[4] Literary theory is a branch of philosophy. Its most vigorous practitioners in the United States have been male. It is no historical accident that the hegemony of the theoreticians and the valorization of theory itself parallels the rise of feminist criticism. While we have been doing literary housekeeping, they have been gazing at the stars. They refuse to bear the burden of the sins of their literary fathers or to make amends for centuries of critical abuse of women writers involving the loss, destruction, bowdlerization, or misevaluation of women's texts, diaries, letters, and biographies.

When feminist critics first forced open the toolshed, they polished and sharpened the rusty spades and hoes and rakes men long since had discarded. They learned history, textual criticism, biography, the recovery of manuscripts. They began to search for and reprint women's works and to study the image of woman in Western art. Many moved into linguistics to get at the origins of oppression in language, while others worked to find the writing of women of color.[5] We were all forced to become historians and biographers and to train ourselves in those disciplines. We devoured theories of female psychology, anthropology, and myth to broaden our grasp of the work of women artists. The more materialist and particular the labor of feminist critics became, the more abstract and antimaterialist became the work of the men (they left in Europe the Marxist origins of structuralism and deconstruction). The more we spoke in moral indignation and anger, the more Parnassian were the whispers of male theorists. If the last conference of the School of Criticism and Theory is any model to go by,[6] soon they will have retreated so far from life and literature that they will be analyzing the songs of birds in the garden of Paradise (Adamic only).

Geoffrey Hartman claims for the theorists that literary criticism is in the wilderness.[7] While one may grant that Hartman's manner is a distinct imitation of John the Baptist, it must be pointed out that the theorists are not in the wilderness at all but in a labyrinthine garden with high hedges that they have constructed themselves. The arrogance of the metaphor indicates the cause of their isolation. If there is one true word in literary criticism, and they are the precursors of their master's voice, the profession is lost. But historians of our difficult era will have little doubt about the social origins of the idea of born-again literary critics. I am reminded of the words of the Victorian aesthetician, Vernon Lee, in a letter to Ethel Smyth. It was bad enough to be a voice crying in the wilderness, she said, but a female philosopher was a "vox clamans" in the closet.[8]

There are some feminist theorists of note, among whom one may cite especially the work of Gayatri Spivak in literature and Julia Lesage in film criticism.[9] Lesage and her colleagues on the film journal *Jump-Cut* have, in fact, made the most revolutionary breakthrough in feminist theory and practice by trying to effect a rapprochement between the left and lesbians. The lesbian-feminist special issue of *Jump-Cut* is a tour de force of brilliant and ground-breaking essays and includes an editorial in which the male editors attempt to deal with what we may call "reparations" for the long battles of the sexes. The writing and publication of these essays is a hopeful sign, but not a victory until feminist critics who are neither left nor lesbian read and debate these issues and bring them into the classroom.

There were no feminist critics speaking at the first meeting of the School of Criticism and Theory at Northwestern University in the spring of 1981, though the intelligent response of Mary Douglas, the anthropologist, to one of the more reactionary papers, was the highlight of the conference.[10] Protest at the omission of feminists was met by the response that there *are* no feminist theorists, at least none whom the men find "interesting." If there is as yet no feminist critical theory that men find interesting, there is no reason to suppose that it is not at this very moment being written; nor is there any reason to suppose that men will ever be as interested as we are in developments in our own field. Recent critical books attacking the hegemony of the theorists ignore both feminists and Marxists or give them a light cuff, while the heavy blows are aimed at theorists of their own sex. We are excluded from their discourse (theorizing is a male activity); consequently, no intellectual intercourse can take place. Even a Marxist critic like Frederic Jameson is loyal to the old boys.[11]

Just as Virginia Woolf predicted both the birth of Shakespeare's sister and our work for her arrival, so one may predict the birth of the feminist critic of genius. She must reject with Virginia Woolf the patriarchal view of literature as a competition with prizes of ornamental pots from the headmaster. The feminist critic is always at odds with the headmaster. She is, as Adrienne Rich argues, "disloyal" to civilization.[12] She must refuse the ornamental pot, even if it is very fashionable and made in France. She must break the measuring rod, even if it is finely calibrated in the literary laboratories at Yale. We shall have a theory of our own when our practice develops it. Though I have quoted this many times, it bears repeating: "Masterpieces are not single and solitary births. . . they are the outcome of many years of thinking in common, of thinking by the body of the people, so that the experience of the mass is behind the single voice."[13] Woolf was discussing Shakespeare as the product of history. But her socialist analysis can be extended to criticism as well. By her analysis one can imagine that there were many little Geoffrey Hartmans before there was one big

Geoffrey Hartman, as in literature there were many little Shakespeares before the master himself.

We have already produced feminist critics to match their male counterparts: Annette Kolodny's work on American literature, Lillian Robinson's *Sex, Class and Culture*, Mary Ellmann, Kate Millett, Ellen Moers, Elaine Showalter. Sandra Gilbert and Susan Gubar can outdo Harold Bloom at his own game; Gayatri Spivak speaks as an equal among the French deconstructionists; Julia Lesage challenges film theory. Many lesser-known feminists have worked steadily for new readings and new values in their fields. But even if we were to construct the feminist supercritic from the collective voice of all of them, it is doubtful that the self-appointed priesthood would find her analysis interesting. I suspect that this literary amazon is even now slouching toward Ephesus to be born—the critic who will deliver us from slavery to the canon, from racist, sexist, and classist misreadings. But one can be sure that, welcome as she will be among us, the chosen critics will see her as a false messiah.

I do not think we should surrender easily. It is they and their fathers who excluded and oppressed us and our mothers, they who decided to exclude women writers from what was taught, women students from who was taught. Our historical losses at their hands are incalculable. It is not up to us to beg them to find our work interesting. It is up to them to make reparations: to establish secure women's studies departments, black studies departments, chairs of feminist literary criticism and women's history, to read the work of women and black writers, and to teach it.

If "Lupine Criticism" is an example of a battle within a small area of literary criticism, fought among one's peers, "One Cheer for Democracy, or Talking Back to Quentin Bell" is a direct confrontation with Virginia Woolf's nephew, official biographer, and owner of her literary estate. In his essay "Bloomsbury and the Vulgar Passions," given on a lecture tour of the United States and published in *Critical Inquiry,* Bell once again mocks Virginia Woolf's *Three Guineas* for its feminism and pacifism.[14] He minimizes her contribution to political thought by comparing it unfavorably to a pamphlet by his father, Clive Bell, as well as to E. M. Forster's "Two Cheers for Democracy" and *A Passage to India.* I admire Bell's *Bloomsbury*[15] and am grateful, as are other Woolf scholars, for the painstaking work of his biography and for the publication of the letters and diaries. Because we are dependent on the estate for permission to quote Virginia Woolf, it has been difficult for Woolf scholars to take issue with his analysis without jeopardizing their careers. The year 1982 is the centenary of Virginia Woolf's birth. In the thirties she predicted that in fifty years men would allow women writers free speech. Could she have imagined this deadlock in criticism, this "separate but equal" free speech as it now exists in literary criticism, where feminist critics are excluded from discourse with male theorists?[16] She suffered from these same exclusions herself, was chastised for her feminism all her life, and continues to be chastised after her death. She died, I believe, in an ethical torment over her pacifism in a terrible war. It seems only natural to take up her weapons. Our first target is the shed where the power tools of literary theory have been kept. There is no doubt that in the hands of feminist critics they will transform the study of literature.

Lupine Criticism

It is amusing to imagine what Virginia Woolf would think of an MLA meeting. We know that she despised lectures and did not believe that literature should be taught to middle-class students. She herself lectured only to women and working-class people. She gave lectures to women students and fellow professional women, to the Workers' Education League, and to the Working Women's Co-operative Guild. She refused offers to lecture to men, to men's colleges and universities, and to male-dominated institutions. While she was in Italy, studying Mussolini's fascism firsthand, she refused, with a simple and defiant No, her government's offer of a Companion of Honour, wanting no companionship whatever with the concerns of the British Empire. She refused a degree from Manchester University and, much to the horror of the editor of her letters, Nigel Nicolson, she even refused quite proudly to give the prestigious Clark Lectures at Cambridge, despite the fact that she was the first woman invited to do so. Her editor feels that this act "only weakened the cause of women in general" and confesses he cannot understand why the only prize she ever accepted was a woman's prize, the Femina vie Heureuse prize for *To the Lighthouse*.[17]

We all know why she did it, and why, if she were here today, she would accept the Florence Howe Award for her essays on women writers and refuse any other honors. Lecturing, she wrote, "incites the most debased of human passions—vanity, ostentation, self-assertion, and the desire to convert." We confess all these sins and more; feminist literary criticism seems to demand them at the moment just for defense. "Why not create a new form of society founded on poverty and equality?" Woolf asked.

> Why not bring together people so that they can talk, without mounting platforms or reading papers or wearing expensive clothes or eating expensive food? Would not such a society be worth, even as a form of education, all the papers on art and literature that have ever been read since the world began? Why not abolish prigs and prophets? Why not invent human intercourse?[18]

In the last decade, the Commission on Women and the Women's Caucus of the MLA, with Florence Howe at the helm, and also a vast community of women scholars working together, have undertaken the enormous task of re-evaluating women's work, uncovering forgotten lives and books, reprinting our own literature. Virginia Woolf is our model for this task. We—I say ostentatiously, self-assertively, with some vanity, and a veritable passion to make converts—in this very room are inventing "human intercourse."

Writers like Tillie Olsen and Adrienne Rich have inspired us not only with their creative work but also with their theoretical and historical essays. They continue the work in which Virginia Woolf as a feminist literary critic was engaged, the historical process of thinking back through our mothers.[19] Woolf would take a particular delight in what Mary Helen Washington and her colleagues are doing on black and third world women writers. She would applaud with Suzanne Juhasz the women poets who tell the truth. Loving Katherine Mansfield as she did, and Elizabeth Robins, the forgotten feminist who influenced both Mansfield and Woolf herself, she would rub her hands with glee that Sydney Kaplan and her feminist colleagues are delivering Mansfield's ghost from the hands of the lugubrious Middleton Murry.

We in a new generation of feminist Virginia Woolf criticism have also had the advantage of collective and collaborative work, and we have sustained each other in many trials. Whenever two or three of us are gathered together sharing notes on manuscripts and letters, we feel what Virginia Woolf described in her meetings with her Greek teacher, Janet Case, and with Margaret Llewelyn Davies of the Working Women's Co-operative Guild; we are at "the heart of the women's republic."[20] It is an open secret that Virginia Woolf's literary estate is hostile to feminist critics. There are two taboo subjects: on the one hand her lesbian identity, woman-centered life, and feminist work, and on the other her socialist politics. If you wish to discover the truth regarding these issues, you will have a long, hard struggle. In that struggle you will find the sisterhood of feminist Woolf scholarship.

It all began with Ellen Hawkes's review, "The Virgin in the Bell Biography." She was duly denounced from the pulpit of the English Institute but, despite excommunication, has had a great influence.[21] A group of feminist Woolf scholars protested her expulsion and organized a conference at Santa Cruz. Here Madeline Moore brought together many feminists—Sara Ruddick, Tillie Olsen, and Florence Howe among them. Madeline Moore published many of the papers from the conference in a 1977 special issue of *Women's Studies*.

The MLA Woolf Seminar has been notably feminist in its papers during the last five years. At one meeting, for example, Margaret Comstock chaired a session on *Between the Acts* with papers by Judy Little and Diane Gillespie, later published in *Women and Literature*. Feminists, including Kate Ellis and Ellen Hawkes, spoke at the Princeton Woolf Conference organized by Joanna Lipking. And at the Bucknell Woolf Conference in 1977, Carolyn Heilbrun, Eve Merriam, and the late Ellen Moers spoke. (Here let me note that Ellen Moer's death diminishes us all; *Literary Women* has provided us with tools and structures for building feminist literary criticism.) These conferences and seminars cemented scholarly friendships and set new directions for Woolf studies.

The publications of Woolf's letters and diaries has greatly facilitated our work. Yet the manuscripts of the novels retain the utmost fascination. We organized a special issue of the *Bulletin of the New York Public Library* with papers from the MLA Woolf Seminar on *The Years,* including Grace Radin's rendering of "two enormous chunks" of material removed from the galleys just before the novel went to press, Sallie Sear's essay on sexuality, and Margaret Comstock's "The Loudspeaker and the Human Voice," on the politics of the novel. Woolf's "Professions for Women" turned out to be three times longer and much more forceful than the version published by Leonard Woolf in *Collected Essays.* It has been reprinted by the New York Public Library in Mitchell Leaska's edition of *The Pargiters.*[22]

The original speech "Professions for Women" was delivered in January 1931 to a group of professional women. Preceding Virginia Woolf on the platform was Dame Ethel Smyth, the great English lesbian-feminist composer. Virginia Woolf's pacifism always receded when she spoke as a feminist. Her violent feelings came pouring out in her description of Ethel Smyth: "She is of the race of the pioneers: She is among the icebreakers, the window-smashers, the indomitable and irresistible armoured tanks who climbed the rough ground; went first; drew the enemy's fire and left a pathway for those who came after her. I never knew whether to be angry that such heroic pertinacity was called for, or glad that it had the chance of showing itself."[23]

In our field the icebreakers and window-smashers have been Tillie Olsen, Adrienne Rich, Florence Howe, Ellen Moers, Carolyn Heilbrun. Our work has been made possible because they drew the enemy's fire. Like Virginia Woolf, we acknowledge our debt, half in anger that such belligerence is necessary, half in gladness that they have fought so well. For the last five years much feminist work on Woolf has appeared in *Virginia Woolf Miscellany,* edited, among others, by the indomitable J. J. Wilson at Sonoma State University. The Fall 1979 issue of *Twentieth Century Literature* contains splendid and important work by feminists: Ellen Hawkes's edition of Woolf's early utopian feminist fantasy, "Friendships Gallery," written for Violet Dickinson; Susan Squier and Louise DeSalvo's edition of an early forty-four-page unpublished story about a woman historian; Madeline Moore's edition of the *Orlando* manuscripts; and Brenda Silver's edition of two very important late manuscripts called "Anon" and "The Reader."[24]

Doubtless I have left out much new work, but this list itself is an impressive example of the comradeship and collective effort of feminist Woolf scholarship. You will note that all this work is American. We have escaped the domination of the Leavises' point of view that still prevents many British readers from seeing Woolf as anything but elitist and mad. The exception is Michèle Barrett's edition of Woolf's *Women and Writing.*[25]

Quentin Bell has announced that the "bottom of the barrel" has been reached in Woolf manuscripts, but we are not finished yet. There is a great deal of literary housekeeping to be done. Virginia Woolf wrote to Ethel Smyth about her struggle for recognition as a composer, "Somehow the big apples come to the top of the basket. But of course I realize that the musicians' apple lies longest at the bottom and has the hardest struggle to rise."[26] I find these "Granny Smyth" apples to be tart and tasty indeed and am editing Dame Ethel's letters to Woolf.

What feminist scholars have found in the apples at the bottom of the barrel is a taste of the two taboo subjects, Woolf's socialist politics and her love of women. When the fifth volume of her letters was published, reviewers rushed to reassure readers that Woolf did not really mean it when she wrote to Ethel Smyth, "Women alone stir my imagination."[27] Nigel Nicolson insisted to me that Woolf was only joking. While Quentin Bell is ready to admit privately that *Letter to a Young Poet* and "Thoughts on Peace in an Air Raid" are "more Marxist than the Marxists," his public lecture, "Bloomsbury and the Vulgar Passions," dismisses *Three Guineas* as silly and unimportant.[28]

Quentin Bell is not amused by feminist criticism of Virginia Woolf. He has invented a name for us. He calls us "lupines." There is a particular variety of flower, the lupine, that grows in the American

West, covering the rocky slopes of the Big Horns, the Tetons, and the Wind River Mountains in July. It is electric blue, startlingly erect, and extremely hardy. Perhaps we feminist Woolf critics can survive the patronizing label of British cultural imperialism by appropriating it ourselves. During the struggle for woman suffrage, a patronizing journalist called the most militant of the activists "Suffragettes." After a few weeks of smoldering rage at the insult, the women simply pinned that badge to their own breasts and wore it proudly.

In *Three Guineas* Virginia Woolf suggests that women might wear a tuft of horsehair on the left shoulder to indicate motherhood as a response to male military decorations. Lupine criticism is obviously here to stay. We might as well accept the label and wear it proudly. If the proliferation and hardiness of the flower is any indication of our tenacity, we have a great future. We have not yet ceased to be "prigs and prophetesses," but we have made a start at inventing human intercourse.

Yet achievement and even struggle in common do not come easily. The first of our two volumes of feminist criticism on Virginia Woolf was finished in 1977, but we were unable to find an American publisher. The essays have circulated among feminist critics and have been cited in books and articles in print for years. Because the University of Nebraska Press bought the book from Macmillan/London, the price in America is very high.[29] These incontrovertible economic facts are not lost on young scholars. Virginia Woolf founded the Hogarth Press in order to publish what she wanted to write. Feminists often feel forced by economic realities to choose other methodologies and structures that will ensure sympathetic readings from university presses. We may be as middle class as Virginia Woolf, but few of us have the economic security her aunt Caroline Emelia Stephen's legacy gave her. The samizdat circulation among networks of feminist critics works only in a system where repression is equal. If all the members are unemployed or underemployed, unpublished or unrecognized, sisterhood flourishes, and sharing is a source of strength. When we all compete for one job or when one lupine grows bigger and bluer than her sisters with unnatural fertilizers from the establishment, the ranks thin out. Times are hard and getting harder.

Being an outsider is a lonely life. Virginia Woolf proposed a "Society of Outsiders." Lupine criticism, I think, will only flourish in the collective and in the wild. In captivity, in the rarefied hothouse atmosphere of current academic criticism, it may wither and die. From my last climbing trip in the Wind Rivers, I brought back some wild lupines and carefully transplanted them. My mother warned me that Chicago clay would stifle them, and she was right. Garden lupines are very pretty, and doubtless our colleagues would find us less offensive in the cultivated state. The British label was meant as an insult, and it might be an adjective as well as a noun. If we are going to wear it, sister lupines, let us wear it with wild Woolfian abandon.

One Cheer for Democracy, or Talking Back to Quentin Bell

Quentin Bell, largely responsible for making the Bloomsbury bed, now refuses to lie in it. In his book on Bloomsbury and his biography of his aunt, he provided readers with the materials for what he now calls "false generalizations."[30] "Bloomsbury and the Vulgar Passions" is a deliberately mystifying title that does not clarify the politics of the period, but muddies the waters even more.

Virginia Woolf's clear understanding of the role of the intellectual in relation to the revolution is evident in her title *Three Guineas.* She wants women and the working class to unite against the war, but she does not presume to speak for any but her own class and sex. In "The Leaning Tower" and *Letter to a Young Poet*[31] she insists on organization in one's own class and has faith that the working class can produce its own leaders. Her title, a deliberate play on Brecht's *Threepenny Opera,* exposes the economic origins of the social problems she discusses. Neither pence nor pounds can accurately describe the contributions expected of a woman in her position. Over the years American academics have shared her frustrating experience, signing petitions and writing checks to help in the civil rights movement and the movement to stop the war in Vietnam. Like her, they sought to relieve social ills by imagining free universities like the one Woolf describes in *Three Guineas*.[32] Current feminism grew out of women's efforts to find a place in movements for social change that assumed that race and class and the present war were more important than sex grievances. Woolf was the first to identify the enemy openly as "patriarchy."

Why does Bell choose Keynes's elitist phrase for an essay calculated to reduce the political power of *Three Guineas* to an entirely personal cause? If *Three Guineas* is merely an aunt's elegy for a dead nephew, as Bell argues, is not such ferocious grief a "vulgar passion," too? The phrase is not Bell's; it is the phrase of a man he admires, Maynard Keynes. It is a Victorian upper-class phrase. Few members of Margaret Llewelyn Davies' Working Women's Co-operative Guild would have known what it meant.[33] The phrase itself is heavy with ambiguity, and it is used by Bell in both positive and negative ways. Curiously, it works to the disadvantage of Virginia Woolf either way. It is men like his father, Keynes, and Forster who remain intellectually above the vulgar passions when Bell considers it correct to be so, and men again who are responsive to the vulgar passions of a nation at war, when this is the attitude he admires.

There is a famous point in Bell's biography of Virginia Woolf when the reader, swept along by the swift flow of prose, brisk and cool like an English trout stream in spring, is suddenly thrown into white water. Bell bursts into capital letters. The reader is on the rocks.

> But were we then to scuttle like frightened spinsters before the Fascist thugs? She belonged, inescapably, to the Victorian world of Empire, Class and Privilege. Her gift was for the pursuit of shadows, for the ghostly whispers of the mind and for Pythian incomprehensibility, when what was needed was the swift and lucid phrase that could reach the ears of unemployed working men or Trades Union officials.[34]

To the generation of Thirties intellectuals (John Lehmann was one, and Woolf wrote her scathing *Letter to a Young Poet* to him), Virginia Woolf was "a fragile middle-aged poetess, a sexless Sappho," and "a distressed gentlewoman caught in a tempest." Bell recalls his "despair" as he urged the Rodmell Labour Party to adopt a resolution supporting the united front, when Virginia, who was the local party secretary, turned the debate from the question. He does not call her a skilled politician for manipulating the meeting, on pacifist principle, away from patriotic militarism. He says, indeed, that she was closer to the feeling of "the masses" than he was. "I wanted to talk politics, the masses wanted to talk about the vicar's wife."[35]

But, I venture, it was precisely her "swift and lucid phrases" that annoyed him, for she spoke to the Workers' Education Association, and she wrote in the *Daily Worker* of a different kind of united front: while the capitalist, imperialist patriarchs were waging their wars, workers should join women in an assault on culture. "Trespass," she urged them on the sacred precincts of home front institutions while the warriors are in the field. She was arguing for total subversion of the world of empire, class, and privilege. And among the shadows she pursued most vigorously were young, upper-class male "missionaries to the masses." Take off those "pro-proletarian spectacles," she urged the generation of Auden, Spender, Lehmann, and Bell; if you really want to make the revolution, you must empty your pockets of your fathers' money, you must convert the men of your *own* class.[36] Virginia Woolf took as hard a line on the role of the intellectual in the class struggle as did Lenin or Trotsky. Its ethical imperative is even improved by the addition of feminism to the socialist-pacifist position. Quentin Bell's objections are honest ones, and there were many who agreed with him. He is infuriated by her feminism and enraged by her pacifism, and he fights back like a man.

It is dirty fighting, to be sure. She is dead, and cannot respond like the Lapland witch Gerald Brenan says she was.[37] E. M. Forster was a dirty fighter, too. He said in his Rede Lecture that Woolf was not a great writer because she had no great cause at heart.[38] But we have already put *A Room of One's Own* and *Three Guineas* on the shelf next to Milton, Wollstonecraft, Mill, and Swift, and where is Forster's "Two Cheers for Democracy"? It is an embarrassment. Forster said he would give up his country before he would give up his friend. But that was not at issue. Nobody was asking him to give up his friend.

And *Three Guineas* has some antifascist feminist thuggery of its own. One thing it does not have is "Pythian incomprehensibility." It is a Cassandra cry in the crowd of thirties political pamphlets. No spinsterish whispers either—the loudspeaker blares for all to hear, a withering revolutionary feminist analysis of fascism. The Hitlers and Mussolinis have no monopoly on fascism, she says. The origin of fascism is the patriarchal family. And the daughters of educated men had better root it out of the hearts of their English brothers before the latter rush off to fight foreign fascism.

Men on the left were horrified. But the argument that elements of fascism lurk behind patriarchal power struggles is still too radical for people. It was the subject of Lina Wertmuller's shattering feminist film *Seven Beauties,* and all the Bettelheims came out with their battering rams and big guns to remind us of how long it will be before men will tolerate free speech in women.[39]

During the period covered by the fifth volume of Woolf's letters (1932–35), the political and personal insults that she had received from men were creating the deep sense of grievance that finally burst out in *The Years* and *Three Guineas.*[40] *The Years* itself is the most brilliant indictment in modern literature of the world of empire, class, and privilege, of capitalism and patriarchy. Structurally it is exciting, too, in its portrait of the artist as charwoman of the world. *The Years* was planned as a new form of her opera for the oppressed, alternating chapters of fact and fiction. The documentary chapters have been reprinted in *The Pargiters.* It is too bad that Leonard talked her out of it. He was fearful of mixing fact and fiction. Her fearlessness went into the writing of both books. But she was justifiably terrified of what the male critics would say.

It is doubtful that she would have predicted her nephew's continuing hostility to *Three Guineas.* I believe there is a direct line in English history from the Clapham Sect to Bloomsbury. The anonymous reviewer in the *Times Literary Supplement* who called Virginia Woolf "the best pamphleteer in England"[41] was (consciously or unconsciously) echoing the very words applied to the antislavery pamphlets of her great-grandfather, James Stephen. That Virginia Woolf should have added feminism to the Stephen family causes is the most natural development in the world.[42] Her pacifism was not a "temporary" phenomenon but a firmly held principle of a tripartite political philosophy. It was largely derived from the important and neglected influence of her Quaker aunt, Caroline Emelia Stephen, described by Quaker historians as almost single-handedly responsible for the revival of the practically moribund English Society of Friends in the late nineteenth century.[43] It is true, as Bell says, that Woolf modified her position at the last, actually wanted to join the fire wardens, and appears to have been willing to defend her beleaguered country in "Thoughts on Peace in an Air Raid." I have described these changes of attitude elsewhere.[44]

Bell's essay is written in response to yet another season of bad press for Bloomsbury. Virginia Woolf wrote to him during an earlier one, stating "Bloomsbury is having a very bad press at the moment; so please take up your hammer and chisel and sculpt a great flaming Goddess to put them all to shame."[45] There was certainly a family precedent. When Fitzjames Stephen was hounded out of office for prejudicing the jury in the Maybrick case after a lifetime of legal bullying and misogyny as the "Giant Grim," Leslie Stephen took up his hammer and chisel and sculpted a genial friendly giant in his biography of his brother. Virginia Stephen herself had participated in Maitland's biography of her father, largely to offset the influence of her aunt Caroline, who had mountains of evidence that the great man had a terrible temper.[46]

Did Bell perhaps agree with Mirsky's dismissal of Bloomsbury and Virginia Woolf in *The Intelligentsia of Great Britain,*[47] the "bad press" referred to? He took up his hammer and chisel, but produced no "great flaming Goddess" but a "sexless Sappho," a "distressed gentlewoman caught in a tempest." I suspect in the end we will all come to see Bell's "sexless Sappho" as a true portrait of the artist who equated chastity with creativity. But she will not do as a portrait of the socialist/pacifist/feminist, the "outsider" who "spat out" *Three Guineas* as an original contribution to an analysis of the origins of fascism in the patriarchal family. If she began the book as an elegy for Bell's brother,

Julian, there is nothing unusual in her method in that, for all her work is elegy. Even *A Room of One's Own* is a female elegy written in a college courtyard for the female writers of the past. The narrator has been denied access to the library which contains the manuscripts of the two great male elegies in poetry and prose, Milton's *Lycidas* and Thackeray's *Henry Esmond,* and so she is driven to invent the female elegy. If grieving for Julian Bell's death in Spain forced her to the conclusion that she must speak directly to women of her class, to the mothers, sisters, and wives of the war makers, the public effect of a private sorrow is impressive.

But *Three Guineas* is a stubbornly feminist elegy, singing the sorrows of women under patriarchy, relentlessly repeating itself as history has repeated itself, trying to establish a feminist ethics. To my mind, and to the minds of other feminists, *Three Guineas* is the pure historical product of the Clapham Sect reform movement. It owes much to the "rational mysticism" of Caroline Emelia Stephen's *The Light Arising.*[48] But if the historian can free himself of sex bias, he will see *Three Guineas* in relation to Bertrand Russell's philosophy and to G. E. Moore's *Principia Ethica.* In fact it might be seen as "Principia Ethica Feminina," volume 1.[49]

If Woolf later, in "Thoughts on Peace in an Air Raid," admitted woman's complicity in war and concluded that "we must compensate the man for his gun,"[50] she did not suggest how. Bell thinks she has come close to the vulgar passions (which are now positive) in this essay, and he is disposed to grant her some credit.[51] I thought so too in 1976. But I am now disposed to think that "Thoughts on Peace in Air Raid" is just what the title suggests, a defensive position taken under extreme pressure. The militant feminism of *Three Guineas,* its equally militant pacifism, socialism, and antifascism, are "saddening" and "exasperating" to Bell. Many European and American feminist historians are studying the forms of Italian and German fascism and their relation to the patriarchal family, marriage, and the treatment of women and children, and they have found Woolf's pamphlet a strikingly original and eerily correct analysis.[52] I believe Bell labors under the misconception that feminism is not political—a major mistake—as well as under minor misconceptions that pacifism in World War II was not a respectable political stance (it was certainly not popular) and that Virginia Woolf could not have been much of a socialist because she did not work in Labour Party committees or associate with the working classes. Even when Bell imagines a committee meeting, he sees only Mr. A, Mr. B, Mr. C, Mr. D, and the chairman. I seem to recall that the committee meeting which caused his admirable prose style to flood the gates was chaired by his aunt, Mrs. W, and she prevented him from passing his resolution. It is a long time to hold a grudge.

It is a failure of the imagination to suppose that all pacifists were, like Clive Bell, ad hoc peaceniks for a particular war. Quakers, like Caroline Stephen and Violet Dickinson, Virginia's early mentors, were opposed to all wars.

It seems oddly un-English and more like an American pragmatist or utilitarian argument to judge the quality of a pamphlet by its contemporary effectiveness. James Stephen turned out antislavery pamphlets that failed to stop the slavers. It was not until he had been dead many years that his son finally got an antislavery bill through Parliament. How much immediate effect did Mill's *Subjection of Women* have? Women did not get the vote until 1928, and the conditions of women are still not by any means satisfactory. *Three Guineas* is still read (and this might be a better measure of "effectiveness") by those who hunger for its message, who feel as guilty as Woolf did about fighting for feminism when atrocities and wars demand one's attention. Seeking for the deepest cause of imperialist and capitalist war, she found it in male aggression. She was saddened, but urged women to stop encouraging aggression. I wish she had been more successful.

If effectiveness is the criterion of a pamphlet's success, is there any way of measuring the success of *Three Guineas* in keeping America out of the war when it was published in the *Atlantic* as "Women Must Weep or Unite against the War"? I suppose it is just as possible to imagine that her pamphlet had that power as to assert that Forster's *A Passage to India* had an immense influence in dissuading Britons from their imperialist passions.[53] I do not share Bell's enthusiasm for

A Passage to India. It seems so pale and liberal compared to the radical anti-imperialism and anticapitalism of *Mrs. Dalloway* or *The Years.* Virginia Woolf once described Mrs. Humphry Ward's novels as hanging in the lumber room of literature like the mantles of our aunts, covered with beads and bugles. Well, there is something about E. M. Forster's novels reminiscent of our unmarried uncles' silk pajamas, something elegant, but rather effete. They have not worn well. And Woolf's novels get harder and tougher year by year, ethically unyielding and morally challenging.

Any member of the Women's International League for Peace and Freedom or the Women's Co-operative Guild, as well as many left-wing feminists and many socialists, would have seen Virginia Woolf's ideology as more powerful than the liberalism of Keynes or Forster. For those readers, *Three Guineas* is not forced or unsatisfactory. It was not at the time, as Bell implies, nor is it now, a political irrelevance.[54] It is hard to believe that the world is as neatly divided into hawks and doves as Bell would have us believe, and that one changes feathers over every war. Some of us imagine Virginia Woolf as a great blue heron anyway, and she describes herself as a misfit, an outsider. As for her ability to feel the vulgar passions, to hear the demotic voice, let Bell read the song of the caretaker's children in *The Years.* It is the voice of the colonial chickens come home to roost. The full measure of *Three Guineas'* effect is yet to be weighed, for it deals with older, more universal, and more deeply rooted social ills than the Spanish fascism that prompted it. Her intent reminds me of a surrealist poem by Laura Riding:

> She opens the heads of her brothers
> And lets out the aeroplanes
> "Now," she says, "you will be able to think better."[55]

9

Quentin's Bogey

One of Virginia Woolf's most iconoclastic gestures in *A Room of One's Own* was her description of the portrait of God the Father in *Paradise Lost* as "Milton's Bogey," a frightening figure which blocked women's "view of the open sky" and consequently was responsible for much of misogynistic British culture's suppression of women artists.[1] Some readers believe that because later in the text Woolf refers to Milton's bogey again in the phrase "for no human being should shut out the view," that Woolf is referring to Milton himself (*Room,* p. 118). But it seems to me that it is typical of Woolf's method to attack the divinity of the Christian godhead in just such a sidelong manner, to deflate the patriarchal God into the Victorian paterfamilias who is the object of her rage in so much of her writing. He is "the large and imposing figure of a gentleman, which Milton recommended for my perpetual adoration" (*Room,* p. 39). Some of Woolf's savage irony appears to have been inherited by her nephew Quentin Bell (see "A 'Radiant' Friendship" [*Critical Inquiry* 10 (June 1984): 557-066]). For he calls me a "personage"(558) in the same tone of voice in which Woolf calls God a "gentleman." Though some feminist readers understand her attack on the poem, the poet, and its progenitor and muse as a portrait of the Christian patriarchal trinity which is the great inhibitor of women's writing, they are troubled by her earlier description of the "sublimity" of Milton's writing. It is possible, I suggest, that sublimity was not a quality she valued, for she asks, "Has any great poem ever let in so little light upon one's own joys and sorrows?"[2]

In a famous essay, later a chapter in the classic work of feminist criticism *The Madwoman in the Attic,* called "Milton's Bogey: Patriarchal Poetry and Women Readers," Sandra Gilbert argues that "Milton's bogey" is made deliberately ambiguous by Woolf and may refer to

202 † WRITING PRACTICE

Milton himself, Adam, or Satan. She argues that "the allusion has had no significant development."[3] But, of course, the previous reference to "the large and imposing figure of a gentleman, which Milton recommended for my perpetual adoration" makes it clear that Woolf's bogey is Milton's patriarchal god. That she later calls him a "human being" may be wicked and perverse, but it is a brilliant undercutting of patriarchal divinity. The allusion is also developed in several ways throughout *A Room of One's Own,* and the reader who puts the pieces together has perhaps caught the "little fish" she promises her readers in the beginning. Where Milton's bogey blocks Woolf's view of the open sky, her aunt's legacy "unveiled the sky" to her; money freed her to look at "reality" (*Room,* p. 39; and see p. 5). The second development of the figure is the phantom form of "J——H——." Jane Harrison's ghostly presence does not block the view of the open sky: "As if the scarf which the dusk had flung over the garden were torn asunder by star or sword—the flash of some terrible reality leaping."(17) Harrison herself, and her great scholarly feminist work on preclassical Greece, is suggested here as having the opposite effect from Milton's bogey. She *unveils* reality and is held up as a model for women. The third development of the theme is the "loneliness and riot" of Woolf's vision of Margaret Cavendish, Duchess of Newcastle— the writer as madwoman, "plunging ever deeper into obscurity and folly": "Evidently the crazy Duchess became a *bogey* to frighten clever girls with" (65; emphasis mine). Virginia Woolf had been a clever girl, and she feared mental instability. The woman writer as madwoman certainly frightened her. She saw Margaret Cavendish's mind "as if some giant cucumber had spread itself all over the roses and carnations in the garden and choked them to death." (ibid.) There is a distinct relationship between Milton's patriarchal bogey and the giant cucumber. Patriarchy covers sky and earth with phallic images preventing women's vision and growth. The woman writer's power is inhibited by Milton's version of the forbidding Christian God who suggests that writing is a male prerogative; and if that doesn't inhibit her enough, a female bogey is invented to show her the woman writer's madness and folly.

I suggest that this reading would support and strengthen the thesis of Gilbert's essay and also its brilliant successor, Christine Froula's "When Eve Reads Milton."[4] Froula argues that Milton's success in *Paradise Lost* is based on his invocation of God the Father as his muse. She is troubled about whether Woolf means that Milton's bogey is the poem or Milton himself, since Woolf uses the words "human being." I suggest that the arrogance of Milton's patriarchal invocation of God as his authority is matched by Woolf's feminist deflation of the divinity of that figure. A bogey is not only a phantom figure of fright; "bogey" also means "imaginary partner," as in the figure of Colonel Bogey (that is how Woolf uses the word when Colonel Pargiter's mistress in *The Years* calls him "bogy.")[5] If God is Milton's imaginary partner in *Paradise Lost*—and Froula proves that he is—the poem claims to be as authoritative as the Bible. When Woolf says that women writers think back through their mothers, and invokes Jane Harrison as muse and mentor, she sets up a feminist alternative to the patriarchal tradition.

The interesting question here is, Where did Woolf get the idea to use the word *bogey* to mean god? I suggest that, like many of her most potent antipatriarchal ideas, the source was in the works of Jane Ellen Harrison, whose fleeting appearance in the text of *A Room of One's Own* represents a world of female "reality" as opposed to the phantom projections of patriarchal religion. From *Prolegomena* to *Themis* to *Epilegomena* to *Alpha and Omega,* Harrison was concerned with discovering the roots of classical Greek religion in earlier spirits created by more "matriarchal" societies. She studied the gods as manifestations of *keres,* figures she defined as spirits, demons, ghosts, gorgons, and *bogeys.* After reading Emile Durkheim, she described these ghostly spirits as projections of the collective human tribe. "Bogey" is a word which turns up very often in her books. Feminists were delighted by her descriptions of Zeus and the Olympians as a version of the Victorian patriarchal family. Woolf's description of the God of *Paradise Lost* as a gentleman bogey is merely an appropriation of Harrison's term from its ancient Greek context to the context of English patriarchal culture.[6]

Why do I begin my response to Bell's attack on me by reference to two feminist critics? Perhaps it is a superstitious move, like scratching the initials of the Blessed Virgin Mary on my schoolgirl essays. Perhaps it invokes the blessing of some powerful figures in my own discipline on the difficult task of explaining yet again to Quentin Bell how his Virginia Woolf is different from our Virginia Woolf. His Woolf is a bogey which frightens American women readers. Our Woolf is a bogey which frightens British male readers. Perhaps the next generation of Woolf critics is sharpening even now the stars and swords which will rip away the veils and give us a real Virginia Woolf.

This is the tale of two bogeys, two phantom figures of Virginia Woolf. One figure, created by Quentin Bell in his 1972 biography, is a modern madwoman in the attic, a fragile, unstable, hysterical suicide, a minor British novelist, ranked somewhere below E. M. Forster as a writer of fiction, historically important because she was Leslie Stephen's daughter and a member of the Bloomsbury group. Quentin Bell's bogey is an Ophelia of the Ouse, a woman who is a failure as a woman, a cautionary figure who warns readers of the terrible consequences when, as Woolf said of "Judith Shakespeare," genius is "caught and tangled in a woman's body" (*Room,* p. 51). Like the Duchess of Newcastle and the cucumbers, this Woolf frightens clever girls. The *Oxford English Dictionary* says that a bogey is a phantom or devil invented by nurses to frighten children. Quentin Bell's bogey, the artist as mad, less than woman, frightens women readers. In "Tintinnabulations" (chap. 7, above), the essay which moves Bell to "confute" my work, I describe the biography:

> Since we are all attached to our families, Bell is not to be blamed for being as a biographer less a good nephew than a good son . . .
>
> By stressing how alien to him was Virginia Woolf's kind of femaleness and by de-emphasizing or disapproving of a lifetime of political engagement, Bell has provided two different sets of symptoms from which the literary doctors may make their diagnoses. One leads to the production of a female cult and its subsequent denunciation by a new generation of Queenie

Leavises. The other leads to her exclusion from the literary/ historical canon on the grounds of "aloofness" or "having no great cause at heart," as Forster claimed . . .

Bell has given her an extended family setting that branches out a bit beyond Bloomsbury. But where is that solitary, strange, antisocial woman who valued privacy so highly that she made it the first principle of her aesthetic? One sees all her nests, their furniture in detail with learned labels on every stick and straw. But where is the Virginia Woolf who wrote novels—that great blue heron of a writer, in flight, alone? She once complained that biography, like sculpture, was all head and shoulders, that one would never know from the biographies of great men "that they had a body between them." The Bell view of Virginia Woolf is from the opposite angle and shows her only from the neck down and in the bosom of her family. This is often the trouble with biographies of great women; one never knows what kind of heads graced their feminine shoulders, and sometimes one can hardly see them at all in the family album. Much of Woolf's best writing attacked private property and the family, and she considered herself an outsider to it all.[7]

My analysis is perhaps unjust; certainly, from Bell's point of view, it *is* unjust. But I would argue, to use Woolf's words—written of a critic who praised Ivan Turgenev at the expense of Honoré de Balzac— that my criticism of Bell is "necessarily and sincerely unjust."[8] It is unfair, I admit, to wish that Quentin Bell were Richard Ellmann. But Woolf scholars envy Joyce scholars; for, however much Joyceans may quarrel with Ellmann's interpretations, he has written an intellectual biography—Joyce the artist and Joyce the thinker are inextricably intertwined. A portrait of Joyce in the bosom of his family, a Paris exile and modernist, which measured him according to an abstract notion of true manhood, which judged his masculinity as related to, say, his loss of sight—Joyce as son, husband, and father—would certainly not do justice to his genius. A biographer who wished to make a portrait of the artist as an emotional cripple could paint Joyce the man in his relations with people. An equally intellectual and more political Woolf can be found in recent essays and books by American critics. Brenda Silver's edition of Woolf's reading notebooks, for instance, goes a long way toward helping scholars recreate Woolf the thinker.[9] But this book is a tool; it has none of the seductive storytelling power of Bell's official narrative. It is modest and unassuming and does not claim that the portrait of the intellectual, the voracious reader, the original thinker, the autodidact with a chip on her shoulder, which emerges from her well-researched pages, is meant to supplant Bell's bogey-woman.

When Woolf was attacked from the left by Dmitri Mirsky in the 1930s and branded an elitist, she wrote to her nephew, perhaps even then imagining him as her future biographer, asking him to sculpt her as a "great flaming goddess." I read this request as both playful and serious. Knowing his interest in politics, she was asking for an image of herself that would emphasize her socialism, feminism, and pacifism, would recognize the devastating critiques of capitalism and imperialism in her novels and essays, and would separate her from the upper-class, elite Bloomsbury Mirsky condemns. The image of Woolf as frigid snob, invalid lady, or mad witch, which Bell sculpted in his elegantly written book, is a political statement of his rejection of Woolf as a political writer.

Marcus' bogey, that "marxist," mystical, and feminist Virginia Woolf created by the so-called lupine critics, myself among them, obviously frightens Bell as much as his ice sculpture of the Snow Maiden frightens us. If he were to accept Marcus' bogey, he would have to revise his version of his own life as well as his versions of his parents and Bloomsbury. Mr. Bell knows perfectly well that my use of the word marxist to describe Woolf as a triple-thinker and to compare her to Walter Benjamin is meant to describe her mind and her fiction, not, as the word is used in his culture, to denote a card-carrying member of a Communist party. He has had ample space in the *Virginia Woolf Miscellany* to chastise me for my grammar and usage.[10] Bell announces another word which waves threateningly at him from the shores of America, a white flag next to the red one of "marxist." That word is *mystical.* What will he think of Madeline Moore's book *The Short Season between Two Silences,* which is subtitled *The Mystical and the Political in the Novels of Virginia Woolf*? What will he make of Catherine Smith's study of Woolf's relation to the history of British women mystics, especially Jane Lead, included in my third collection of essays on Woolf?[11] Given the contempt with which he dismisses Woolf's Quaker aunt, Caroline Emelia Stephen, in his essay, what will be his response to my long study called "The Niece of a Nun: Virginia Woolf, Caroline Stephen, and the Cloistered Imagination" in *Virginia Woolf: A Feminist Slant*?[12] Not only do I believe that Caroline Stephen was an important Quaker philosopher, I also believe that she and Violet Dickinson between them shaped the young Virginia, despondent after her father's death, into a serious professional writer and that, by helping to get her reviews published in the *Guardian*, they set her on course. Not only was the legacy of her aunt, which "unveiled the sky" to the narrator of *A Room of One's Own*, a financial gift which assured her of income while trying to write; it was a female spiritual legacy which profoundly affected her writing. In my essay I argue as well that Woolf took her famous lighthouse image from an essay written by her aunt.

Bell's objections to these feminist readings are that they put women at the center of Woolf's life. Woolf, in *A Room of One's Own*, is, to my mind, the first modern socialist feminist critic. She articulates in that work a feminist aesthetics of social commitment. And in her statement, "We think back through our mothers," if we are women writers, she argues a theory of women's influence on women which applies equally well to herself (p. 79). That feminist critics are following her example in analyzing Woolf upsets Bell. Why is he so upset?

As a biographer, he is somewhat justified in disliking a portrait contradictory to his own. But he is more than a biographer. He is the owner of the Virginia Woolf Literary Estate. He owns, with his sister, as unearned income, a lifetime of Woolf's literary labor. He controls what will be published or not published, and when. He chooses the editors of her work. He and her publishers collect fees for the quotation of her words. Not only does he own and control the literary labor of his aunt, he also, to some extent, owns and controls the labor of his aunt, he also, to some extent, owns and controls the labor of aunt, he also, to some extent, owns and controls the labor of literary critics, who must ask him for permission to quote from Woolf's works— and some, though not all, must pay for the use of those words. That this ownership shapes scholarship is undeniable.

Another example of the power of the literary estate is the fact that seven volumes of her early journals have yet to be published. In " 'As Miss Jan Says': Virginia Woolf's Early Journals," Louise DeSalvo asks

> how the literary and scholarly world might respond to the fact that seven volumes of journals of James Joyce, written from his fifteenth year through his twenty-seventh year, which pro- ided, among other things, a day-by-day record of a period of his adolescence during which a mother surrogate died and which documented his reading of fifty or so books that he alluded to in his maturity, in addition to thirty unpublished essays written when he was in his twenties, existed and had not yet been published.

DeSalvo answers that these documents would be considered essential to understanding the artist's intellectual development.[13] And in Woolf's case, we do not have them.

Bell's "confutation" of my work is an attempt to personalize a debate which has enough natural polarities to rage forever—male/female, old/young (well, fairly young), British/American, biographer/literary critic, English "intellectual aristocracy"/American leftist, and so on. Fortunately, I can erase misogynist/feminist from the list, for, though only a few veteran Woolf critics will notice it, Bell, between the lupine dashes, agrees that Woolf was a feminist. The reader may be perplexed by my joy at his aside. But Bell has asserted so many times that Woolf was *not* a feminist, that the Woolf critic who has followed his remarks is astounded at this reversal of position. (The most recent example was an interview in the *Guardian* where Bell and his wife, Olivier, editor of Woolf's diaries, declared once again, "She wasn't a feminist and she wasn't political."[14]) Though Bell does not offer his change of mind as a gracious concession to a decade of Woolf scholarship on this side of the Atlantic, I will accept it as such on behalf of my sister scholars, who will breathe a collective sigh of relief.

It is always an obstacle to creative work to be constantly arguing with an authoritative male voice which asserts as truth what you know to be false. One gets a critical crick in one's neck from straining to convince him, and standing on the literary barricades shouting across the Atlantic is beginning to get boring. We can straighten up now that one of those burdens is off our backs. But our discourse is still not a conversation between equals. Though Bell elevates me in his text to "a person of great charm and ability," and describes his pain at having to put in her place "so influential a personage," both "person" and "personage" convey the negative message: not a recognized Woolf scholar—rather, a woman intruder who invents a Virginia Woolf whose image contradicts his own factual portrait. Charm is a quality which has never been attributed to me before, thank heaven, and the word would shock my colleagues, students, and family. I hope Professor Bell will never mention it again, as it could damage my reputation and seriously compromise my next battle with the dean over establishing a women's studies program.

I could reply to Bell on his own terms as a charming and able person, a "personage" whose opinions are valued by many. Once his occupation is gone, as mine is in his text, so is the reader's respect. The reader would read "dilettante" and be done with it. But that will not close the gap. (An eye for an eye, an I for an I, a "p" for a "p," or " 'Here we go round the mulberry tree,' " as Woolf says in *Three Guineas*.[15]) I could, alternatively, be polite. "The distinguished biographer of Virginia Woolf . . . " But he says I have written of his biography with "contempt"; so he will suspect me of being disingenuous. Oh, dear, yes, this discourse, this dialogue, must have a plot. Bell began his essay in the voice of Shakespeare—the Shakespeare of the history plays. His tale of Woolf's friendship with Margaret Llewelyn Davies is the main plot, while his quarrel with me is Falstaff's subplot. But I protest. I'm not ready for Mistress Quickly. I could have replied in the voice of his aunt's "Judith Shakespeare," but it is so obvious that much more work will have to be done by women before she "put[s] on the body which she has so often laid down" (*Room*, p.

118). I did reply as one voice among feminist critics reading Woolf reading Milton. But even that stance is problematic. Feminist criticism is now, in the United States at least, a respectable discipline, and white feminist criticism based on certain psychological, poststructural, or gynocritical models is no longer marginal. Yet socialist feminist criticism is still marginal, and I would argue that it ought to maintain its marginal status and its Woolfian outsider's "freedom from unreal localities."[16] I will therefore not match Mr. Bell quote for quote.

Bell asserts that since I argue that Woolf thinks like a "marxist" and also that she was influenced by several women, this should result necessarily in my finding a host of card-carrying women who influenced Woolf. One thing has nothing to do with the other. I am also puzzled by Bell's portrait of Woolf's friendship with Margaret Llewelyn Davies. Does he mean to show me that this is how it should be done? Though he is obviously familiar with my work, he fails to refer to two long essays in which I did at length and in detail exactly what he does here. My study of the influence of Margaret Llewelyn Davies on Woolf (along with a portrait) appears in the issue of the *Bulletin of the New York Public Library* devoted to revaluation of *The Years*; a further portrait appears in my sequel, "Pargetting the Pargiters," also in the *Bulletin of the New York Public Library*.[17] There I quote Margaret's praise of *The Years*: "Of course the book would appeal to me no end on account of peace and anti-humbug and justice."[18] I claim that Margaret was one of the models for Mary Datchet and Eleanor Pargiter. My version of the friendship differs considerably from Bell's. He writes with pity for poor Virginia and as if pity for the poor mad artist and friendship with Leonard were the only possible motivation for Margaret Llewelyn Davies' concern for Woolf.

I will not bore the reader with my version of Bell's other argument, regarding the two versions of the essay for the introduction to *Life As We Have Known It*. Though Bell ignores it, my essay "No More Horses: Virginia Woolf on Art and Propaganda" compares the two texts in detail.[19] I do have a suggestion about why Leonard Woolf did not print the last, best version in *Collected Essays*, and the reason is not an artistic but a political one. I suggest that Leonard Woolf,

collecting the essays during the repressive 1950s, might have decided that the less political Virginia Woolf looked, the better for her
reputation.

As for my concern with Woolf's politics, I am certainly not alone:
see the essays by Bernice Carroll, Naomi Black, Brenda Silver, and
Laura Moss Gottlieb. In addition, Woolf is taken very seriously as a
political thinker by Dale Spender.[20] *Three Guineas* is becoming increas-
ingly important in studies of women and pacifism. Madeline Moore's
new book, mentioned earlier, takes Woolf's socialism and feminism
for granted, and Susan Squier's forthcoming *Virginia Woolf and the
Politics of the City* takes a similar stance.

Marcus' bogey, Virginia Woolf as the "great flaming goddess" of
modern socialist feminism, may block the scholarly sky for a few
years as a historical necessity. But she will fade away when she has
served her purpose as the invisible companion of women writers. I
do not think we have even begun to explore her complexities. I have
before me three reviews Woolf wrote for the *Times Literary Supplement* in 1918. We know very little about the radical 1917 Club to
which she belonged, but it is clear from her diary that she spent a
great deal of time there. Reviewing Meriel Buchanan's *Petrograd: The
City of Trouble, 1914–1918,* Woolf shows a remarkable command of
and interest in the historical details of the Russian Revolution—for
someone who was "not political." The editor of the *Times Literary
Supplement* obviously thought Woolf was political enough to review
these books. Woolf rebukes the diplomat's daughter for claiming that
Aleksandr Kerensky declared himself dictator and also for an unfair
account of the Kornilov affair. "Unlike personalities," Woolf writes,
"politics cannot always be elucidated by the clever intuition which
Miss Buchanan in her purely descriptive chapters shows herself well
able to command." She points out that the book is full of gossip and
does not fulfill the introduction's promise of a view from " 'the man
in the street.' "[21] While she stresses the morally "earnest" tone of
Ernest Belfort Bax's socialist memoirs and compares his destructive
fervor to his evangelical forebears, there is no irony in her conclusion:
"He looks forward to a time when the working classes of the world

will be united in such an international society that the struggle of race with race will be forever impossible."[22] I think this was a belief she shared with Bax, though she would have found his antifeminism as abhorrent as the lack of emotion in his socialism.

Her review of *The Village Priest,* Russian stories by Elena Militsina and Mikhail Salikov, is really an essay on the ideal of brotherhood in Russian literature and an attempt to understand why English literature has no comparable "deep sense of human suffering": "However much we may wish to follow the Russian example, we cannot say 'brother' to a stranger in England." "The truth is that if you say 'brother' you must say it with conviction, and it is not easy to say it with conviction."[23] Bell does not believe in a mystical and political Virginia Woolf. Here in this early essay she is both, admiring the conviction of the Russians when they write of brotherhood, longing for a way to practice it herself. The Russians succeed

> because they believe so passionately in the existence of the soul. . . . And that alone is important: that living core which suffers and toils is what we all have in common. We tend to disguise or decorate it; but the Russians believe in it, seek it out, interpret it, and, following its agonies and intricacies, have produced not only the most spiritual of modern books but also the most profound.[24]

As Woolf found this passionate politics in the Russians, we modern feminist readers find sisterhood and soul in her fiction and essays. I doubt, *pace* Quentin Bell, that, ingenious as we are, we would be able to find it if it weren't there. An American of my generation is perfectly capable of saying "Brother" with conviction. Let me end this response by saying "Brother" to Quentin Bell.

A THEORETICAL PERSPECTIVE
††††

10

Still Practice, A/Wrested Alphabet: Toward a Feminist Aesthetic

> *Louvinie's tongue was clipped out at*
> *the root. Choking on blood, she saw*
> *her tongue ground under the heel of*
> *Master Saxon. Mutely she pleaded for*
> *it, because she knew the curse of her*
> *native land. Without one's tongue in*
> *one's mouth or in a special spot of*
> *one's own choosing, the singer in*
> *one's soul was lost forever to grunt*
> *and snort through eternity like a pig.*
> —Alice Walker, *Meridian*

In *Between the Acts* Woolf uses Ovid's telling of the Procne and Philomel myth as an appropriate metaphor for the silencing of the female, for rape and the male violence against women which are part of patriarchal and fascist wars. I see her as Procne to Philomel's text, the socialist feminist critic as reader of the *peplos,* the woven story of her silenced sister's rape.[1] The reading of the weaving is a model for a contemporary socialist feminist criticism. It gives us an aesthetics of political commitment to offer in place of current theories based in psychology or in formalism.

The voice of the nightingale, the voice of the shuttle weaving its story of oppression, is the voice which cries for freedom; an appropriate voice for women of color and lesbians, it speaks from the place of imprisonment as political resistance. The voice of the swallow, however, Procne's voice, is the voice of the reader, the translator, the middle-class feminist speaking for her sisters: in a sense, the voice which demands justice. The socialist feminist critic's voice is a voice of revenge, collaboration, defiance, and solidarity with her oppressed sister's struggle.

She chooses to attend to her sister's story or even to explicate its absence, as Virginia Woolf told the story of Shakespeare's sister.

A Room of One's Own is the first modern text of feminist criticism, the model in both theory and practice of a specifically socialist feminist criticism. The collective narrative voice of *A Room of One's Own* is a strategic rhetoric for feminist intellectuals. It solves the problem, moral and intellectual, of being one's sister's keeper, one's voiceless sister's voice.[2] Woolf has transformed the formidable lecture form into an intimate conversation among female equals.[3] Men are excluded. Shakespeare is important to *A Room of One's Own* because he is used as a barrier to the text for the male reader. In order to gain entry to the closed circle of female readers and writer, the male reader must pass a test, give the correct password; he must agree that Shakespeare's gender has nothing to do with his greatness. Shakespeare himself retold the story of Procne and Philomel in *Titus Andronicus,* and in it there is an even clearer statement of the role of the critic.[4]

In *Titus Andronicus,* Shakespeare explores the rape victim as a "speaking text" and the problem of how to read her to its bloodiest degree. Lavinia is a "map of woe" to be read by her father and nephew. She is gang-raped by the sons of her father's captive in war. Not only is her tongue cut out but her arms are cut off to prevent her writing her tale. Her "peplos" is a bloody napkin (a reminder of the bridal sheet stained only the night before), and she makes bodily gestures and signs to her father: "But I, of these, will wrest an alphabet,/And by still practice learn to know thy meaning" (3.2.44–45). With her stumps, Lavinia points to the Procne and Philomel story in her nephew's Ovid and writes the names of her rapists in the sand with a stick held between her teeth. The story is not a pretty one, but it does give us a vivid image for the feminist critic and her relation to oppressed women. *A Room of One's Own* is *still practice,* a reading of the signs, the dumb show of silence of all the women between Sappho and Jane Austen who wrote in sand with a stick between their teeth. It tries to "wrest an alphabet" from the "speaking text" of women's bodies. This concept of "still practice," the patient struggle to "read" the body of the text of the oppressed and silenced, is a

model for feminist criticism. It demands the suppression of the critic's
ego in a genuine attempt at explicating the signs of the subject, her
body, her text. It is a frustrating activity which must include, as in
the case of Titus, a recognition of one's own complicity in the silencing
of the subject. The focus of the critic must fix on forms foreign to the
common practices of communication and art, as Titus reads Lavinia's
sand-writing and Procne interprets Philomel's message in the tapestry.
The white woman critic must be careful not to impose her own alphabet
on the art of women of color; the heterosexual critic must not impose
her own alphabet on the lesbian writer. She must learn to read their
languages. The alphabet she wrests from these signs may spell out
Woolf's "little language unknown to men." Lavinia's lament written
in the sand, the picture in Procne's peplos, not only ask for interpretation, they demand action. Thus, the socialist feminist critics' desire
to change the world as well as the hearts and minds of readers is
included in their challenge. Reading that "map of woe," the history
of women artists and makers, in this way reverses the current practice
of much literary criticism, where the initial act of the critic is an
aggressive forced entry into the text of the writer with a reading of
one's own, and a subsequent silence regarding the impulse to political
action as a result of one's reading. "Still practice" is not always still,
not entirely pacifist, for certainly Procne and Titus, on reading these
texts of sister and daughter, are moved to violent revenge. A revolutionary criticism would perhaps insist that it is the critic's role to follow
Procne and Titus in redressing the wrongs committed against the
violated victim. We are at the very least forced to recognize that the
suppression of women's writing is historically and psychologically
directly related to male sexual violence against women, that men have
cut out the tongues of the speaking woman and cut off the hands of
the writing woman for fear of what she will say about them and about
the world. If we arrest the alphabet we wrest from the tapestry and
translate the voice of the stick in the sand, the poem is a four-letter
word, $R A P E$. The unwritten poems of Philomel and Lavinia, the
stories of their lives before they were brutalized as women and as
poets, are tragically lost. Woman is thus imaginatively fixed on a point

which conflates her art with man's perception of her sexuality. Because man wishes to repress her power to accuse him and to remake the world, he has also repressed all her powers of celebration and limited her expression to the depiction of the scene of raping and the naming of her oppressors. Male patriarchal writing, in its aggressiveness, often rings with guilt for its history of robbing women of language and art. These stories reinforce a vision of one primal scene in the history of woman in which both her sexual power and her creative power are attacked and destroyed. Her desire and her art are intimately related in their suppression. She writes on sand or weaves cloth for the reader who can see something other than the printed page as a text.

In "Aristotle's Sister," Lawrence Lipking laments the lack of a woman's poetics, imagining Aristotle's sister Arimneste and inventing a poetic for her, as well as reintroducing us to Madame de Staël's radical proposals for a community of readers reading society as well as literature.[5] Lipking is sympathetic to such a project, but his "poetics of abandonment" merely fits his women's "theory" into the existing male hierarchical structure, where it is clearly less important than men's. It does have the advantage, however, of extending, the range of the male critic's possibilities for study into the fiction of feeling and the reading practice of women. Like the ubiquitous recreations of the androgyne in art (always as a feminized male) in the 1890s in response to the last wave of European feminism, this proposal extends the range of male critical action into the female. The opposite figure, the mannish woman, was given no such liberating exposure, in life or art. Yet the feminist critic who concentrates on male texts, like Nina Auerbach, is often seen as a trespasser on male territory.

Elaine Showalter, in her discussion of Jonathan Culler and Terry Eagleton's attempts at feminist criticism, asks "But can a *man* read as a woman?"[6] and points out their essentialist bind in trying to imitate a *woman's* reading practice, as if this were an eternal Platonic state undetermined by class, time, history, gender, ethnicity, or place, as well as their confusion about what has become clear to feminist critics, that any number of women's readings may not be feminist readings. Showalter asks the male would-be feminist to confront what reading as a man entails, to surrender his "paternal privileges." Otherwise, she claims, "we get a phallic 'feminist' criticism that competes with women instead of breaking out of patriarchal bounds" (143). The unexamined paternal privilege of Lipking's poetics of abandonment leads him into this trap. *We valorize the victim at our own peril.* The suffering posture of the abandoned woman is appealing to the phallic feminist because the absent male is at the center of the woman writer's text. But, as Judith Newton argues, feminist criticism has abandoned the posture of seeing history as a story of "individual and inevitable suffering." Literary texts are, for this kind of committed criticism, "gestures toward history and gestures with political effect," and feminist criticism is "an act of political intervention, a mode of shaping the cultural use to which women's writing and men's will be put."[7] Lipking's tragic essentialism focuses on eternal victimization, ignoring the fact that the power relations which construct gender do change over time. Victimization here seems to be woman's natural condition. Elevating sexual victimization as a woman's poetics is a political act of phallic feminism which robs women of a sense of agency in history. Women have certainly gnashed their teeth and torn their hair and written good poems about it, but one could offer instead a feminist aesthetics of power with, say Judith beheading Holofernes and Artemisia Gentileschi's depiction of the scene as its paradigm. Or an aesthetics of maternal protection, an aesthetics of sisterhood, an aesthetics of virgin vengeance (from the Amazons to Joan of Arc to Christabel Pankhurst), an aesthetics of woman's critique of male domination. Any one of these structures of literary history would have the virtue of melting the current thinking of the virtuous subjugated woman and the eternally dominating male. Such a brilliantly overdetermined and insistently feminist reading of men's female literary monsters as powerful, in Nina Auerbach's *Woman and the Demon,* is far more valuable as a political tool for changing gender relations, however much she may resist the intended meanings of Victorian men, than the ethos of suffering and romantic love which haunts Lipking's nostalgic vision.[8] Auerbach's re- and misreadings urge her own readers to similar subversive acts.

Challenging and revising the canon is often an effective weapon in a campaign of criticism as political intervention. The most challenging critique of the canon comes from feminism, hence one's shock at the omission of such a critique from the *Critical Inquiry* canon issue. (Lillian Robinson's essay, invited but not published by that journal, appears in *Tulsa Studies in Women's Literature*).[9] The use of four new texts in my women's studies course leads me to believe, perhaps too optimistically, that our students' intellectual lives will be less shadowed by Milton's and other patriarchal bogeys than our own. Barbara Taylor's *Eve and the New Jerusalem* makes clear that there always was a feminism at the heart of British socialism, but male historians left it out. Marta Wiegle's *Spiders and Spinsters* exposes the ethnocentricity of our cultural studies. How deflated is Greek myth when seen in the context of world mythology, how interesting the place of women and goddesses in non-Western cultures or the lore of American Indians. And the Bankier and Lashgari *Women Poets of the World* gives any would-be poet a rich and exciting heritage in which to place herself.[10] Any young woman dipping into this extraordinary volume has a poetic past of glorious words belonging to her sex, perhaps a *cliterologos* to think and write back through her many singing mothers. At her age I had only Sappho, Emily Dickinson, and Amy Lowell, and felt I had to choose an ethnic heritage for a writing identity rather than a gendered one. An important event in the history of women's literature is the publication of *Inanna.*[11] It may take several generations before Inanna as the cliterologos becomes flesh in the hearts and minds of readers or on the pages of a Norton Anthology of Literature, but her advent is a prologue to an emancipation proclamation for a whole sex. Scholars are not satisfied with the popular paperback text, but it has caused such a stir that a more authentic scholarly version of these fragments is sure to emerge from the controversy. It is Inanna's anteriority which is part of her aura, many centuries before the Hebrew biblical narrative. Given the chronological nature of patriarchal thinking, an authentic *Inanna,* when read before Homer or the Hebrew and Christian biblical narratives, will cause Eve's firstness to fade, and young women will read aloud to one another Inanna's stirring celebration of the power of her vulva under the apple tree: "Rejoicing at her wondrous vulva, the young woman Inanna applauded herself." The celebration of female sexuality is one of the wonders of this text. No guilt, no blame, no bearing of children in sorrow. In fact, this first written female epic has little to say about either motherhood or chastity; it stresses instead a powerful ethos of sisterhood and a sexuality both oral and genital. It presents a heroine who is politically powerful and sexually free. When Inanna demands that her brother fashion for her both "a throne and a bed" from the wood of the tree of life, which she has saved from the flood, female sexuality speaks as a blessing, not a curse, a sign of power, not a sin. Our students may then see the Greeks and Judeo-Christian biblical scribes as patriarchal revisers of a reality and a literature in which women were powerful. They will start to explore this first hanged goddess who descends into hell and rises again after three days as a prototype and will begin to ask *why* succeeding cultures inscribed, over and over again, female sexuality as evil.[12]

To return to Lipking's Arimneste, it appears probable that she could not read. However sympathetic male critics are to women, they never seem able to acknowledge that throughout history patriarchy has denied women (and many men) access to the tools which make it possible to create written works of art or written criticism of culture. Women have nevertheless produced and reproduced culture. Until male critics acknowledge their own patriarchal privilege, built on centuries of violent suppression of women's art, they will see Arimneste as a shadow of Aristotle. Her fate was doubtless the fate of Freud's female patients or Marx's daughters or Tolstoy's wife—Woolf's Shakespeare's sister is less a fiction than we suppose.

Let us imagine a different scene. Let us suppose that Aristotle and his ilk were unhappy in the communal culture of family and kinship; unhappy with their roles as sons and husbands and fathers; that to escape a culture in which art, work, religion, ritual, and community life were intertwined, they separated themselves out by gender and class from women, slaves, and children; they then defined an art and a way of thinking which denied the connection between art and work, as higher and better than the household arts, and made themselves its priests. Women continued to make pots, weave cloth, cook and serve food, prepare religious festivals, and sing the songs of their oral tradition among themselves in their own space. Lipking's most shocking statement is the one he puts into Arimneste's mouth, that she achieves "a momentary sense of not being alone," "through sharing the emotions of loneliness and abandonment"(77). If I read this correctly, he means that the woman artist achieves the radical sense of intimacy between speaker and listener and the effect of the interconnected nature of human relations because and only because her lover has left her. Certainly women have written great poems on this theme, but to define a specifically female poetics in these terms seems to deny the very existence of a female culture.

We could imagine another aesthetics, call it Penelope's, which grew out of a female culture. Lipking says that Arimneste's "cannot compete, of course, with her brother's tradition." Penelope's aesthetics doesn't wish to compete: is antihierarchical, antitheoretical, not aggressively exclusionary. *A real woman's poetics is a poetics of commitment, not a poetics of abandonment.* Above all, it does not separate art from work and daily life. Penelope weaves her tapestry by day and takes it apart by night. Could Aristotle destroy his lectures and start over again each day? This model of art, with repetition and dailiness at the heart of it, with the teaching of other women the patient craft of one's cultural heritage as the object of it, is a female poetic which women live and accept. Penelope's art is work, as women cook food that is eaten, weave cloth that is worn, clean houses that are dirtied. Transformation rather than permanence is at the heart of this aesthetic, as it is at the heart of most women's lives.

History is preserved not in the art object, but in the tradition of *making* the art object. Alice Walker's "Everyday Use" is the perfect modern example of Penelope's poetic in practice. Penelope's poetic is based on the celebration of the intimate connection between art and the labor which produced it. The *boeuf en daube* or the embroidered robe is not produced to survive eternally. It is eaten, it is worn; culture consists in passing on the technique of its making. Stories are made to be told, songs to be sung, and in the singing and the telling they are changed. Both "Penelope's aesthetics" and Procne's role as reader of her sister's text are rooted in the material base of female experience. A formalist criticism privileging the printed text cannot deal with the basic premises of this practice. The physical production of the work of art, studies of textual revision, censorship (by the poet and her editors, publishers, etc.), the historical conditions of the writing, biography, all the old-fashioned methodologies of literary history—as well as the new ones that deal with maternal subtexts in women's fiction, or mother-daughter relations—can contribute to a new criticism which presumes that a female culture has been produced and reproduced throughout history. As Dale Spender writes of women's ideas:

> We *can* produce knowledge, we have been doing so for centuries, but the fact that it is not part of our traditions, that it is not visible in our culture, is because we have little or no influence over where it goes. We are not the judges of what is significant or helpful, we are not influential members in those institutions which legitimate and distribute knowledge. We are women producing knowledge which is often different from that produced by men, in a society controlled by men. If they like what we produce they will appropriate it, if they can use what we produce (even against us) they will take it, if they do not want to know, they will lose it. But rarely, if ever, will they treat it as they treat their own.[13]

The same is true for women's works of art. Sandra Gilbert and Susan Gubar have written eloquently on the anxiety a woman writer feels in a patriarchal society when the pen is equated with the penis. Ovid's *Procne and Philomel* and Shakespeare's *Titus Andronicus* give us a mythos which explains the female artist's fear. Here is a poem by a sixteenth-century French woman, Catherine des Roches, who overcomes her anxiety, as I would argue most modern women writers have, by keeping a hand in both worlds. Penelope's spindle protects the writer as she attempts the pen:

To my Spindle

My spindle and my care, I promise you and swear
To love you forever, and never to exchange
Sweet domestic honor for a thing wild and strange,
Which inconstant, wanders, and tends its foolish snare.

With you at my side, dear, I feel much more secure
Than with paper and ink arranged all around me,
For, if I needed defending, there you would be,
To rebuff any danger, to help me endure.

But, spindle, my dearest, I do not believe
That, much as I love you, I will come to grief
If I do not quite let that good practice dwindle

Of writing sometimes, if I give you fair share,
If I write of your goodness, my friend and my care,
And hold in my hand both my pen and my spindle.[14]

Reading as Desire I

Virginia Woolf believed that a woman's reading group was revolutionary; and in her edition of *Virginia Woolf's Reading Notebooks,* Brenda
Silver describes a lifetime of intellectual and political obsession with
reading and notetaking which belies the biographers' portrait of a
lady.[15] Her attitude (reading as desire) is perhaps best expressed in
this letter to Ethel Smyth:

> Sometimes I think heaven must be one continuous unexhausted
> reading. It is a disembodied trance-like intense rapture that used
> to seize me as a girl, and comes back now and again down
> here, with a violence that lays me low . . . the state of reading
> consists in the complete elimination of the *ego*; and its the ego
> that erects itself like another part of the body I dont dare to
> name. [L 2915]

It seems pointless to argue whether women are better readers than men because of their receptiveness and openness to the text. What is important is that Woolf saw gender as determining the roles of writer, speaker, and reader and privileged the female versions of these acts as more democratic than the male. Given contemporary male critics' descriptions of ravishing the text and deconstructionists' search for points of entry into the text, Woolf's critical "still practice" as the enraptured reader, egoless and open to the text, rather than aggressively attacking it, is consistent with the goals of feminist philosophy. The reader's desire to be enraptured by the writer, which Woolf celebrates, is very different from contemporary criticism's assertion of intellectual superiority over writers and books. It is difficult to imagine an American formalist deconstructive critic being laid low by a book. Woolf's imagined embrace of the common reader and the common writer comes from a desire for shared pleasure.

By the use of obscurantist language and labeling, formalist critics batter the text and bury it. They assert their egos and insult their own readers by making them feel ignorant. Much as they criticize anti-intellectual bourgeois society, they add to popular contempt for art and thought by alienating readers even further. Their jargon, the hieroglyphics of a self-appointed priesthood, makes reading seem far more difficult than it is. In an age of declining literacy, it seems suicidal for the supposed champions of arts and letters to attack and incapacitate readers.

The language of current theoretical writing is a thicket of brambles; the reader must fight her way into it, emerging shaken and scratched. Those survivors in the central clearing congratulate themselves on being there and class everyone on the other side of the bushes as a coward or an intellectual weakling. Bleeding and exhausted from their struggle, they invent a new hierarchy, with theorists at the top, vying to be scientists and philosophers. Literary criticism and theory are somehow tougher and more rigorous than other forms of literary study. It is an ironic turn of events when one declares that a socialist feminist criticism should defend its old enemies, the very bibliographers, editors, textual scholars, biographers, and literary historians who wrote women writers out of history to begin with. But without the survival of these skills and the appropriation of them, women will again lose the history of their own culture. Theory is necessary and useful, but it is not superior to other literary practice or immune to historical forces. Despite its birth in the left-wing beds of Europe, it has grown in practice to be an arrogant apolitical American adolescent with too much muscle and a big mouth. As theorists constrict the world of readers and writers to ever-tinier elites, the socialist feminist critic must reach out to expand and elasticize that world to include the illiterate, the watchers of television, the readers of romances, the participants in oral cultures—in short, our students.

When male theorists practice a feminist criticism, as Elaine Showalter brilliantly argues in "Critical Cross-Dressing," they are giving their abstract theory a body. One is as reluctant to lend them the materiality of our reading practice as ballast as one is to see good feminist critics throw that materiality overboard to soar in the high ether of theory with the men. If we are good enough to steal from, we are good enough to get published, get tenure, get grants. The male critics who find our work so interesting have put remarkable little effort into seeing that we survive professionally to write it. When a famous Yale professor who *is* the establishment refuses to recognize his power, in fact defines himself as an outsider, feminist critics have little hope of institutional comfort.[16] I agree with Gayatri Spivak that our marginality is important—but there is very little room in the margins when that space has been claimed by Marxists and theorists of all stripes. With all this jostling in the margins, who is in the center? Shari Benstock, discussing the appendixes to Joanna Russ's *How to Suppress Women's Writing,* suggests that academic feminist critics are not marginal in the least, compared to black outsiders or writers excluded from the academy.[17] Yet a hierarchy develops within feminist criticism itself. Are certain forms of feminist criticism more acceptable to the patriarchy? Obviously, yes. Are certain forms of feminist criticism more marginal than others? Obviously, yes. Note that Elizabeth Abel's feminist issue of *Critical Inquiry*[18] contains essays by several left-wing women. Yet none of them explicates a theory of socialist feminist or Marxist feminist criticism. Women of color and lesbians are working on their own theories of feminist criticism. A socialist feminist criticism which wishes to include them must overcome separatist notions of "more marginal than thou," and offer an umbrella of sisterhood under which to shield many writers who feel that their privileged, straight, white sisters are not sisters at all. Yet it must also have the courage to explicate its own tenets and assert its presence in public.

Shari Benstock challenges us: "Feminist criticism must be willing to pose the question of the *differences within* women's writing. . . .Feminist criticism must be a radical critique not only of women's writing but of women's *critical* writing." She calls for us to "inscribe the authority of our own experience" (147) and to question the assumptions of that authority. I am not sure that she realizes how dangerous this project can be. My own career began with such critiques of feminist criticism,[19] and I am sure that old-girl networks exist. Some feminist journals have "better" reputations than others. Star feminist critics perform their acts on platforms all over the country. The only difference is that we like what they have to say, and fall asleep less easily than at a male critic's lecture. Judith Newton says that she wouldn't have the "hubris" to criticize Gilbert and Gubar. It is not hubris but a pledge to our collective future as practicing critics to point out differences in theory and practice. I am sure that Sandra Gilbert and Susan Gubar would be the first to insist that such sisterly criticisms of their work be offered, for they continue to write, to grow, and to change. If feminist criticism has taught us anything, it has taught us to question authority, each other's as well as our oppressors'.

Benstock assumes a willingness on the part of feminist critics to change their practice which may be as utopian as my wish for a historically sound, materially based, theoretically brilliant socialist feminist criticism. I assure her that several of my feminist colleagues who agree with my analysis have nevertheless urged me to delete some of the following remarks. Standing on tiptoe, under an umbrella, in the margin of the margin, can we really engage in dialogue with each other? But there are some cases in which theorists ignore scholarship at their peril.

In "Making and Unmaking in *To the Lighthouse*," Gayatri Spivak

places a Derridian box over the text and crushes and squeezes everything to fit.[20] Like Cinderella's stepsister cutting off a piece of her foot
to fit the glass slipper, this technique distorts the text. This reading
cannot encompass Woolf's celebration of celibacy in Lily Briscoe. So
the text is distorted to allow Spivak to see Lily's painting as analogous
to gestation, with Mr. Ramsay an agent to complete the painting. That
the text actually exults in Lily's *refusal* of Mr. Ramsay is ignored.
The sexual and grammatical Derridian allegory of the copula, in which
the painting is the predicate of Mrs. Ramsay, imposes a male structure
which simply doesn't fit on a female text. The biographical reading
of the "Time Passes" section as Woolf's "madness" depends entirely
on Quentin Bell and is not only not an accurate picture of Woolf's
mental states, but far from feminist criticism. The footnotes do not
cite a single feminist reading of Woolf. Yet there is no more perfect
example of "still practice" than Spivak's essay on, and translation of,
an Indian revolutionary writer's story in *Critical Inquiry*.[21]

Peggy Kamuf's suggestive essay "Penelope at Work: Interruptions
in *A Room of One's Own*" also fails to keep faith with its subject.[22]
The politics of the footnote is the subject of another essay, but it is
clear from Kamuf's reading of Woolf through Foucault, Descartes, and
The Odyssey (like Spivak's reading through Derrida and Freud), that
the critics reject the role of common reader to Woolf's common writer,
and that they also reject the notion of a community or collective of
feminist criticism.[23] It is not "still practice," and it does not try to
wrest a woman's alphabet from the woman writer but spells her
message in the letters of canonical criticism. More important, Spivak
and Kamuf reject explicitly Woolf's role as foremother of feminist
criticism in *A Room of One's Own*. There she outlines "thinking back
through our mothers" as writing practice for feminist critics as well
as novelists, and shows us how to do feminist criticism. By refusing
to accept their role as inheritors of this tradition established by Woolf,
seeing her only as a writer whose texts are decoded with male tools,
whose premises they dare not enter without the support of male
systems, they assert themselves as superior and isolated from their
subject as well as from those other critics who have seen themselves

as descendants of Woolf, the feminist critic. In *A Room of One's Own* Woolf stakes out the territory for the practice of feminist criticism, includes the history of women writing before her, and prophesies the future. But these critics deny the authority of female text. By taking father-guides to map the labyrinth of the female text, they deny the motherhood of the author of the text. These readings reinforce patriarchal authority. By reading Woolf through Foucault, Kamuf names Foucault's critique of the history of sexuality as more powerful than Woolf's. By reading Woolf through Derrida, Spivak serves patriarchy by insisting on a heterosexuality which the novel attacks by privileging chastity in the woman artist. The critic takes a position which is daughter to the father, not daughter to the mother. Is Woolf so frightening to the female critic, are her proposals so radical, that she must provide herself with a male medium through whom to approach the text? What they seem unable to accept is their own daughterhood as critics to Woolf's role as the mother of socialist feminist criticism. One of the major points of *A Room of One's Own* is the clear injunction to the audience of female students to avoid male mentors, the assertion with the story of Oscar Browning that the British academic world is a male homosexual hegemony which needs to deny women to stay in power. Woolf says when turned back from the university library, "Never will I wake those echoes again." Why does the female critic wake those echoes? What one asks of Peggy Kamuf is an interrogation and revision of the methods of her male mentors from the perspective of feminism, an effort to include her work in the feminist dialogue with theory and criticism, to historicize and contextualize her compelling readings of texts.

I suggest that the course Woolf proposes, if taken seriously as intellectual and political action, is often too difficult for women trained by men to do. In effect, the critic says to the writer, "I cannot face your female authority without a male guide; I cannot face the historical fact, the interrupted woman writer, without interrupting the woman telling me the story of woman's oppression." There is a way of being a feminist critic without insisting on the role of daughter of Derrida or *femme de Foucault,* a way of accepting and exploiting the marginality of women and of feminist literary criticism. It is a way described in *Three Guineas* as the alternative institution built by women and working-class men. The critic must join the Outsiders' Society. I am not denying the brilliance of Spivak and Kamuf as critics. It is because I have learned from them that I want to ask them to reject male formalist models for criticism. I do not even claim that a pragmatic historical feminist criticism is the only way to read a text. Yet I am hopeful that a materialist "still practice" may emerge.

I would also like to see a more sisterly relationship develop between feminist theorists and feminist scholars. At present the scholars generously acknowledge the theorists, but the theorists, like their brothers, follow the fashionable practice of minimalism in footnoting, often slighting the years of scholarship, textual editing, and interpretation without which their own work could not begin. This is a denial of the place of one's own work in literary history, asserting as virgin births interpretations which have ancestry. As Virginia Woolf claimed of art that "masterpieces are not single and solitary births," so one may claim that criticism itself has a familial and cultural history. Perhaps theorists, like the characters in Oscar Wilde's plays, want to be orphaned. It increases the cachet of avant-gardism. A look at feminist interpretations of Virginia Woolf's madness would have altered Spivak's reading of the "Time Passes" section of *To the Lighthouse.* It does not seem necessary for Peggy Kamuf cavalierly to dismiss the importance of the historical authenticity of Héloïse's letters to Abelard in her brilliant *Fictions of Feminine Desire.*[24] That their authenticity is questioned is surely part of the historical suppression of the idea or evidence of female desire. Whether Héloïse wrote the letters or the Portuguese Nun was a man is of interest to the argument about female desire. Why this defensive bristling at the historical nature of our enterprise as well as its collectivity? Who profits when departments of literature reward theorists more than scholars? As Virginia Woolf wrote, one must beware of the headmaster with a measuring rod up his sleeve. Who set us in competition with one another, and for such small stakes? The prize is only, as Woolf dryly remarks, an ornamental pot. There is also a real problem, which I do not wish to minimize, for left-wing feminist critics, regarding whether our Marxism or socialism is mediated through men. Certainly Jameson, Saïd, and Eagleton do not make things any easier for us. (Eagleton has now added feminism to his repertoire, and Elaine Showalter has discussed his appropriation and Jonathan Culler's in "Critical Cross-Dressing." Saïd's critique of racism can only benefit from a concurrent reading of sexism and their interrelation. Jameson's Marxism resists feminism from its presentation as a totalizing system. While one does not wish to supplant it with an equally totalizing feminism, this remains a fruitful area of inquiry, as opposed to recent moves toward the totalizing of Lacanian psychoanalysis.)

What would a truly socialist feminist criticism look like? We do have some examples in Virginia Woolf and Sylvia Townsend Warner. What Sylvia Townsend Warner calls the "backstairs or pantry-door" marginality of the feminist critic is a position to be prized and protected. Yet the practice and recent production of theory professionalizes the feminist critic and makes her safe for academe. But I am not sure if it is worth giving up Procne's Bacchic vine leaves for an academic robe. The writing practice of some new theory is often heavily authoritarian, deliberately difficult, and composed in a pseudoscientific language which frightens off or intimidates the common reader. If criticism is reading, then contemporary theorists often move too aggressively and too fast for "still practice." If we are really worried about how few of our students read, how can we write essays which deny our *own* readers the pleasures of reading? A new feminist alphabet which we wrest from the text and arrest in our criticism should not be an imitation of the Greek or Latin by which older generations of critics declared themselves priests of art and culture, superior to the mass of ordinary readers. As feminisms proliferate, it is clear that there is no monolithic feminist practice. We are still in struggle with language and theory, as the "wrest" in my title suggests. Where we "arrest" the logos from a phallocentric alphabet, we are stopping it in its tracks, fixing it in a female gaze, as the male has fixed the female image. Yet as we are also taking this alphabet into our own custody, we need not make an unreadable criticism. A demotic female tongue may surely be spelled out in which criticism is conversation, as in *A Room of One's Own*. Let yourselves go, feminist critics. Wind Bacchic vine leaves in your hair, as Procne did when she went to find her sister. How can we read the message of the tapestry, the words scraped on the sand, if our own tongues practice patriarchal criticism, wars of words? Openness to the text and sharing conversation with our readers is not as intellectually safe as a formal practice, distanced from the desire Woolf sees embodied in the act of reading. Here is a critic speaking in such a voice, aware of her place in the history of feminist criticism. Intimacy between the woman writer and reader, reproduced by that reader for her reader, is not always easy. The white heterosexual critic often fears such an intimacy with black, Chicana or lesbian writers, and class can constitute a serious obstacle. It is not surprising that it is in nonacademic works where the principle of "still practice" or reading as desire is beautifully practiced, most recently in Rachel Brownstein's *Becoming A Heroine*, Joanna Russ's *How To Suppress Women's Writing*, and Alice Walker's *In Search of Our Mothers' Gardens*.[25]

We are now fortunate to have in print, tucked away in the back of her *Collected Poems*, Sylvia Townsend Warner's 1959 Peter Le Neve Foster Lecture delivered to the Royal Society of Arts as a sequel to *A Room of One's Own*.[26] The year 1959 was a low point for Woolf's reputation, and Townsend Warner was reviving a "lost" book by her imitation of it, and by asking to have Leonard Woolf introduce her. Sylvia Townsend Warner was a poet, novelist, historian of early music, a lesbian, and a leftist (a long-time member of the Communist Party). Her feminist fantasy novel *Lolly Willowes* (1929) is as brilliant as *Orlando* and has had a small but faithful audience of admirers. "Women as Writers" is not a seductive sapphistry like *A Room of One's Own*, but in its own dry, wryly ironic way it continues the work of its predecessor as feminist criticism. It modestly apprentices itself (we might say daughters itself to its mother text) and brings up to date the history of women writers. Like Woolf, Warner opens with doubts about the subject chosen for her, a technique which forces the audience to participate in the lecture and makes them responsible for the subject.

"Even when people tell me I am a lady novelist, it is the wording of
the allegation I take exception to, not the allegation itself. . . . Suppos-
ing I had been a man, a gentleman novelist, would I have been asked
to lecture on Men as Writers? I thought it improbable." "It would
appear," she goes on to say,

> that when a woman writes a book, the action sets up an extrane-
> ous vibration. Something happens that must be accounted for.
> It is the action that does it, not the product. It is only in very
> rare, and rather non-literary instances, that the product—*Uncle
> Tom's Cabin,* say, or the *Memoirs of Harriet Wilson*—is the
> jarring note. It would also appear that this extraneous vibration
> may be differently received and differently resounded. Some
> surfaces mute it. Off others, it is violently resonated. It is also
> subject to the influence of climate, the climate of popular opinion.
> In a fine dry climate the dissonance caused by a woman writing
> a book has much less intensity than in a damp foggy one.
> Overriding these variations due to surface and climate is the
> fact that the volume increases with the mass—as summarized
> in MacHeath's Law:
>
>> One wife is too much for most husbands to hear.
>> But two at a time sure no mortal could bear.
>
> Finally, it would appear that the vibration is not set up until a
> woman seizes a pen. She may invent, but she may not write
> down. MacHeath's Law explains why the early women writers
> caused so little alarm. They only went off one at a time. [*Col-
> lected Poems of Sylvia Townsend Warner,* pp. 256, 266]

Townsend Warner adds her own footnotes to *A Room's of One's
Own*'s name-dropping (the lecture's oblique purpose was to supply
students with the names of women writers) from Mother Goose to
Lady Murasaki. Her iconoclastic opinions are "I doubt if Pope would
have laid so much stress on Lady Mary Wortley Montagu being dirty
if she had not been inky"; too much is made of Dr. Johnson on women
preachers and not enough of his support of Fanny Burney; Jane Aus-

ten's "immediacy" keeps a bookful of rather "undistinguished characters" alive; George Eliot is a lecturer and an edifier—"it seems to me that George Eliot insisted upon being a superlative Mrs. Trimmer" (270). Like Woolf's socialist insistence on the importance of money and the material circumstances of the artist, Townsend Warner's analysis emphasizes class and economics. She sees the difference between the nineteenth-century writer and the modern writer in terms of the first's being hampered by an attribution of moral superiority, while the second is hampered by "an attribution of innate physical superiority." "There is, for instance, bi-location. It is well known that a woman can be in two places at once; at her desk and at her washing-machine. . . . Her mind is so extensive that it can simultaneously follow a train of thought, remember what it was she had to tell the electrician, answer the telephone, keep an eye on the time and not forget about the potatoes" (267–68).

Her one positive assertion about women as writers is that they are "obstinate and sly."(267) Her examples of good clear writing are Florence Nightingale's medical reports, a recipe for custard (perhaps in tribute to Woolf's descriptions of the dinners in her lectures), a fifteenth-century letter about apoplexy, a fourteenth-century Norfolk mystic's "I Saw God in a Point," and Frances Cornford's poem, describing a Cypriot mother breastfeeding her baby. Obstinate and sly as the writers she discusses, Sylvia Townsend Warner equates women outsiders with Shakespeare, climbing into the castle of literature through the pantry window. "It is a dizzying conclusion, but it must be faced. Women, entering literature, entered it on the same footing as William Shakespeare" (271). That's as daring a rhetorical trick as any Virginia Woolf ever penned. Because they have had no training, women writers share with Shakespeare a "kind of workaday democracy, an ease and appreciativeness in low company," and an ear for common speech. She advocates the tradesman's door as an alternate entrance to literature, citing the success of Aphra Behn. Writing is now an acceptable trade, except among the upper classes. "Suppose that a royal princess could not tear herself from the third act of her tragedy in order to open a play-centre. People would be gravely put out, especially the men who had been building the play-centre, men who have taught their wives to know their place, and who expect princesses to be equally dutiful" (273).

Since most women writers are middle class, she says, their writing reflects middle-class virtues. She longs for a woman Clare or Burns or Bunyan. Like Woolf, she urges the working-class woman to write: "A working class woman may be as gifted as all the women writers I have spoken of today, all rolled into one; but it is not part of her duty to write a masterpiece." Like Woolf's eloquent peroration to the women absent from her lecture because they are washing up the dishes, Townsend Warner ends with a leap out of the cozy class and cultural world of her audience:

> It may well be that the half has not yet been told us: the unbridled masterpieces, daring innovations, epics, tragedies, works of genial impropriety—all the things that so far women have singly failed to produce—have been socially not sexually debarred; that at this moment a Joan Milton or a Françoise Rabelais may have left the washing unironed and the stew uncared for because she can't wait to begin.

In twenty-five years feminist critics have shown that indeed the half was not told us of our heritage in women writers. Princesses are not yet writing plays, but the works of black people and other minorities are being rediscovered, written, and read. *But Some of Us Are Brave*[27] and the Mexican-American collections published by Arte Publico Press at the University of Houston make clear that both artists and critics of subject peoples have voices. Many a stewpot has burned, and many a man has learned to iron or gone unpressed to his job since then. We all have our own candidates for Joan Milton and Françoise Rabelais. My Joan Milton is Mary Daly; yours may be the early mystic Jane Lead. My candidate for Françoise Rabelais is June Arnold; yours may be Zora Neale Hurston. Because Judith Shakespeare is not only Radclyffe Hall but all the silenced women of history, the continuing work of the critical task of keeping this heritage alive and broadening its base across race, class, and national prejudice is part of what Woolf meant by "thinking back through our mothers."

After Townsend Warner, *A Room of One's Own* was rewritten and reinterpreted by Mary Ellman in *Thinking about Women*, Adrienne Rich in *On Lies, Secrets and Silence*, Tillie Olsen in *Silences*, Carolyn Heilbrun in *Reinventing Womanhood*, Lillian Robinson in *Sex, Class and Culture*, Joanna Russ in *How To Suppress Women's Writing*, and Alice Walker in *In Search of Our Mothers' Gardens*.[28] They consciously paid tribute to Woolf and pushed the barriers further back to include as many women writers as possible. It was less than a decade ago that Lillian Robinson read a working woman's diary to an audience of outraged scholars and called it literature. What these writers have in common with Woolf and Townsend Warner as well as the mute inglorious Joan Miltons whose writing they value is obstinacy and slyness. They speak intimately to the reader, and they are amusing and witty. One after the other they have climbed in the pantry window of literary criticism, taking note of the muddy footprints of their predecessors. In this way literary criticism moves from one generation to the next, affirming its mothers' works and moving them along.

Reading as Desire II

Virginia Woolf's description of the rapture she experienced in "a state of reading" with its "elimination of the ego" equates reading with the female erotic. Reading is desire, and in *To the Lighthouse,* Woolf explicates a practice of gender-different experiences in descriptions of Mr. Ramsay and Mrs. Ramsay as readers. There was, of course, a special thrill associated with reading in Woolf's mind, since she had been so often forbidden to read, assured that it had contributed to her mental instability and might cause further breakdowns. Books, both erotic and dangerous, were also material objects to be treated with care. Woolf often bound books, set type, and performed all the other physical tasks in the making of books. Such an intimate relationship to the material production of one's work is rare for novelists, though poets have often stayed close to type and paper. Woolf suggests that there is clearly a female aesthetic of reading (very different from

contemporary feminist arguments about the resisting reader or even
Nina Auerbach's claim, in *Woman and the Demon,* that Victorian
women deliberately misread portraits of evil, witchlike women (as
figures of power), opposed to a male, aggressive, egotistical and
abstract aesthetic, which desires to conquer and control the book or
use it for the aggrandizement of the self.

Adrienne Monnier, who owned the Paris bookshop Les Amis des
Livres, across from Sylvia Beach's Shakespeare and Co., described
women's reading as enacting the desire to recall the mother's voice
reading to one as a child. This is certainly true for Woolf and for
Colette. One may argue then, that the female reading experience is
*erotic, dangerous, and expressive of the desire to merge with the
mother.* The book, which a woman treats with such care, is the
mother's body. Adrienne Monnier described a woman's attitude toward
books and reading:

> She will not experience the need, like a masculine reader, to
> own her favorite authors in beautiful and lasting edi-
> tions. . . . She will prefer to keep the ordinary editions that were
> the very ones she read first, and she will surround them with
> kind attentions; she will cover them with fine patterned
> paper . . . it is not she who will have the nasty habit of writing
> in the margins. . . . The fact of writing in the margins is further-
> more specifically masculine. Yes, it is curious, a man . . . often
> corrects the author, he underlines, he denies, he opposes his
> judgment; in fact, he *adds himself to it.* A woman remains
> silent when she does not like something, and when she detests
> something *she cuts it out.*[29]

Colette describes the book-lined shelves of her mother's house as
like the protective lining of the womb. She recalls choosing books in
the dark as if feeling along the keyboard of a piano, taking sensuous
delight in the colors and textures of the bindings. As a child she chose
her fairy tales by their illustrations, and she compares the text of a
story to Walter Crane's illustrations: "The large characters of his text
linked up picture with picture like the plain pieces of net connecting

the patterns in lace."[30] Her pleasure in books was physical, and like Woolf she took special delight as a writer in beautiful paper and well-designed pens. She uses the female images of sewing, embroidering, or lace-making to describe books: "Beautiful books that I used to read, beautiful books that I left unread, warm covering of the walls of my home, variegated tapestry whose hidden design rejoiced my initiated eyes." Jean Rhys also associated reading with her mother's sewing, the reading eye with the eye of a needle and the "I" of identity:

> Before I could read, almost a baby, I imagined that God, this strange thing or person I heard about, was a book. Sometimes it was a large book standing upright and half open and I could see the print inside but it made no sense to me. Other times the book was smaller and inside were sharp flashing things. The smaller book was, I am sure now, my mother's needle book, and the sharp flashing things were her needles with the sun on them.[31]

When Rhy's nurse, Meta, caught her reading the *Arabian Nights,* she told her that her eyes would fall out if the kept reading so much, leaving only the pupils, "like heads of black pins." Rhys's most persistent memory of her mother captures her stirring jelly with one hand and reading Marie Corelli's sensational *The Sorrows of Satan* with the other. Anna reads *Nana* in *The Voyage in the Dark,* its lurid jacket depicting a dark girl sitting on the knee of a bald gentleman as much of a context to the story as her clothes are to her body: "The print was very small, and the endless procession of words gave me a curious feeling—sad, excited, frightened. It wasn't what I was reading, it was the look of the work, blurred words going on endlessly that gave me that feeling." (*Voyage,* p. 9) The male text (God/Phallus/Logos) remains illegible even when it tells in such graphic detail the fate of Anna's own female body.

Colette was forbidden to read Zola by her father, though her mother said "There are no such things as harmful books" (*My Mother's House and Sido,* p. 37). She stole a Zola novel and fainted with shock at its graphic description of childbirth. Her mother comforted her, telling of her own difficult birth and reassuring her that she was loved more because she had caused so much pain and had been so reluctant to leave the womb. Colette wrote:

> Books, books, books. It was not that I read so many. I read and re-read the same ones. But all of them were necessary to me. Their presence, their smell the letters of their titles and the texture of their leather bindings. Perhaps the most hermetically sealed were the dearest. I have long forgotten the name of the author of a scarlet-clad Encyclopedia, but the alphabetical references marked upon each volume have remained for me an indelible and magic word: *Aphbicecladiggalhymariod-phorebstevanzy.* [35]

This practically unpronounceable neologism (perhaps Colette is the mother of feminist critical neologisms) recalled for Colette the magic experience of reading. It is a grunt or groan of pleasure, a made-up word like the little alphabets mothers create when they teach their children to speak and to read, a secret sound of baby-talk, the little language never translated from their privacy by mothers and children. If we use Kristeva's concept of the difference between the symbolic and the semiotic, in which the semiotic is laughter, rhythm, sounds without meaning, that which is outside of discourse, and attribute the semiotic (as she does not) to the babble of babies and mothers, to erotic sighs and to fearful gasps of breath, we may define a female aesthetic of reading as "semiotic" as opposed to a male "symbolic" aesthetic, with fixed meanings and "correct" orderly relations between words and meanings. Colette's word *Aphbicecladiggalhymariod-phorebstevanzy* could well stand for the recovery of the mother's body in a book, a cliterologos for speaking in the female tongue.[32]

Perhaps the most disturbing evocation of the difference between men and women reading is chapter 19 ("The Window") of *To the Lighthouse*. The polarized reading experiences reflect the polarization of the sexes in Victorian marriage, each partner living and feeling at the furthest possible point from the other, each desiring confirmation but expecting denial. In the total dialectic of sex the denial is given—he will not speak to her; she will not tell him she loves him—"Say anything, she begged, looking at him, as if for help. He was silent" (184).[33] "A heartless woman he called her; she never told him she loved him. . . . But she could not do it; she could not say it" (185). He, however, *needs* her to be inarticulate (for that is how he defines the feminine) as much as she needs his gruff, negative criticism (for that is how she defines the masculine): "That is what she wanted—the asperity in his voice reproving her" (184); "He could say things—she never could. So naturally it was always he that said the things, and then for some reason he would mind this suddenly, and would reproach her" (185). The polarization of silence and speaking as female and male respectively seems to privilege the male voice of Mr. Ramsay as he paces, reciting male poets, while in fact the text privileges Mrs. Ramsay's silence as more humane and intelligent. In chapter 19 her silence allows her to read not only her husband's mind, but the minds and motivations of all the other characters as well, from *their* point of view, not as a projection of her own desires or ego. Mr. Ramsay has no such insight into others' feelings. Mr. Ramsay "reads" the sight of his wife reading to James as "fortifying" and "satisfying" his energy for work: "He was safe, he was restored to his privacy" (52, 53). His reading is accompanied by many physical actions, like his pacing, gesturing, and reciting aloud. He weeps; he fidgets, twirls his hair, slaps his thigh, and laughs. Both his reading and his projection of a voice which speaks *only to himself* into the space and hearing of others are aggressive, self-dramatising performative activities, reassuring himself of his dominance and mastery over his wife, children, and guests. Their silence gives him a great space in which he may hear the echo of his own voice and shore up his ego. Lily thinks "he was acting, this great man was dramatising himself," and "it was horrible, it was indecent" (277). Mrs. Ramsay thinks "all this phrase-making was a game . . . for if she had said half what he said, she would have blown her brains out by now" (106).

Mr. Ramsay's readings of people and books are aggressive, intrusive male actions meant to take all he needs into himself, with no thought for others' needs. Mrs. Ramsay's readings go out of the self into the mind of the author or sympathize with the feelings of others. Her reading is a privileged female way of being, and the narrator suggests that her mental experiences are far deeper and more profound than Mr. Ramsay's logical progression along the alphabet, with his intense fear of rational "blundering" and his habit of mind which compares doing philosophy with the misplaced valor of a military massacre.

As in Rhys's memory, the mother's needles are a set of nonphallic pens for the woman writer. Woolf recovers her mother as Mrs. Ramsay knitting the brown stocking and reading Shakespeare's sonnets. The text of *To the Lighthouse* is tricky in its representation of reading by gender, and this is one of the reasons it so vividly seems to represent Victorian relations between men and women, that idealization whose subtext was a fear of woman's deep relation to eros and death. Like Mr. Ramsay, who reads to judge, the critic must be open to rereading: "That's fiddlesticks, that's first-rate, he thought, putting one thing beside another. But he must read it again. He could not remember the whole shape of the thing. He had to keep his judgment in suspense" (180). His reading is analytical, while hers is experiential. The reader suspends judgment when the narrator describes Mrs. Ramsay not reading but speculating about reading. (How ironic is this passage, we ask? Irritably, we fidget like James being measured for the stocking; what is the *tone* of this passage?):

> Books, she thought, grew of themselves. She never had time to read them. Alas! Even the books that had been given her and inscribed by the hand of the poet himself: "For her whose wishes must be obeyed". . . . "The happier Helen of our days" . . . disgraceful to say, she had never read them. And Croom on the Mind and Bates on the Savage Customs of Polynesia ("My dear, stand still," she said)—neither of these could one send to the Lighthouse. [43]

She is inscribed as a siren. The inscriptions claim Mrs. Ramsay romantically from the male point of view as tyrant and femme fatale, as muse, the inscribed, not the inscriber. Just how "disgraceful" is it that she does not read contemporary male poets? She is the practical housewife, but the stocking she knits is too short. She is idealized by poets, but Mr. Carmicheal is not in the least taken in by her. The ellipses, the quotation marks, the capitalization of Mind and Savage Customs, the parenthetical "My dear, stand still,"—all work to claim complexity and irony as part of Mrs. Ramsay's image, to ask us to "suspend judgment," to reread her seemingly casual choices about what to read and what not to read. As one who interrupts herself thinking, she is one of Woolf's privileged characters. The whole issue of rereading the canonical texts is at stake here since both are rereaders, aptly pointing attention to a major concern of feminist critics at the moment, whether to reread the classics from a feminist perspective or to read new work by women. Mrs. Ramsay's reading practice is certainly not "feminist."

Later, as Mr. Ramsay watches her reading, "he wondered what she was reading, and exaggerated her ignorance, her simplicity, for he liked to think that she was not clever, not book-learned at all. He wondered if she understood what she was reading. Probably not, he thought. She was astonishingly beautiful" (182). The reader knows what Mr. Ramsay does not know, that she has been reading Elizabethan and Jacobean poetry, that she is astonishingly sensual and astonishingly bright. While he has been reading Sir Walter Scott and thinking "The whole of life did not consist in going to bed with a woman," she has had an erotic, almost orgasmic experience in reading:

> "Nor praise the deep vermilion in the rose," she read, and so reading she was ascending, she felt, on to the top, on to the summit. How satisfying! How restful! All the odds and ends of the day stuck to this magnet; her mind felt swept, felt clean. And then there it was, suddenly entire; she held it in her hands, beautiful and reasonable, clear and complete, the essence sucked out of life and held rounded here—the sonnet. [181]

Mr. Ramsay, Mrs. Ramsay, and the reader are united in this chapter, in that we are all *rereading*. Mrs. Ramsay comes into the room where her husband is reading. "First she wanted to sit down in a particular chair under a particular lamp. But she wanted something more, though she did not *know,* could not *think* what it was that she wanted" (176). "So she turned and felt on the table beside her for *a* book. . . . And she opened the book and began reading here and there *at random* . . . " (178; italics added). The irrationality of her instinctual desire for Shakespeare (rather than modern poets, philosophers, or anthropologists) is stressed. But her pleasure in the text seems in part due to its familiarity. She goes to it almost blindly like a lover, as she responds to the third stroke of the lighthouse beam, anticipating both pain and pleasure. Mr. Ramsay returns to Scott to reaffirm his faith in his own work, upset that Charles Tansley "had been saying that people don't read Scott any more." He is "weighing, considering, putting this with that as he read" (177). But he is really worried about his own books: "will they be read, are they good, why aren't they better, what do people think of me?" The experience of rereading is comforting to his ego. It makes him feel "vigorous." Louise De Salvo and Maria Di Battista have written about the importance of Scott to Leslie Stephen and analyzed Woolf's relation to misreading "poor Steenie's drowning and Mucklebait's sorrow." But what interests me here is that Mr. Ramsay "forgot himself completely (but not one or two reflections about morality and French novels and English novels . . . " (180). But he does not really forget himself. His pleasure (laughing, crying, arguing) is as melodramatic as the text he is reading, a heavily plotted romantic historical novel. Reading is performing in a drama whose lines he knows by heart, and he also knows its conclusion: "Well, let them improve upon that, he thought as he finished the chapter. He felt that he had been arguing with somebody, and had got the better of him." When a man rereads the patriarchal plot, the text seems to say, "his own position [becomes] more secure."

When the feminist critic, the third rereader of this triangular text, rereads *To the Lighthouse,* she is confronted by many problems. Recursive reading for both genders reaffirms their most stereotypical qualities. Mr. Ramsay reads like a soldier on the battlefield, emerging "roused and triumphant." Mrs. Ramsay reads "like a person in a light sleep. . . . She was climbing up those branches, this way and that, laying hands on one flower and then another" (181), in a sensual trance. Does the text simply represent extreme gender polarization through reading? Does the text merely privilege Mrs. Ramsay's erotic reading experience? Don't we admire Mr. Ramsay in some way for being able to mend his wounded ego by reading Scott? Don't we sympathize for a second with the fragility of the male ego? Don't we fear that the total self-annihilation of Mrs. Ramsay's submission to the text may be very dangerous?

Though Woolf does describe reading, in her diary, as an erotic experience, the pleasure of "being laid low by a book"; as a critic she also forgot herself completely, like Mr. Ramsay, while remembering to exercise her critical faculties on the question of the difference between the French and the English novel. Mr. Ramsay is a very public reader. One can read him reading by watching his gestures, but Mrs. Ramsay reading "grew still like a tree which has been tossing and quivering and now, when the breeze falls, settles, leaf by leaf, into quiet" (177). This kind of private sensual experience is her secret life. Her reading of poetry is a form of "still practice." As a public reader, a mother in the patriarchy, she reads aloud the sentence of her own doom and that of all women, to James, in the story of "The Fisherman and His Wife," while everyone "reads" her picture in the window with James as the classic madonna and child of Western patriarchy. There is only one moment which suggests that she is aware of her own role in helping James through his oedipal stage by teaching him to reject her. As she finishes the story she begins to worry about her other children and imagines their deaths. Then, in a new paragraph, the text reads ambiguously, "But she did not let her voice change in the least as she finished the story, and added, shutting the book, and speaking the last words as if she has made them up herself, looking into James's eyes: 'And there they are living still at this very time' " (94).

While in this passage Mrs. Ramsay plays the public reader for a patriarchal audience, she feels guilty throughout the story about the power she exercises over everyone. Not only does the fairy tale crudely tell James that fathers are sensible and women are power-mad—the housewife, Ilsabil, wants to be God—it brings out Mrs. Ramsay's guilt at playing god by arranging marriages and dominating the lives of everyone around her—her family, her guests, and the sick people she visits. Her hesitation, "She did not let her voice change in the least" over the housewife's punishment, the return forever to the hovel of her powerlessness, suggests that she is aware of her own hunger for power, and is willing to learn a lesson as well as to teach one to James.

As *private* reader, Mrs. Ramsay lets herself go completely, and is preparing for a lover:

> And dismissing all this, as one passes in diving now a weed, now a straw, now a bubble, she felt again, sinking deeper . . . and she fell deeper and deeper . . . and those words . . . began wash- ing from side to side of her mind rhythmically, and as they washed, words, like little shaded lights, one red, one blue, one yellow, lit up the dark of her mind, and seemed leaving their perches up there to fly across and across, or to cry out and to be echoes . . .

Like Cam in the drafts of *To the Lighthouse* and the narrators of "Professions for Woman" and *A Room of One's Own*, Mrs. Ramsay is a mermaid, and reading is swimming into the unconscious. She is submerged in water, but her mind is also a body of water with the words washing back and forth. Words (which are fish in the other texts) are here both lights and birds. Illogical as the possibility of birds or lights flying around in the depths of the ocean is, the passage does convey a rhythmic, rocking, womblike atmosphere, as if the reader were a baby, flying and swimming inside the womb, returning phys- ically to the womb, as Mrs. Ramsay reads:

> she felt that she was climbing backwards, upwards, shoving her way up under petals that curved over her, so that she only knew this is white, or this is red. She did not know at first what the words meant at all.
>
> Steer, hither steer your wingèd pines, all beaten Mariners
>
> She read and turned the page, swinging herself, zigzagging this way and that, from one line to another as from one branch to

another, from one red and white flower to another. [178–79]

Like William Browne's figure of the "wingèd pines" ("The Siren's Song" is by William Browne of Tavistock, 1591–1643), the boat as a flying tree, Woolf's image of Mrs. Ramsay reading as a flying mermaid, fish/woman/bird, swimming and flying from word to word in the text, is extremely original. She is the siren-mermaid. She is also moved by the lines "Yet seemed it winter still, and, you away, / As with your shadow I with these did play" (182), and yet the shadow in Shakespeare takes an ominous shape as it relates to her husband: "But through the crepuscular walls of their intimacy, for they were drawing together, involuntarily, coming side by side, quite close, she could feel his mind like a raised hand shadowing her mind" (184).

While one reads this passage as Mrs. Ramsay feeling threatened by her husband's mind, it also suggests that she is attracted by it. And, given the predominance of Shakespeare in Virginia Woolf's life as a reader, as well as the number of Elizabethan references in her written texts, we may read the shadow mind as the one which most threatened and challenged her. "Shakespeare," the name for the poets in the anthology, was Mrs. Ramsay's secret lover, whom she met clandestinely when opening the pages of his poems. "Shakespeare," as the figure of the collective historical artist, was also Virginia Woolf's secret lover. How different from Harold Bloom's description of the relationship between a male writer and his great predecessor as a struggle for mastery is Woolf's description of swimming down into "Shakespeare's" text and flying out of it as a winged mermaid. But Shakespeare is here significantly contextualized with other poets of his age. He is not an individual but an historical period in English literature, foreshadowing the invention of Shakespeare's sister in *A Room of One's Own* and Woolf's claim that "There is no Shakespeare" in her attack on individual genius toward the end of her life.

The female reading aesthetic as we have been reading it in women's texts is erotic, a sensual experience of return to the mother's womb, and a dangerous secret experience of loss of self, a *jouissance* of profound desire. Crudely put, Mr. Ramsay reads to find himself; Mrs. Ramsay reads to lose herself.

Yet, we ask, are these kinds of reading necessarily derived from gender? What are the moral implications of their reading? Is the secret reader a better person? William Empson was disturbed by *To the Lighthouse.* He wrote in 1931: "If only (one finds oneself feeling in re-reading these novels), if only these dissolved units of understanding had been co-ordinated into a system; if only, perhaps, there was an *index,* showing what had been compared with what, if only these materials for the metaphysical conceit, poured out so lavishly, had been concentrated into crystals of poetry that could be remembered, how much safer one would feel."[34] The male critic or rereader of texts places himself outside the triangle of reading in *To the Lighthouse.* He wants the figure to work like William Browne's—wingèd pines = boat, not like the complex diving and flying mermaid. He wants to know what is what, and for it to stay permanently fixed in a reading. He wants *To the Lighthouse* to be *Ulysses,* and the critic's role the matcher of exact resemblance to exact resemblance. Woolf is thrilled by the lack of safety she feels as reader, reproduces this excitement as a woman's experience of reading in her novel, and encourages her reader to enjoy a similar unsafe reading. Thus the quotations are not identified, and Shakespeare merges into William Browne. She dissolves differences between great and minor texts, defining the reading pleasure in the sensuous experience of words, not in the knowledge of who authored them. She deliberately shatters the "crystals of poetry" and does not allow even the polarities of gender to form a set of perfect opposites from which the reader may make a metaphysical conceit. Obviously she read Mr. Empson, for she provided a wonderful mock index to *Orlando.* But an index to *To the Lighthouse* such as Empson desired might put it on the patriarchy's Index of Feminist Books, to be conveniently lost at some future point in history. It seems somehow a condition of their marriage that Mr. Ramsay cannot read Mrs. Ramsay. So it seems somehow fitting that Mr. Empson could not remember Virginia Woolf. There is an index to *To the Lighthouse.* It is, as Lily Briscoe says, "nothing that can be written in any language known to men." It is the narrative of merger with the mother, the lost object of desire, a semiotic sound like Colette's *"Aphbicecladdig-*

galhymariodphorebstevanzy." Reading it is perhaps what Shakespeare meant by "still practice."

And yet the reader remains troubled by the dialectics of reading and
rereading in this now canonical text for feminist critics. Valorizing
Mrs. Ramsay may cause us as much trouble as it does Lily Briscoe.
Mrs. Ramsay's emotional reading practice and Mr. Ramsay's rational
performative reading may stall us again in essentialist categories of
female and male. Perhaps that old Neptune figure, Mr. Carmichael
(Shakespeare's brother? a modern William Browne of Tavistock?), can
help us out here, as he could always see through Mrs. Ramsay. Is
the gender question really a genre question? Perhaps the text is merely
privileging anthologies of poetry over Scott's novels as "better reads."
Why does Mrs. Ramsay not experience the "immasculation" of Judith
Fetterley's resisting reader? Does she recognize that these poems use
her against herself to denigrate female difference? Nina Auerbach
might argue that she enjoys being monster/mermaid because it gives
her an experience of power. What about the reader who cannot distinguish the origin of the quotations? Was Woolf a snob in league with
well-educated minds, appealing to a select group of "rereaders,"
superior to those who are simply common readers and cannot trace
the allusions? William Browne's "The Siren's Song," which causes
Mrs. Ramsay to swoon and sub/merge is about the very seductive
role into which the male poets' dedications (which she won't read)
have cast her. Does she identify with the siren-speakers to entrap the
sailors in love/death? Or is Mrs. Ramsay's reading reverie Virginia
Woolf's "love/death by drowning," an enactment of reunion with her
dead mother by reading? If so, Cam's sub/merging reverie on the boat
in the last chapter, imagining a glorious underwater world, is a reading
of her mother's death. Mrs. Ramsay may also be working out, in the
"real" context of the delayed trip to the lighthouse, what women's
role has been in relation to the epic tradition, both literary and historical,
to men and their voyages in ships, their attribution of shipwreck to
female sexuality (as in *The Odyssey*), and the accusation that Mr.
Ramsay's career would have been more brilliant if not for her. If
woman cannot travel on the sea in flying trees, does she make her

own "voyage under" as a mermaid? Are those "wingèd pines," like the triple stroke of the lighthouse beam, signs of submission to the phallus or a sign of her role as phallic mother in the Victorian family? Any of these readings is "unsafe," and perhaps *To the Lighthouse* in its gendered reading scenes enacts a reading practice which is not like Shakespeare's "still practice" at all, but rather like the seductive dynamic between the sirens and the sailor in the poem. Reading beckons us to unsafe experience:

> Then come on shore,
> Where no joy dies till Love hath gotten more.

Mrs. Ramsay unsettles and destablizes both reading and rereading despite the emphasis on gender difference in the text, as if difference itself and gendered reading are as "historical" and outmoded as the madonna and child Lily remakes in her abstract triangle of the family romance. The critic is reminded that the very "still practice" she has privileged must certainly be deconstructed.

In *To the Lighthouse* Woolf unsettles private and public reading practices and destablizes them at the personal and cultural levels (reading versus rereading) by setting up a gender dichotomy, which also is a genre dichotomy, between the novel and the poem. If fiction is for the male public reader and poetry for the female private reader, which is privileged? Since Mr. Ramsay reads as we do as critics, he is also a producer of texts as well as a reader. The text which Mrs. Ramsay produces is James's safe passage through the oedipal complex. Mr. Ramsay reads *against* desire, to suppress its urges. Mrs. Ramsay reads *to* desire, "till love hath gotten more." This reader is haunted by the word "more." Does it signify death?

Notes

Chapter 1

1 This essay, which appeared in *Bulletin of the New York Public Library* in fall 1974, predates the lively feminist debate over androgyny in Carolyn Heilbrun's *Toward a Recognition of Androgyny* and the issue of *Feminist Studies* devoted to this topic. I still believe that the androgynous ideal does not help women. It often extends the range of male sexuality into the feminine but continues to regard the extension of female sexuality into the historical masculine as perverse. Virginia Woolf's tentative remarks about androgyny in *A Room of One's Own* have been taken out of context by some readers and hardened into a philosophy which is not consistent with the rest of her work. *Orlando* is not an androgyne, but male for the first half of the book and female for the second, for very specific historical reasons.

2 Mario Praz, *The Romantic Agony,* trans. Angus Davidson, 2d ed., (London and New York: Oxford University Press, 1970), p. 216.

3 Ibid., p. 312.

4 See Philippe Jullian, *Dreamers of Decadence: Symbolist Painters of the 1890s* (New York: Praeger, 1971), and also his *The Symbolists* (London: Phaidon, 1973).

5 Oscar Wilde, *Salomé,* illus. Aubrey Beardsley, trans. Lord Alfred Douglas (New York, Toronto, and London: Dover, 1967). Originally published by Elkin Mathews and John Lane (London, 1894).

6 The long-handled powderpuff dominates the right-hand corner of the drawing, as if Beardsley is suggesting to fellow necrophiliacs that there is sex after death.

7 The 1973–74 production of the opera at the Metropolitan in New York, with Grace Bumbry, had Salomé pierced by the spears of the soldiers in a rather sexually symbolic death, not in the spirit of the play. But then Salomé's costume is a glittering, jeweled version of Moreau's Tattooed Salomé, and she is played as an older, sexually experienced vampire-woman, really Herodias, not the young tormented virgin of Wilde's play.

8 Richard Ellmann, *Golden Codgers: Biographical Speculations* (London: Oxford University Press, 1973), pp. 39–59.

9 Ibid., p. 58.

10 Ibid., p. 57.

11 Jullian, *Dreamers of Decadence,* p. 37.

12 The scene in which she asks Herod for a silver charger (representing

both the cold, glittering moon and an enlarged coin, the price of her own chastity) is grimly humorous. Herod sighs with relief at the modesty of her request, encourages her to demand more, then recoils with horror at her slow command that he give her the head of the prophet.

13 Ellmann, *Golden Codgers,* p. 40.

14 The paintings of the period show a fascination with severed heads, not only John's but those of Orpheus and Medusa. See *Dreamers of Decadence;* Klimt's *Salome* as a reincarnation of Judith; also, Kubin's *Black Flowers,* with the head of a man on a water-lily pad, with a woman in the background; and Moreau's *Thracian Girl Carrying the Head of Orpheus.*

15 Jean Paladihle and José Pierre, *Gustave Moreau,* trans. Bettina Wadia (New York: Praeger, 1972), see particularly pp. 99–118.

16 Ibid., p. 99.

17 Ibid., p. 99.

18 See Elizabeth Robins, *Both Sides of the Curtain* (London: Heinemann, 1940). Miss Robins (1862–1952), Ibsen actress and later playwright, novelist, and feminist, was for brief but intense periods of time closely associated with both Henry James and Bernard Shaw. In the early 1890s Oscar Wilde was her friend and confidant. He warned her repeatedly against getting involved with Beerbohm Tree and other actor-managers who might exploit her. She described in her diary Oscar Wilde's "smooth-shaven, rather fat face, rather weak; the frequent smile showed long, crowded teeth, a rather interesting presence in spite of certain objectionable points." In their first conversation he told her, "England is a garden. England is a growth. Boston is an invention. New York is a piece of dry goods on a counter." He visited Miss Robins at her boardinghouse, introduced her to his theatrical friends and to society, subscribed to her Ibsen productions, and much later contributed to a fund for a silver tea set given her in honor of her Ibsen work. (The sugar bowl was inscribed to Hedda Gabler, not a sweet woman, but the greatest role she played in London.) Wilde helped her out of legal difficulties.

19 See *Black and White* 5 (May 11, 1893), p. 290.

20 Jullian, *Dreamers of Decadence,* p. 257.

21 See Aubrey Beardsley, *Collected Drawings,* ed. Bruce S. Harris, with an appreciation by Arthur Symons (New York: Bounty, Crown, 1967). A sense of Beardsley's conception of evil in intellectual women may be seen in his drawings of a Wagnerian audience, his hatred and fear of political women in his drawings for *Lysistrata.* Again this is a case of a complete misreading of the play. Aristophanes wrote a warm, largely comic, very human play about women who withdrew their sexual favors from men in order to obtain peace. In the play, the women suffer from the loss of sex, their husbands, and their children. They are not Amazons, but ordinary women, and they win. Beardsley's suggestions of lesbianism, his gigantic penises, are inappropriate, to say the least. (Laurence Housman did a contemporary translation of the play for the Women's Suffrage Movement [London: The Woman's Press, 1911] which is witty and amusing, not pornographic.)

22 Jorge Luis Borges, "About Oscar Wilde" in *Oscar Wilde: A Collection of Critical Essays,* ed. Richard Ellmann (Englewood Cliffs: Prentice-Hall, 1969), p. 174.

23 "Lord Alfred Douglas on *Salomé*" (extracts from a signed review in *Spirit Lamp,* May 1893), in *Oscar Wilde: The Critical Heritage,* ed. Karl Beckson (London: Routledge & Kegan Paul, 1970), p. 139.

24 "William Archer on *Salomé*" (signed review, "Mr. Oscar Wilde's New Play," in *Black and White* #5, May 1893), in Beckson, *Oscar Wilde: The Critical Heritage,* p. 142.

25 Strauss's father, on hearing the music, said, "It is exactly as if one had one's trousers full of maybugs." See Norman Del Mar, *Richard Strauss: A Critical Commentary on His Life and Works* (London: Barrie and Rockliff, 1962), and also William Mann, *Richard Strauss: A Critical Study of the Operas* (London: Cassell, 1964).

26 Del Mar, *Richard Strauss,* p. 245.

27 Ibid., p. 250.

28 See ibid., p. 283. Romain Rolland wrote to Strauss:

> Oscar Wilde's Salome is not worthy of you. It is not that I do this piece the injustice of putting it in the same category as the majority of modern lyric dramas which are solemn trifles or whose symbolism is sleep-inducing. Despite the pretentious archness of its style there is an incontestable dramatic power; but its atmosphere is sickening and stale. . . . It is not a question of bourgeois morals, it is a question of healthiness. The same passions can be healthy or unhealthy according to the artists who experience them and the characters in whom they are incarnate. The incest of Die Walküre is a thousand times healthier than conjugal and lawful love in these rotten Parisian comedies, the names of which I should prefer not to mention. Wilde's Salome and all those who surround her, save only that brute of a Jochanaan, are unhealthy, unclean, hysterical or alcoholic, oozing with a perfumed and mundane corruption. It is in vain that you transfigure your subject by multiplying a hundredfold its energy, and enveloping it in a Shakespearean atmosphere; it is in vain that you have lent emotional tones of a moving nature to your Salome; you surpass your subject, but you cannot make one forget it.

29 See Sir Thomas Beecham, *A Mingled Chime* (New York: Putnam's, 1943) for a description of censorship troubles in 1911.

30 See O. G. Brockett, "J. T. Grein and the Ghost of Oscar Wilde," *Quarterly Journal of Speech* 52/2 (1966): 131–38. The calling in of eminent physicians to testify on moral and political questions as well as on aesthetic propriety, while reminiscent of Oscar Wilde's trial, was also a tactic of the foes of feminism in England and was used effectively to oppose women's suffrage. Dimly as they understood the play, the accusers sensed some connection between Salomé

and the New Women who were demanding the vote. Wilde's impeccable feminist connections and opinions were well known.

31 Mann, *Richard Strauss,* pp. 50–51. Mann calls Salomé a "hysterical nymphet" and explains her actions as psychologically realistic in view of her need for a father at the time of her adolescent crisis.

32 Jullian, *Dreamers of Decadence,* p. 254.

33 Ibid.

34 Oliver M. Sayler, *The Russian Theatre* (New York: Brentano's, 1922), p. 154. Sayler acclaims the lack of a sense of shame or morbidness in the Russian interpretation of Wilde's play. "He takes his art frankly and openly, stepping over and beyond the half-mood, middle ground of the *double entendre* of the French and other Europeans, apparently without ever recognizing its presence. Thus he emerges on the other side, unfettered by any moral or other entangling considerations, with his mind and his imagination and his feelings free to react as they will in the presence of works of art" (pp. 152–53). Sayler speaks of "the rhythmic control of the human body" in this Cubist production and the "austere attitude toward the passions which saves the Kamerny *Salome* for tragedy. . . . They have achieved tragedy not by restraint but by self-effacing unrestraint . . . the entire performance is intensely impersonal and at the same time hotly and passionately intimate—a paradox which is possible only with artists and audiences who view their art honestly."

35 Yeats even uses Wilde's image of the woman's foot: "Why must those holy, haughty feet descend / From emblematic niches?" (*Collected Plays* [New York: Macmillan, 1953], p. 396). And Emer dances around the head of Cuchulain.

36 Thomas Mann, "Wilde and Nietzsche," in Ellmann, *Oscar Wilde: A Collection of Critical Essays,* p. 171.

Chapter 2

This essay first appeared in *Bulletin of the New York Public Library* (Winter 1976).

1 The text used here is the Norton paperback edition of *Diana of the Crossways* (New York, 1973), with an introduction by Lois Fowler (hereafter cited as *Diana*). I have also used J. A. Hammerton's *George Meredith: His Life and Art in Anecdote and Criticism* (Edinburgh: John Grant, 1911), Lady Butcher's *Memories of George Meredith,* (New York: Scribner's, 1919), and *The Letters of George Meredith,* ed. C. L. Cline (3 vols, Oxford: Clarendon, 1970). The most interesting essays on *Diana of the Crossways* are Jan B. Gordon's "Internal History and the Brainstuff of Fiction," in *Meredith Now,* ed. Ian Fletcher (New York: Barnes and Noble, 1972) and a chapter in Gillian Beer's *Meredith: A Change of Masks; A Study of the Novels* (London: Athlone, 1970). Diane Johnson's *The True History of the First Mrs. Meredith and Other Lesser Lives* (New York: Knopf, 1972) is an original attempt at a new

biographical form, but it is not very useful on the subject of Meredith himself.

2 *The Letters of Caroline Norton to Lord Melbourne,* ed. James O. Hoge and Clarke Olney (Ohio State University Press, 1974). See also the Scholars' Facsimile edition of selected works of Caroline Norton, edited and with an introduction by James O. Hoge and Jane Marcus.

3 Alice Acland, *Caroline Norton* (London: Constable, 1948).

4 *Letters of Caroline Norton,* pp. 1438–39.

5 Christopher Lasch and William Taylor, "Two 'Kindred Spirits': Sorority and Family in New England, 1839–1846," reprinted in Lasch, ed., *The World of Nations* (New York: Knopf, 1973). Feminists generally cite Carroll Smith-Rosenberg, "The Female World of Love and Ritual," in regard to women's friendships.

6 Virginia Woolf, *Second Common Reader* (New York: Harcourt, Brace, 1960), p. 179.

7 *Diana,* p. 186.

8 E. M. Forster, *Aspects of the Novel* (New York: Harcourt, Brace, 1956), p. 90.

9 Woolf, *Second Common Reader,* p. 212. For a discussion of the way Virginia Woolf's life imitates *Diana,* see chapter 4 below, "Thinking Back through Our Mothers."

10 *Letters of Caroline Norton,* p. 964.

11 George Meredith, *Essay on Comedy,* ed. Wylie Sypher (Garden City: Doubleday, 1956), p. 32.

12 Adeline Sergeant, writing in *Temple Bar* (June 1889).

13 Quoted in Hammerton, *George Meredith,* p. 237.

14 *Cinderella* was published as no. 31 in the Folklore Society Series (London: D. Nutt, 1893).

15 Available in various English translations in the 1880s.

16 Another interesting tribute to Clio is in Virginia Woolf's novel *The Years,* where Colonel Pargiter appears to be drawn directly from Lord Larrian, missing fingers and all; there is a deathbed scene, but no Diana to see Mrs. Pargiter safely into the other world.

17 Hammerton, *George Meredith,* p. 16.

18 See n. 1, above.

Chapter 3

This essay appeared in the *Bucknell Review,* 24/1 (1978).

1 Hardwick's Dorothy Wordsworth essay is an exercise in pure nostalgia:

"She lived his life to the full"; "We are no longer allowed such surrenders and absorptions as the Wordsworth brother and sister lived out. The possibilities for this kind of chaste, intense, ambitious, intellectual passion are completely exhausted"; "This is the way for gifted, energetic wives of writers to a sort of composition of their own, this peculiar illusion of collaboration." Hardwick's ambivalence is difficult for the reader here. She feels nostalgic about the form of the victim's subjugation, and yet she blames the victim for not freeing herself. She is envious and judgmental at the same time. It is Dorothy's fault, somehow, that society could not encourage the growth of the female imagination. For a clearer judgment, see Virginia Woolf's essay in *Second Common Reader.* Hardwick blames Dorothy Wordsworth for not taking risks, for not generalizing, and most of all for not telling in her journal the details of personal life with "the great men."

2 Elizabeth Hardwick, *A View of My Own* (New York: Farrar, Strauss & Cudahy, 1962), p. 35.

3 One objects to the slur against the profession of women teachers. The history of the profession is an honorable one, as Virginia Woolf points out. Teaching and writing were for centuries the only respectable female professions. Chastity and morality were requirements for entrance and subsequently for mockery. Jokes about governesses from women writers share the dominant culture's scorn for women.

4 *New York Review of Books* (March 20, 1975), p. 31.

5 Elizabeth Robins, *Ibsen and the Actress* (London: Hogarth, 1928).

6 See chapter 2, above.

7 For a more detailed discussion of the politics of *Mrs. Dalloway,* see my "Middlebrow Marxism: *Mrs. Dalloway* and the Masses," *Virginia Woolf Miscellany* 5 (Spring/Summer 1976).

8 For clues to Hardwick's feelings about mothers, see her novel *The Ghostly Lover* (New York: Harcourt, Brace, 1945), a Southern gothic tale about a heroine lost "in that lonely, confused corridor of the female lie." Marian, the heroine, has been abandoned by her mother and abandons her in return, is very critical of rational women (there are some vicious portraits of women scholars in a New York dormitory), and is condescending to emotional women. The ghostly lover is a young man who tells the heroine of his lusty exploits with black women and pays the bill for her year of study in New York. Marian's last encounter is with a beautiful, embittered Eastern intellectual woman who says, "Where is she now? that old slut, the Revolution!" but is scooped up by her parents at the station. Marian, free of family and of lovers, we are to believe, is free alone.

Chapter 4

1 Letter of Virginia Woolf to Ethel Smyth, March 29, 1931, with permission of Nigel Nicolson (who is editing the letters), Quentin Bell and the Berg Collec-

tion, Astor, Lennox and Tilden Foundation, New York Public Library, for this and subsequent letters to Ethel Smyth.

2 *New Statesman,* October 16, 1920.

3 See Walter Benjamin, *Illuminations,* ed. Hannah Arendt (London: Collins, 1973), and *Reflections,* ed. Peter Demetz (New York: Harcourt Brace Jovanovich, 1978).

4 For a discussion of *A Room of One's Own* and *Three Guineas* as "the propaganda of hope and the propaganda of despair," see chapter 5, below.

5 Letter of Virginia Woolf to Ethel Smyth, Berg Collection.

6 Virginia Woolf, "On Not Knowing Greek," *Collected Essays,* vol. 1 (London: Hogarth, 1966).

7 Virginia Woolf's obituary for her aunt Caroline Stephen, the Quaker visionary whom she called "Nun," is reprinted here in full from the *Guardian,* April 21, 1909, with permission of Quentin Bell. While it makes a rather long note, it is unlikely to be collected elsewhere and will provide the student with hints for the sources of Woolf's spiritual vision, the ascetic, moral, practical, and political "religion" which informs her writing. Woolf's "communion of saints" was a conspiracy against the aggressive godlessness of Leslie Stephen and Leonard Woolf—it was a political and antipatriarchal piety in which the materialist worship of solid objects and solid flesh could be combined with the visionary rhapsodies of a Greek chorus demanding justice from the gods. Caroline Stephen left her niece a larger legacy than the money for a room of her own; she gave her an English feminist religious context and history in which to extend the rhapsodic single voice into a chorus of voices. (Another aunt whose influence is worth studying is Lady Henry Somerset, whose impetuous marriage to a homosexual lord who soon left her to chase boys in Italy brought disastrous scandal on her head, not his—an example which may have saved her niece from marrying Lytton Strachey. Lady Henry Somerset then devoted herself to social work and became the active leader of the Temperance Movement in Britain, an important sphere for women's expression of political ideas and organization.)

> The death of Caroline Emelia Stephen will grieve many who knew her only from her writing. Her life had for years been that of an invalid, but she was wonderfully active in certain directions—she wrote, she saw her friends, she was able occasionally to read a paper to a religious Society, until her final illness began some six weeks ago. Her books are known to a great number of readers, and it is not necessary here to dwell upon their contents. The *Service of the Poor* was published in 1871, *Quaker Strongholds* in 1890, *The First Sir James Stephen* in 1906, and *Light Arising* in 1908. A few words as to her life and character may interest those who had not the happiness of knowing her personally. She was born in 1834, and was the daughter of Sir James Stephen, Under-Secretary for the Colonies, and of his wife, Jane Catherine Venn, daughter of the Rector of Clapham. She was educated,

after the fashion of the time, by masters and governesses, but the influence which affected her most, no doubt, was that of her father, always revered by her, and of her home, with its strong Evangelical traditions. Attendance upon her mother during her last long illness injured her health so seriously that she never fully recovered. From that date (1875) she was often on the sofa, and was never again able to lead a perfectly active life. But those who have read her *Quaker Strongholds* will remember that the great change of her life took place at about this time, when, after feeling that she "could not conscientiously join in the Church of England Service" she found herself "one never-to-be-forgotten Sunday morning . . . one of a small company of silent worshippers." In the Preface to that book she has described something of what the change meant to her; her written and spoken words, her entire life in after-years, were testimony to the complete satisfaction it brought her.

Her life was marked by little outward change. She lived at Malvern for some time, but moved in 1895 to Cambridge, where she spent the last years of her life in a little cottage surrounded by a garden. But the secret of her influence and of the deep impression she made even upon those who did not think as she did was that her faith inspired all that she did and said. One could not be with her without feeling that after suffering and thought she had come to dwell apart, among the "things which are unseen and eternal" and that it was her perpetual wish to make others share her peace. But she was no solitary mystic. She was one of the few to whom the gift of expression is given together with the need of it, and in addition to a wonderful command of language she had a scrupulous wish to use it accurately. Thus her effect upon people is scarcely yet to be decided, and must have reached many to whom her books are unknown. Together with her profound belief she had a robust common sense and a practical ability which seemed to show that with health and opportunity she might have ruled and organised. She had all her life enjoyed many intimate friendships, and the dignity and charm of her presence, the quaint humour which played over her talk, drew to her during her last years many to whom her relationship was almost maternal. Indeed, many of those who mourn her to-day will remember her in that aspect, remembering the long hours of talk in her room with the windows opening on to the garden, her interest in their lives and in her own; remembering, too, something tender and almost pathetic about her which drew their love as well as their respect. The last years of her life among her flowers and with young people round her seemed to end fittingly a life which had about it the harmony of a large design.

8. Virginia Woolf, "The Eccentrics," *Athenaeum* (April 25, 1919), pp. 230–31.

9 Readers will perhaps recognize what the woman Co-operator was like from D. H. Lawrence's portrait of Mrs. Morel in *Sons and Lovers.* In 1927 Margaret Llewelyn Davies wrote an introduction to Catherine Webb's *The Woman with the Basket: The Story of the Women's Co-operative Guild*

published by the Manchester Co-operative Guild. Here Margaret Llewelyn Davies uses the same terms, calling the Co-operators "this republic of women," and "individual heroines of the home." She quotes a letter from a middle-class visitor to the 1916 conference, and from its style we may well assume that visitor was Virginia Woolf: 'It seemed as if the working women of England were gathered together and become articulate. Working women were addressing working women about the questions which interest them, and not to have shared their experiences seemed, for the first time, perhaps, to set a woman, or even a man, apart in a way that was curiously humiliating. Certainly no middle-class woman could speak with anything like the knowledge and conviction with which these women spoke on one subject after another.'

10 See my "*The Years* as Greek Drama, Domestic Novel and Götterdämmerung," *Bulletin of the New York Public Library* (Winter 1977), pp. 276 – 301, and "Pargetting the Pargiters," ibid. (Spring 1977), pp. 416–35.

11 This and subsequent letters from Ethel Smyth to Virginia Woolf are quoted by permission of Letcher and Sons for the Smyth Estate, and the Berg Collection, Astor, Lennox and Tilden Foundation, New York Public Library.

12 See chapter 2, above.

13 In Washington State University at Pullman library containing the collection of Leonard and Virginia Woolf's books.

14 Christopher St. John, *Ethel Smyth* (London: Longmans Green, 1959) pp. 229–30. The next quotation is from p. 232.

15 See " 'No More Horses' " (chapter 5), the two essays on *The Years,* and "The Snow Queen and the Old Buccaneer," *Virginia Woolf Miscellany* (Winter 1977).

16 See Virginia Woolf, "Professions for Women," in The Pargiters: *The Novel-Essay Portion of* The Years, ed. Mitchell A. Leaska (New York: New York Public Library and Readex Books, 1977).

17 Ethel Smyth, *Female Pipings in Eden* (London: Peter Davies, 1934).

Chapter 5

This essay has its origins in a 1974 *MLA* talk and was first printed in the 1976 Woolf issue of *Women's Studies.*

1 Virginia Woolf, *Three Guineas* (New York: Harcourt, Brace, 1973, Harbinger Paperback), p. 170 (hereafter *TG*). First published by Hogarth in London and Harcourt, Brace in New York, 1938. The paperback does not reprint the photographs, which were so central to the book's argument, that appeared in the original editions. In May and June, 1938, the *Atlantic Monthly* published a condensed version under the title "Women Must Weep—Or Unite against the War," which clearly identified it as an antifascist document written from a feminist and pacifist point of view. The contributors' column stated that "her essays, especially *A Room of One's Own,* have endeared her to all militant members of the gentle sex."

2 "Middlebrow," letter written but not sent to the *New Statesman;* in Virginia Woolf, *The Death of the Moth* (New York: Harcourt, Brace, 1942), pp. 176–86.

3 Virginia Woolf, *A Writer's Diary,* ed. Leonard Woolf (New York: Harcourt Brace Jovanovich, 1954; hereafter *AWD*), p. 266. Numbers in this paragraph refer to pages in *AWD.*

4 Virginia Woolf, *Collected Essays,* ed. Leonard Woolf, 4 vols. (New York: Harcourt, Brace, 1967), 3:231. Since, in the cases noted in this essay, the editor did not always choose to reprint the last revised version of the author's essays or to supply the necessary information about original publications, the reader is advised to check earlier collections of essays as well as the periodical in question.

5 Rebecca West, "Autumn and Virginia Woolf," in *Ending in Earnest* (New York: Doubleday, 1913), pp. 208–13.

6 Quentin Bell, *Virginia Woolf: A Biography,* 2 vols. (New York: Harcourt Brace Jovanovich, 1972), 2:186.

7 See Christopher Caudwell, *Pacifism and Violence: A Study in Bourgeois Ethics* (New York: Oriole). Quentin Bell in *Bloomsbury* sees pacifism as both an aesthetic and an ideology as the one defining characteristic of the group. See also H. B. Parkes, "The Tendencies of Bergsonism," in *Scrutiny* (1936), pp. 407–24, for a discussion of Bergsonism as a philosophy which may be used to justify withdrawal from life; although the discussion is of Proust, and of Bergsonism as "the philosophy of an invalid," because Woolf was much influenced by this philosophy through her reading of Jane Harrison, this study is applicable.

8 St. John, *Ethel Smyth,* p. 233. In *The Fortnightly Review* (1891), p. 677, Millicent Garrett Fawcett, in "The Emancipation of Women," (an answer to Frederick Harrison's earlier essay which had called for better-educated house-wives), wrote: "In the time of Mrs. Hannah More, it was unwomanly to learn Latin; Sydney Smith tried to reassure the readers of the *Edinburgh* eighty years ago that the womanly qualities in a woman did not really depend on her ignorance of Greek and Latin, and that a woman might even learn mathematics without "forsaking her infant for a quadratic equation."

9 See the Winter 1977 issue of the *Bulletin of the New York Public Library* for revaluations of *The Years* by several critics, Woolf's galleys of the novel cancelled at the last moment, and an essay on "The Pargiters," the unpublished first version of the novel with the interspersed documentary chapters.

10 The "snub" to Queenie Leavis ascribed to Woolf in *AWD* as the cause of her vicious attack on *Three Guineas* and its author was Woolf's refusal to answer Mrs. Leavis' letter praising her introductions to *Life As We Have Known It* and enclosing a copy of a review in *Scrutiny.* Woolf sent it to Margaret Llewelyn Davies on September 6, 1935, saying "I don't know her, but am told that she and her husband represent all that is highest and dryest at Cambridge. So I rather feel from reading her article; but I suppose she means well, and

I'm glad that she should feel sympathetic in her high and dry way to our book" (Manuscripts of V. W.—M. Llewelyn Davies correspondence, Sussex University Library). In "Lady Novelists and the Lower Orders," *Scrutiny* (1935), pp. 112–32, Queenie Leavis asks why books about the working class haven't "resulted in technical originality and locally authentic writing?" "No amount of observation of the district-visiting kind, however conscientious and however creditable to the industry and heart of the novelist, will produce a convincing substitute for adequate response to the quality of working-class life." She praises Grace Lumpkin's 1933 *To Make My Bread* as "better propaganda because better literature" and compares the novels under review with passages from the cooperative working women's letters. The novels have a "nauseating sentimentality" because they see the workers only as symbols of capitalist exploitation, while Woolf as an artist responded to the quality of life in the writing of real workers. Leavis praises Woolf for recognizing the rich language and culture of the British working class, but like Woolf in *The Years* she sees the dangers which threaten it in the cinema and the loudspeaker. Later that year, reviewing Dorothy Richardson, Leavis called Woolf's feminism dated and *A Room of One's Own* crude. "The demand for mass rights" she wrote "can only be a source of embarrassment to intelligent women, who can be counted on to prefer being considered as persons rather than as a kind. . . . " The Leavises and *Scrutiny* have been responsible for forming the taste of several generations of readers. The false choice demanded by pitting Lawrence against Woolf, the reiteration of Woolf's snobbery and elitism, and the denial of her appeal to ordinary readers on the basis of her birth has deprived many of the experience of finding pleasure in the radical politics, moral strength, and aesthetic experimentation of Woolf's fiction.

11 "By freedom from unreal loyalties is meant that you must rid yourself of pride of nationality—religious pride, college pride, school pride, family pride, sex pride—Directly the seducers come with their seductions to bribe you into captivity, tear up the parchment; refuse to fill up the forms" (*TG*, p. 80). Woolf also demands "that you help all properly qualified people, of whatever sex, class or colour, to enter your profession" (80). Some things will take care of themselves, for "we can scarcely doubt that our brothers will provide us for many centuries to come, as they have done for many centuries past, with what is so essential for sanity, and so invaluable in preventing the great modern sins of vanity, egoism and megalomania—that is to say ridicule, censure and contempt" (82). She warns women of the dangers of professional life: loss of the senses, competition, greed. The professional who has lost his humanity is "only a cripple in a cave." Woolf describes with an outsider's knowledge what "uneasy dwelling places," what "cities of strife" are the old and rich universities for both women and the working class. *Their* new college should teach "Not the arts of dominating other people; not the arts of ruling, of killing, of acquiring land and capital" (34). See *The Workingmen's College, 1854–1904,* ed. J. Llewelyn Davies (London: Macmillan, 1904) for similarities between Woolf's ideas on education and those of F. D. Maurice.

12 Contemporary reviews of *Three Guineas* are in themselves worth a

study. I quote in full *Time and Tide*'s defense, because Woolf wrote to Margaret Llewelyn Davies that it had saved her the trouble of preparing her own response. (*Time and Tide,* June 25, 1938, pp. 887–88):

> Mrs. Woolf's best-seller, *Three Guineas,* descending on the peaceful fold of the reviewers, has thrown them into that dreadful kind of internal conflict that leads to nervous breakdown. On the one hand there is Mrs. Woolf's position in literature: not to praise her work would be a solecism no reviewer could possibly afford to make. On the other hand there is her theme, which is not merely disturbing to nine out of ten reviewers but revolting. There are things which should be ignored and she has not ignored them. There are faces that should remain behind a veil—or at any rate a yashmak—and she has dragged the veil away. A terrible sight. Indecent, almost obscene.
>
> The appalling struggle of most of the reviewers to combine respect and loathing is only too evident in their phrases. On the whole, I award the palm to Mr. Graham Greene for his review in *The Spectator.* While paying all the obligatory lip service to Mrs. Woolf's genius, he contrived to slip in a suggestion that her thesis was out of date, her voice shrill, her outlook provincial and her experience over sheltered.
>
> The only reviewer, as far as my reading goes, who gave up the struggle and frankly went all out in two columns of sheer passionate exasperation was Mr. G. M. Young in the *Sunday Times.* Mr. Young's exasperation was buttressed by page references calculated to induce readers to believe that he could substantiate each point of his attack in detail. Well—I looked them all up. Inaccurate, said he, quoting Mrs. Woolf as making statements she never could or would have made, besides perverting into literalness flights which were obviously intended to be figurative and symbolic. "Belated sex-egoism," he exclaimed, "a pamphleteer of 1905; agnostic, radical, pacifist and feminist." He, at least, has got it out of his system. I should think he is in no danger of a nervous breakdown.

Graham Greene (*The Spectator,* June 17, 1938, p. 112) pokes fun at Woolf's analysis of "woman's influence" as a refined form of prostitution, saying "It is all a little reminiscent of that good man who would rather have given his daughter poison than a copy of *The Well of Loneliness.*" He is absolutely mystified by the fact that she does not regard chastity as woman's highest virtue and is genuinely dismayed by a woman's refusal to see that physical chastity is her real virtue. More interesting to modern readers, however, are the responses of women, to whom the book is addressed. K. John ("The New Lysistrata," *New Statesman* and *Nation,* June 11, 1938, pp. 995–96) praises the book but feels that most women do not "deserve all these bouquets" and that many women are not pacifists by nature; some have the violence of Queen Victoria in them, and some are even fascists. "There is no questioning the justice of Mrs. Woolf's demands, or the beauty of her gospel," she writes, but feels that Woolf is too bitter on lecturers, as "personal charm" is one of Woolf's own best qualities. Louise Bogan (*New Republic,* September 14, 1938, pp.

164–65) titles her piece "The Ladies and Gentlemen" and says that, noble as Woolf's motives are, the elegance of style and class of the writer are to be questioned. "Upper-middle-class Englishwomen, thus fenced off, are to erect, upon the class-consciousness and class education dinned into them from the first moment they were dangled before the nursery fire, a moral pattern so severe that it has never been adhered to by anyone who was not by nature an artist or a saint." She asks Woolf to forget that she is a lady and "go on being an artist," for her position has allowed her, unlike the rest of us, to concentrate on pure ends, not means.

13 Virginia Woolf's own attitude toward revolution may be found in a review of T. D. Beresford's novel *Revolution* in the *Times Literary Supplement,* January 27, 1921, p. 58 (not in *Collected Essays*).

> If the reader finds something amiss—he will probably blame the subject. He will say that revolutions are not a fit subject for action. And there he will be wrong—He means that to write a book about what is going to happen in England when Isaac Perry proclaims a general strike and the army refuses to obey its officers is not a novelist's business—Yet the fault cannot lie with revolutions. Tolstoy and Hardy have proved, revolutions are fine things to write about if they have happened sufficiently long ago. But if you are impelled to invent your own revolution, half your energy will be needed to make sure it works. . . . We find ourselves tempted to suggest alternatives, and seriously wish to draw Mr. Beresford's attention to the importance of the cooperative movement which he appears to overlook. . . . As Lady Angela plays we cannot help thinking about a possible policy for the left wing of the Labour Party. We want Mr. Beresford to turn his mind to that problem, directly the Chopin is over. In short, we want him to give us facts, not fiction.

14 London: L. & Virginia Woolf, 1931; with introduction by Virginia Woolf. The editor of the *Yale Review* (44) describes Woolf as the author of *A Room of One's Own* who "turns her mind here to women of the working class." In a footnote he gives the membership of the English Women's Co-operative Guild in 1930 as 70,000.

15 Woolf praises the working-class women in her introduction, "not down-trodden, envious and exhausted, they are humorous and vigorous and strongly independent." In the Woolf-Davies correspondence cited above, Woolf's concern politically and morally with the Women's Co-operative Guild is demonstrated. She arranged lectures on venereal disease, wondering to her friend why some working women objected and some wept, since they were the class most affected by it. Woolf explained her "impertinence" in writing *Three Guineas* to her fellow feminist (July 4, 1938) "to sit silent and acquiesce in all this idiotic letter signing and vocal pacifism when there's such an obvious horror in our midst—such tyranny, such Pecksniffism—finally made my blood boil into the usual ink-spray." She answered Miss Davies' objection to "verbosity"; "One has to secrete a jelly in which to slip quotations down people's throats—

and one always secretes too much jelly." She was glad she roused G. M. Young's rage and said the book was for the "common," "reluctant," and "easily bored" reader, not for the convinced. She praised the Co-op women for taking a much more radical stance than the Labour Party. As early as 1920 Woolf read Mrs. Layton, one of the writers in *Life As We Have Known It,* praising the style except when it was "too like a book" and a feeling that "she hushes things up a little." (July 21, 1920). In July 1930 she still had grave doubts about her own paper on the Guild's being suitable for an introduction to the book. She asked for permission to change the names to make it fictional for the *Yale Review,* since the editor had said Americans were "in the dark" about cooperation. "Can you trust me to make the thing blameless? I don't suppose any Guildswoman is likely to read the *Yale Review.*" On July 27 she wrote that Leonard had given his oath that "it will be quite all right about America," that she would rewrite the essay for the book, and asked what the women felt, "Do they want their things to appear in print? Are they all alive?" On September 14 she sent a revised version back to Miss Davies, saying that she would withdraw her essay if it would "give pain and be misunderstood." "The difficulty with impressions is that if you once start altering from the best of motives everything gets blurred and out of proportion." On October 10 she responded to the working women's criticism of her essay: "Vanity seems to be the same in all classes. But I swear that Mrs. Burton shall say exactly what she thinks of the appearance of me and my friends and I wont think her unsympathetic. Indeed I wish she would—what fun to hand her a packet of our letters and let her introduce it." Woolf was appalled by "the terrific conventionality of the workers." "I don't think they will be poets or novelists for another hundred years or so. If they can't face the fact that Lilian smokes a pipe and reads detective novels, can't be told that they weigh on an average 12 stone—which is largely because they scrub so hard and have so many chilidren [sic]" then, Woolf felt, they weren't facing reality. She was depressed that the workers were taking on the "middle class respectabilities" which artists had worked so hard to throw off. "One has to be 'sympathetic' and polite and therefore one is uneasy and insincere." In February 1931 she offered her royalties to the Women's Guild, as the *Yale Review* had paid her "handsomely"; "I should only feel I was paying my due for the immense interest their letters gave me." Most important, she confessed that she had now, when reading proof, come round to Miss Davies' view that she had "made too much of the literary side" of her interest. "I tried to change the tone of some of the sentences to suggest a more human outlook," and she added the sentence about cigarettes, "a little blue cloud of smoke seemed to me aesthetically desirable at that point." In June Woolf wrote that she was relieved by the "generous" and "appreciative" letters of the working women, but she agreed with Margaret Llewelyn Davies' sister-in-law that she was the wrong person as a writer to "get people interested in the women's stories." The Yale University Press rejected the book for America as "rather far from the experience and interest of possible readers here," but Woolf said that young English intellectuals found the letters "amazing." She reported much later (July 1937) that there were 395 copies left, "I wish we could bring out another volume. The young are all on the side of the workers, but naturally know nothing whatever about them." Leonard Woolf may perhaps have only remembered the fuss and printed the first version of the essay, but I think it may be argued that the essay itself became a cooperative venture, and the last version was Virginia Woolf's own best version.

16 Perhaps Leonard Woolf was leaving some clues behind him when in *A Calendar of Consolation* (London: Hogarth, 1967) he quoted the proverb, "Go down the ladder when you choose a wife, up when you choose a friend," and Gorky on Tolstoy's determination to tell the truth about women only when he had one foot in the grave.

17 Virginia Woolf, "The Leaning Tower," in *The Moment and Other Essays* (New York: Harcourt, Brace, 1948), p. 154.

Chapter 6

Versions of this paper were read at NEMLA, 1976, and Pioneers for Century III, April, 1976. It was published in *Feminist Studies* 4/1 (1978).

1 In *by a Woman writt,* ed. Joan Goulianos (New York: Bobbs-Merrill, 1973), p. 24.

2 Elizabeth Robins, *Ancilla's Share: An Indictment of Sex Antagonism* (London: Hutchinson, 1924; Westport, Conn.: Hyperion, 1976); Virginia Woolf, *A Room of One's Own* and *Three Guineas.* Quotations are from Harcourt, Brace, & World editions, 1957 and 1966.

3 See Elizabeth Robins, *Way Stations* (New York: Dodd, Mead and Company, 1913) for a collection of feminist essays. Her other novels are *George Mandeville's Husband, The New Moon, The Open Question, Below the Salt, The Magnetic North, The Dark Lantern, Come and Find Me, The Florentine Frame, Where Are You Going To?, The Messenger of the Gods,* and *The Secret That Was Kept.* She published Henry James's letters to her as *Theatre and Friendship* (London: Jonathan Cape, 1932) and her memoirs, *Both Sides of the Curtain;* Leonard Woolf wrote an introduction to her *Raymond and I* (New York: Macmillan, 1956). Virginia and Leonard Woolf had published her *Ibsen and the Actress.* Elizabeth Robins is discussed in *Shaw and the Actresses* by Margot Peters (New York: Doubleday, 1980) and The Women's Press, London and the Feminist Press, New York have reprinted Robins' suffrage novel, *The Convert,* with an introduction by Jane Marcus. My dissertation (Northwestern University, 1973) is a biography of Elizabeth Robins.

4 Woolf, *A Room of One's Own,* pp. 68–69.

5 See "Profile of Leon Edel," *New Yorker,* March 13, 1971, where he mocks Robins, Wilberforce, and the rest home for women. In the Robins Collection, Fales Library, New York University, is a letter from Edith Wharton to Elizabeth Robins urging her to help him in his work on Henry James because of his piety toward "the Master." She did.

6 Trekkie Parsons has been very generous in allowing me to cite from Elizabeth Robins' letters and papers. Letters from Virginia Woolf to Elizabeth

Robins in the Humanities Research Center, University of Texas at Austin, and in the Berg Collection, New York Public Library, urge her to write her memoirs and bring manuscripts; Woolf chooses the title for *Both Sides of the Curtain.*

7 Robins, *Ancilla's Share,* p. 204.

8 Ibid., pp. 85–86.

9 Ibid., p. 104.

10 *Times Literary Supplement,* May 29, 1924, p. 343. The remarks about Woolf occur in the review of *Three Guineas.*

11 *Times Literary Supplement,* June 17, 1920. Since this review by Virginia Woolf has not been collected, I reprint it in full:

New Novels
The Mills of the Gods

Miss Elizabeth Robins must be used by this time to being told that she writes like a man. What the reviewers mean is that a page of her writing has the kind of bare brevity which marks the talk even of undergraduates. The idea may be commonplace, the knowledge superficial, but it stands unpalliated by superfluous phrases. For this aspect of her art there can be nothing but praise. If you miss a sentence you will not find that a slight variety of the same thing offers you another chance of understanding. You must read even the first story, which is the worst in the book, The Mills of the Gods (Thornton Butterworth, 7s. net), with attention. You will find yourself stopping to have another look at the fine hard fabric before passing on.

Therefore, one pays Miss Robins the compliment of formulating one's case against her; and what is our case against her? Only that she is pre-war writer. At the end of each of the seven series one can pencil a date—any date between 1895 and 1910 will do; the date that is quite out of the question is the date 1920. It was between those years that old English houses were so very old: that strong men went gold digging in the Yukon, and Italian counts of satanic disposition lived upon the tops of mountains with beautiful wives. In those days there were suffrage raids, and butlers, and haunted houses. Houses, indeed, played a very large part in life; and life itself was a great deal more at the mercy of coincidence and mystery than it is now. Life, in short, was somehow different. But that is not true. Life is precisely the same; and our charge against Miss Robins amounts simply to this—that, misled largely by her strong dramatic sense, she has backed certain human qualities which dropped out of the race and neglected others which are still running. So, at least, we define the queer sense we have after being impressed and interested—that all this happened a very long time ago. If there had not been a war we should not have felt this with anything like the same force. The war withered a generation before its time. Yet among the pre-war writers we do not know many who do their job with Miss Robins' efficiency, or give us the assurance, at all times so comfortable, that, although the story may be of no great concern, the mind behind it is exceptionally robust.

12 When still Viriginia Stephen she wrote to Violet Dickinson (May 1905), "I have been reading Miss Robin's [sic] book *[A Dark Lantern]* all the evening, till the last pages. It explains how you fall in love with your doctor, if you have a rest cure. She is a clever woman, if she weren't so brutal." *The Letters of Virginia Woolf* (6 vols.), 1:1888–1912, ed. Nigel Nicolson, asst. ed. Joanne Trautmann (New York: Harcourt Brace Jovanovich, 1975), p. 190. Virginia Stephen's review appeared in the *Guardian,* May 24, 1905, p. 899:

A Dark Lantern. By Elizabeth Robins. Heinemann. 6s.

Of this novel it can be said without exaggeration that every page interests. If such a thing were possible, it might almost be added that it is too interesting, or, perhaps that the interest it excites is not quite of the right quality. Miss Robins has the gift of charging her air with electricity, and her readers wait for the expected explosion in a state of high tension. This is partly due to the fact that she is always in earnest—that she is one of the few novelists who can live in their characters. But it is also true that her work would be finer if its intensity were, not less, but, so to speak, diffused over a greater surface. As it is, she is too closely interested in her characters to be able to take a dispassionate view of them. A character like that of Garth Vincent, for instance, comes near failure because of this tendency to a kind of passionate concentration on the part of the novelist. He is one of the many versions of Rochester. The argument applied once more by Miss Robins seems to be that, if you want a man to be excessively masculine, you have only to take certain of the conventional masculine qualities and develop them to the desired strength. The result has overpowering effects within the covers of the novel; but, outside, the hero is more melodramatic than impressive. In the woman's character Miss Robins shows far more sense of propor-tion, and we protest that if Miss Katherine Dereham had met Mr. Garth Vincent under normal conditions she would not have allowed herself to take him seriously. A great part of the book is devoted to the medical details of a nervous breakdown and a rest cure, in which Mr. Garth Vincent is the doctor in attendance. Here, too, Miss Robins seems to have had some purpose in her mind which leads her to insist, rather more emphatically than is artistic, upon the faults of hospital nurses and the incidents of physical illness. The defects of the book seem to us to be the persistent atmosphere of the sick room; of morbidity, whether of body or mind; and the lack of a sense of humour. But there can be no doubt that few living novelists are so genuinely gifted as Miss Robins, or can produce work to match hers for strength and sincerity.

13 Robins, *Ancilla's Share,* p. 175.

14 Ibid., p. 49.

15 Woolf, *A Room of One's Own,* pp. 31–32. I discuss Woolf's response

to Oscar Browning in "Taking the Bull by the Udders: Sexual Difference in Virginia Woolf, A Conspiracy Theory," in *Virginia Woolf and Bloomsbury: A Centenary Celebration,* (London: Macmillan, 1987). For a full discussion of Woolf's treatment of Brontë's anger, see my "Daughters of Anger, Material Girls," in *Women's Studies* 1988, ed. Gina Barecca, *Last Laughs: Hate and Humour in Women's Writing.*

16 *A Room of One's Own,* pp. 34–35.

17 Goulianos, *by a Woman writt,* pp. 27–28.

18 *A Room of One's Own,* p. 92.

19 For a discussion of Woolf's politics and feminism, see chapter 5, above, and Naomi Black's "Virginia Woolf and the Women's Movement," in *Virginia Woolf: A Feminist Slant,* ed. Jane Marcus (Lincoln: University of Nebraska Press, 1983).

20 For a revaluation of *The Years,* see the Spring 1977 and Winter 1977 issues of the *Bulletin of the New York Public Library,* including my "*The Years* as Greek Drama, Domestic Novel and Götterdämmerung," and "Pargetting the Pargiters: Notes of an Apprentice Plasterer."

21 See chapter 5, above.

22 Woolf's draft of "Professions for Women," in *The Pargiters,* ed. M. Leaska.

23 Vera Brittain, "A Woman's Notebook," *Nation and Athenaeum,* vol. 48 (January 31, 1938), p. 571.

24 Letter from Virginia Woolf to Ethel Smyth, January 24, 1931, Berg Collection, New York Public Library; quoted by permission of Quentin Bell. Dame Ethel's letters to Woolf, in this period of Woolf's relationship with Vita Sackville-West, have several blanks and may have been destroyed because of their personal nature.

25 This quotation and those following through the next nine paragraphs are from the draft of "Professions for Women," which is now available in Leaska's edition of *The Pargiters.* For an analysis of the artist as fisherwoman, see *Virginia Woolf and the Languages of Patriarchy.*

26 Robins, *Ancilla's Share,* p. 138.

27 Ibid., p. 172.

28 Woolf, *Three Guineas,* p. 141.

29 Robins, *Ancilla's Share,* p. 152.

30 Woolf, *A Room of One's Own,* p. 94.

31 Robins, *Ancilla's Share,* p. 62.

32 Ibid., p. 51.

33 Ibid., p. 118.

34 Ibid., p. 116.

35 Ibid., pp. xliv–xlv.

36 Woolf, *A Room of One's Own,* p. 103.

37 Robins, *Ancilla's Share,* pp. 311–12.

38 Ibid., p. 275.

39 Woolf, *A Room of One's Own,* p. 57.

40 See letters from Gerald Duckworth to Elizabeth Robins, Robins Collection, Fales Library, New York University.

41 Woolf, *Letters,* 1:189.

42 Jane Marcus, "Some Sources for *Between the Acts*" in *Virginia Woolf Miscellany* (Winter 1977), pp. 1–3.

43 Barbara Charlesworth Gelpi and Albert Gelpi, eds., *Adrienne Rich's Poetry* (New York: W. W. Norton, 1975), p. 71.

44 Hortense Calisher, "No Important Woman Writer," in *Women's Liberation and Literature,* ed. ELaine Showalter (New York: Harcourt Brace Jovanovich, 1971), p. 230.

45 Typescript, Robins Collection, Fales Library, New York University. The Rede Lecture is reprinted in *Recollections of Virginia Woolf by Her Contemporaries,* ed. Joan Russell Noble (London: Owen, 1972).

46 Letter from Virginia Woolf to Ethel Smyth, September 21, 1930, Berg Collection, New York Public Library.

Chapter 7

1 Bell, *Virginia Woolf,* 1972.

2 Allen McLaurin, *Virginia Woolf: The Echoes Enslaved* (Cambridge, 1973).

3 Elaine Showalter, *A Literature of Their Own: British Women Novelists from Brontë to Lessing* (Princeton: Princeton University Press, 1977).

4 Samuel Hynes, *The Auden Generation: Literature and Politics in England in the 1930s* (New York: Viking, 1977).

5 Ellen Hawkes, "The Virgin in the Bell Biography," *Twentieth Century Literature* 20: 96–113, and "A Form of One's Own," *Mosaic* 8: 77–90.

6 Michael Holroyd, *Unreceived Opinions* (London: Penguin, 1976).

7 *Vogue,* January 1973.

8 Only volume 1 of Woolf's *Diary* contains hostile notes and does not inform the reader when passages have been left out.

9 For a discussion of Woolf's left-wing politics and feminism, see Bernice A. Carroll, " 'To Crush Him in Our Own Country,' " *Feminist Studies* 4 (1978):

99–131; Alex Zwerdling, "*Mrs. Dalloway* and the Social System," *PMLA* 92 (1977): 69–82; Jane Marcus, "Middlebrow Marxism," pp. 4–5; Winter 1977 issue of *Bulletin of the New York Public Library,* particularly the article by Margaret Comstock; and Lillian S. Robinson, "Who's Afraid of a Room of One's Own?" in Louis Kampf and Paul Lauter, eds., *Politics and Literature* (New York, 1972), pp. 354–411, and in Robinson's *Sex, Class and Culture.*

10 For a discussion of music as an influence, see McLaurin, *Virginia Woolf,* and Jane Marcus, "Enchanted Organ, Magic Bells: *Night and Day* as a Comic Opera," in Ralph Freedman, ed., *Virginia Woolf: Revaluation and Continuity, A Chorus of Voices* (Berkeley: University of California Press, 1979).

11 *Times Literary Supplement,* May 27, 1977.

12 *Athenaeum,* April 25, 1919, pp. 230–31, uncollected.

13 *Times Literary Supplement,* April 4, 1918.

14 Virginia Woolf, *Moments of Being,* ed. with introduction by Jeanne Schulkind (London: Hogarth, 1976).

15 Hermione Lee, *The Novels of Virginia Woolf* (London: Methuen, 1977), and Avrom Fleishman, *Virginia Woolf: A Critical Reading* (Baltimore: Johns Hopkins University Press, 1975).

16 Thomas S. W. Lewis, *Virginia Woolf: A Collection of Criticism* (New York, 1975); John Lehmann, *Virginia Woolf and Her World* (New York: Harcourt Brace Jovanovich, 1976); Virginia Woolf, *Freshwater,* ed. Lucio Ruotolo (New York: Harcourt Brace Jovanovich, 1976).

17 Virginia Woolf, *Books and Portraits: Some Further Selections from Her Literary and Biographical Writings,* ed. Mary Lyon (London: Hogarth, 1977).

18 Robin Majumdar and Allen McLaurin, *Virginia Woolf: The Critical Heritage* (London: Routledge & Kegen Paul, 1975).

19 George Spater and Ian Parsons, *A Marriage of True Minds: An Intimate Portrait of Leonard and Virginia Woolf* (London: Hogarth, 1977).

20 Roger Poole, *The Unknown Virginia Woolf* (Cambridge: Cambridge University Press, 1978).

21 Jane Lilienfeld, " 'The Deceptiveness of Beauty': Mother Love and Mother Hate in *To the Lighthouse," Twentieth Century Literature* 23 (1977): 345–76.

22 Phyllis Rose, *Woman of Letters* (New York: Oxford University Press, 1978).

23 Jean O. Love, *Virginia Woolf: Sources of Madness and Art* (Berkeley: University of California Press, 1977).

24 Mitchell Leaska, *The Novels of Virginia Woolf from Beginning to End* (New York: John Jay, 1977).

25 *The Diary of Virginia Woolf, 1920–1924,* ed. Anne Olivier Bell, assisted

by Andrew McNeillie (London: Hogarth, 1978).

26 Ibid., p. 340.

Chapter 8

1 Two of the papers delivered at that meeting have since been published: Mary Helen Washington, "New Lives and New Letters: Black Women Writers at the End of the Seventies," *College English* 43/1 (January 1981): 1–11; and Florence Howe, "Those We Still Don't Read," *College English* 43/1 (January 1981): 12–16.

2 See *Women's Studies Quarterly* 9/3 (Fall 1981), particularly the reprint of speeches by Adrienne Rich, "Disobedience Is What the NWSA is Potentially About," pp. 4–6; and Audre Lorde, "The Uses of Anger," pp. 7–10.

3 See Annette Kolodny, "Dancing through the Minefield: Some Observations on the Theory, Practice, and Politics of a Feminist Literary Criticism," *Feminist Studies* 6/1 (Spring 1980); 1–25; and Judith Gardiner's response, "Marching through Our Field," in the following issue. Gardiner distinguishes between liberal, radical, and socialist feminist critics. Gayatri Spivak's unpublished "A Response to Annette Kolodny" is an even stronger critique of Kolodny's position. She writes: "To embrace pluralism (as Kolodny recommends) is to espouse the politics of the masculinist establishment. Pluralism is the method employed by the *central* authorities to neutralize opposition by seeming to accept it. The gesture of pluralism on the part of the *marginal* can only mean capitulation to the center."

4 Dame Ethel Smyth's story of her struggle against the masculine establishment in music is told in *Female Pipings in Eden.* A revival of her work has begun: several papers were delivered at the First National Congress on Women and Music at New York University in March 1981; her memoirs have been reprinted, *Impressions That Remained* (New York: Da Capo, 1981), with a new introduction by Ronald Crichton; and Da Capo Press has also reprinted the score of her *Mass in D* for soli, chorus, and orchestra, with a new introduction by Jane Bernstein.

5 See Gloria T. Hull, Patricia Bell Scott, and Barbara Smith, eds., *But Some of Us Are Brave: Black Women's Studies* (Old Westbury, New York: Feminist, 1982).

6 The conference, entitled "A Controversy of Critics," was sponsored by the School of Criticism and Theory at Northwestern University in May 1981.

7 Geoffrey Hartman, *Criticism in the Wilderness: The Study of Literature Today* (New Haven: Yale University Press, 1980).

8 Quoted by Ethel Smyth in *Maurice Baring* (London: Heinemann, 1937), p. 206.

9 See Gayatri Spivak, "Feminism and Critical Theory," *Women's Studies International Quarterly* 1/3 (1978): 241–46, "Three Feminist Readings: Mc-

Cullers, Drabble, and Habermas," *Union Seminary Quarterly Review* 35/1–2 (Fall–Winter 1978–79): 15–38. The essays by Julia Lesage are "Subversive Fantasy in *Celine and Julie Go Boating*," *Jump-Cut* 24–25 (March 1981): 36–43, which deals with the semiotics of body language and domestic space, "Dialectical, Revolutionary, Feminist," *Jump-Cut* 20 (May 1979): 20–23, and "Artful Racism, Artful Rape: D. W. Griffiths' *Broken Blossoms*," *Jump-Cut* 26 (May 1981). See also the entire lesbian-feminist special issue of *Jump-Cut* (24–25 [March 1981]), especially its bibliography, p. 21; Ruby Rich's analysis of the teacher in girls' schools playing the roles of "good cop" and "bad cop" in her study of *Maedchen in Uniform*, "From Repressive Tolerance to Erotic Liberation," pp. 44–50; and Bonnie Zimmerman's discussion of lesbian vampire films, "Daughters of Darkness: Lesbian Vampires," pp. 23–24.

10 Julia Lesage uses Mary Douglas' *Purity and Danger: An Analysis of Concepts of Pollution and Taboo* (London: Routledge & Kegan Paul, 1966) as a theoretical construct for the analysis of *Celine and Julie Go Boating* (see n. 9, above); this theory was also very useful to Marina Warner in her analysis of female heroism in *Joan of Arc* (New York: Knopf, 1981).

11 See Gerald Graff's *Poetic Statement and Critical Dogma* (Evanston: Northwestern University Press, 1970), and *Literature against Itself* (Chicago: University of Chicago Press, 1979); Frank Lentricchia's *After the New Criticism* (Chicago: University of Chicago Press, 1980); Frederic Jameson's *The Political Unconscious: Narrative as a Socially Symbolic Act* (Ithaca: Cornell University Press, 1981); and Terry Eagleton's "The Idealism of American Criticism," *New Left Review* 127 (May–June 1981): 53–65, which reviews Lentricchia and Jameson and surveys the field. Eagleton notes that these critics refuse to discuss gender and maintain sexist attitudes, but his own review does not mention the brilliant work done by feminist critics in the United States in the last decade, nor has Eagleton's work itself deviated from male discourse, despite its Marxism. If Annette Kolodny's espousal of the pluralist position from the margin may be seen as a capitulation to a misogynist power structure, Jameson's Marxist pluralism, in its refusal to deal with gender, should show those tempted to follow Kolodny's lead that male bonding transcends theoretical enmities and is more primary among American critics than the issues that divide them intellectually.

12 Rich, "Disobedience," p. 5.

13 *A Room of One's Own*, pp. 68–69, 110.

14 Quentin Bell, "Bloomsbury and the Vulgar Passions," *Critical Inquiry* 6/2 (Winter 1979): 239–56.

15 Quentin Bell, *Bloomsbury* (London: Weidenfeld & Nicholson, 1968).

16 Recent contributions to feminist critical theory include Myra Jehlen, "Archimedes and the Paradox of Feminist Criticism," *Signs: Journal of Women in Culture and Society* 6/4 (Summer 1981): 575–601; and Nina Baym, "Melodramas of Beset Manhood: How Theories of American Fiction Exclude

Women Authors," *American Quarterly* 33/2 (Summer 1981): 123–39. See also the special issue of *Critical Inquiry* (8/2 [Winter 1981]) edited by Elizabeth Abel, called *Writing and Sexual Difference,* with essays by Elaine Showalter, Mary Jacobus, Margaret Homans, Susan Gubar, Nancy Vickers, Nina Auerbach, Annette Kolodny, Froma Zeitlin, Judith Gardiner, Catherine Stimpson, and Gayatri Spivak; but note the lack of a socialist-feminist theoretical essay.

17 Nigel Nicolson's introduction to *Woolf: Letters,* vol. 5, *The Sickle Side of the Moon,* pp. xi–xvii, is a sustained attack on Woolf's politics and feminism. Carolyn Heilbrun's feminist review of this volume appears in *Virginia Woolf Miscellany* (Spring 1980): 4, and Nicolson's reply in *Virginia Woolf Miscellany* (Spring 1981): 5. See also Jane Marcus, review of *The Sickle Side of the Moon, Chicago Tribune Book World,* November 4, 1979.

18 Virginia Woolf, "Why?" in *The Death of the Moth,* pp. 227–34.

19 See Marcus, *New Feminist Essays on Virginia Woolf,* pp. 1–30.

20 Woolf, *Diary,* p. 146.

21 Hawkes, "The Virgin in the Bell Biography," and "A Form of One's Own."

22 See *Bulletin of the New York Public Library* (Winter 1977); and Woolf, *The Pargiters,* ed. Leaska.

23 Woolf, *The Pargiters,* p. xciii.

24 See *Twentieth Century Literature* 25/3–4 (Fall–Winter 1979). The collection was conceived and edited by Lucio Ruotolo, Stanford University.

25 Virginia Woolf, *Women and Writing,* ed. Michèle Barrett (London: Women's, 1979; New York: Harcourt Brace Jovanovich, 1980).

26 Woolf, *Letters,* vol. 4, *A Reflection of the Other Person,* p. 348.

27 Ibid., p. 203.

28 Bell, "Bloomsbury and the Vulgar Passions," pp. 239–56.

29 See Marcus, *New Feminist Essays on Virginia Woolf. Virginia Woolf: A Feminist Slant* continues the lupine tradition.

30 Bell, *Bloomsbury; Virginia Woolf;* and "Bloomsbury and the Vulgar Passions."

31 Woolf, "The Leaning Tower," pp. 128–54; *Letter to a Young Poet,* Letters Series no. 8 (London: Hogarth, 1939).

32 See Adrienne Rich, "Toward a Woman-Centered University," in *On Lies, Secrets and Silence: Selected Prose, 1966–1978* (New York: W. W. Norton & Co., 1979), pp. 125–55.

33 Virginia Woolf was a lifelong member of the Guild and shared its socialist, feminist, and pacifist politics. See chapter 5, above, and Black, "Virginia Woolf and the Women's Movement," in Marcus, *Virginia Woolf: A Feminist Slant.*

34 Bell, *Virginia Woolf,* 2:186.

35 Ibid.

36 Woolf, "The Leaning Tower," p. 154.

37 Gerald Brenan, *Personal Record, 1920–1972* (London: Jonathan Cape, 1974).

38 E. M. Forster, *Virginia Woolf: The Rede Lecture, 1941* (Cambridge: Cambridge University Press, 1942).

39 See Bruno Bettelheim, "Surviving," in *Surviving and Other Essays* (New York: Knopf, 1979), pp. 275–314; see also pp. 20–33.

40 See Nicolson's attack on Woolf's politics in the introduction to Woolf, *Letters,* 5:xi–xvii.

41 Woolf, *A Writer's Diary,* p. 234.

42 The Stephen family background is discussed in Martine Stemerick's dissertation (University of Texas, 1982).

43 Catherine Smith discusses Caroline Stephen in her forthcoming study of English women mystics. See also Smith, "Jane Lead: The Feminist Mind and Art of a Seventeenth Century Protestant Mystic," in *Women of Spirit: Female Leadership in the Jewish and Christian Tradition,* ed. Rosemary Reuther and Eleanor McLaughlin (New York: Simon & Schuster, 1979), pp. 184–85. Robert Tod is preparing a biography for the English Society of Friends' Quaker biography series; and see Marcus, "Niece of a Nun," in *Virginia Woolf: A Feminist Slant.*

44 Bell, *Bloomsbury.* See also chapter 5, above.

45 Woolf, *Letters,* 5:383.

46 Ibid., 1:148, 151–52, 165, 180.

47 Dmitry Mirsky, *The Intelligentsia of Great Britain,* trans. Alec Brown (New York: Conici, Friede, 1935).

48 Caroline Emelia Stephen, *The Light Arising: Thoughts on the Central Radiance* (Cambridge: W. Heffer & Sons, 1908).

49 Jaakko Hintinkka's "Virginia Woolf and Our Knowledge of the External World," *Journal of Aesthetics and Art Criticism* 38/1 (Fall 1979): 5–14 is relevant here.

50 Virginia Woolf, "Thoughts on Peace in an Air Raid," in *The Death of the Moth,* pp. 243–48.

51 Bell, "Bloomsbury and the Vulgar Passions."

52 See Maria-Antonietta Macciocchi's "Female Sexuality in Fascist Ideology," *Feminist Review* 1 (1979): 59–82.

53 Bell, "Bloomsbury and the Vulgar Passions."

54 Ibid.

55 Laura Riding, "In the Beginning," *Collected Poetry of Laura Riding* (New York: Random House, 1938), p. 358.

Chapter 9

This essay appeared in *Critical Inquiry* 11/3 (Spring 1986) in response to Quentin Bell's "Bloomsbury and the Vulgar Passions" in the previous issue.

1 Virginia Woolf, *A Room of One's Own,* pp. 118, 39; all further references to this work, abbreviated *Room,* will be included in the text.

2 Woolf, September 10, in *A Writer's Diary,* p. 5.

3 Sandra M. Gilbert and Susan Gubar, *The Madwoman in the Attic: The Woman Writer and the Nineteenth-Century Literary Imagination* (New Haven: Yale University Press, 1979), p. 188; and see pp. 187–212.

4 See Christine Froula, "When Eve Reads Milton: Undoing the Canonical Economy," *Criticial Inquiry* 10 (December 1983): 321–48.

5 See Woolf, *The Years,* pp. 7 and 246.

6 See Jane Ellen Harrison, *Prolegomena to the Study of Greek Religion* (Cambridge, 1903); *Themis: A Study of the Social Origins of Greek Religion* (Cambridge, 1912); *Epilegomena to the Study of Greek Religion* (Cambridge, 1921); and *Alpha and Omega* (London, 1915).

7 See chap. 8, above.

8 Woolf, "Winged Phrases," *Contemporary Writers* (New York: Harcourt Brace Jovanovich, 1965), p. 144.

9 See Brenda R. Silver, *Virginia Woolf's Reading Notebooks* (Princeton: Princeton University Press, 1983).

10 See the Fall 1983 and Winter 1983 issues of *Virginia Woolf Miscellany,* ed. J. J. Wilson.

11 See Madeline Moore, *The Short Season between Two Silences: The Mystical and the Political in the Novels of Virginia Woolf* (Boston, 1984), and Catherine F. Smith, "*Three Guineas:* Virginia Woolf's Prophecy," in Marcus, *Virginia Woolf and Bloomsbury.*

12 See Marcus, "Niece of a Nun," pp. 7–36.

13 Louise A. De Salvo, " 'As Miss Jan Says': Virginia Woolf's Early Journals," in Marcus, *Virginia Woolf and Bloomsbury.* The largely phallocentric discourse of *Critical Inquiry* is exemplified in Stanley Fish, "Profession Despise Thyself: Fear and Self-Loathing in Literary Studies," *Critical Inquiry* 10 (December 1983): 349–64. Fish attacks both an essay by Walter Jackson Bate, which deplores an MLA session on Texas lesbian feminists, and a journalist's review of the publication of a scholarly edition (by the New York Public Library and

Readex Books) of *Melymbrosia* (one of the early versions of Woolf's *The Voyage Out*), a volume which received the approval of the MLA Center for Scholarly Editions. What Fish neglects to mention is that the editor of *Melymbrosia* is the highly respected Woolf scholar and Hunter College professor Louise A. De Salvo. Fish sets up a debate in which he is the champion of the blacks, Chicanos, and Texas lesbians maligned by Bate, as well as the champion of scholarly editions contemptuously dismissed by anti-intellectual journalists. He tells us that the journalist in question, Jonathan Yardley, won the Pulitzer Prize, but he does not tell us even the name of the scholar whose work represents several years of meticulous textual study. His argument is framed as an all-male debate between himself, the journalist, and the Harvard professor. If he were really interested in educating Bate, he might have suggested that the work of Texas (and other) lesbian feminists may be found in the journals *Sinister Wisdom, Lady Unique, Feminary,* and *Conditions,* and in publications of the Kitchen Table Press. Furthermore, even a cursory reading of *Melymbrosia,* which is more like an H. G. Wells novel than a Woolf novel, may have suggested a serious questioning of one of the most strongly held tenets of our profession, that the last published text is the best text. *Melymbrosia* is in many ways more interesting than *The Voyage Out,* as *The Pargiters* is a more radical text than *The Years.* The publication of early versions of the work of feminist writers, as well as those of other oppressed groups, may allow us to see a rich body of material from which we may speculate on the power of internal and external forces of censorship plaguing anti-establishment writers.

14 Quentin Bell, *Guardian,* March 21, 1982.

15 Woolf, *Three Guineas,* p. 66.

16 Ibid., p. 113.

17 See my "*The Years* as Greek Drama, Domestic Novel, and Götterdämmerung," and "Pargetting the Pargiters."

18 Margaret Llewelyn Davies, quotations in "Pargetting the Pargiters," p. 435.

19 See chapter 5, above.

20 See Carroll, " 'To Crush Him in Our Own Country' "; Black, "Virginia Woolf and the Women's Movement"; Brenda R. Silver, "*Three Guineas* Before and After: Further Answers to Correspondents," in *Virginia Woolf: A Feminist Slant,* pp. 254–76; Laura Moss Gottlieb, "The War between the Woolfs," in *Virginia Woolf and Bloomsbury;* Dale Spender, *Women of Ideas and What Men Have Done to Them, From Aphra Behn to Adrienne Rich* (Boston, 1982); Dale Spender, ed., *Feminist Theorists: Three Centuries of Key Women Thinkers* (New York, 1983); and Naomi Black, "Virginia Woolf: The Life of Natural Happiness," in *Feminist Theorists,* pp. 296–313.

21 [Woolf], "A View of the Russian Revolution," review of *Petrograd: The City of Trouble, 1914–1918* by Meriel Buchanan, *Times Literary Supplement,* December 20, 1918, p. 636.

22 [Woolf], "A Victorian Socialist," review of *Reminiscences and Reflections of a Mid and Late Victorian* by Ernest Belfort Bax, *Times Literary Supplement,* June 28, 1918, p. 299.

23 [Woolf], "The Russian View," review of *The Village Priest and Other Stories* by Elena Militsina and Mikhail Salikov, *Times Literary Supplement,* December 20, 1918, p. 641.

24 Ibid.

Chapter 10

A shorter version of this chapter appeared in the Spring/Fall 1984 Feminist Criticism issue of *Tulsa Studies in Women's Literature,* ed. Shari Benstock. It has been reprinted in Benstock, *Feminist Issues in Literary Scholarship* (Bloomington: Indiana University Press, 1987). I am grateful to Elizabeth Abel, Judith Kegan Gardiner, Moira Ferguson, Michael King, Mary Mathis, and Sandra Shattuck for their helpful comments on drafts of this paper. The epigraph from *Meridian* was pointed out by Lynda Koolish, who discusses it in her forthcoming "This is Not Romance."

1 I discuss the Procne and Philomel myth in *Between the Acts* in "Liberty, Sorority, Misogyny," in *The Representation of Women in Fiction,* pp. 60–97, ed. Carolyn Heilbrun and Margaret Higonnet (Baltimore: Johns Hopkins University Press, 1982).

2 "Her Sister's Voice," is part of the argument of "Taking the Bull by the Udders."

3 Woolf's deconstruction of the lecture form is discussed in "Taking the Bull by the Udders," and the role of Shakespeare is also taken up in "Sapphistry: Narration as Lesbian Seduction in *A Room of One's Own,*" in my *Virginia Woolf and the Languages of Patriarchy,* (Bloomington: Indiana University Press, 1987).

4 My thanks to Lynda Boose for discussions of *Titus Andronicus.*

5 Laurence Lipking, "Aristotle's Sister," in *Critical Inquiry* 10 (September 1983), "Canons," pp. 61–81. On page 62 Lipking argues that Samuel Butler's *The Authoress of the Odyssey* is regarded as "irredeemably crackpot." For some redeeming features in his "crackpot" theory, see classicist David Grene's introduction to the University of Chicago Press reprint, 1967. Despite my disagreement with Lipking's argument here, I remain grateful for his personal encouragement of my work.

6 Elaine Showalter, "Critical Cross-Dressing: Male Feminists and the Woman of the Year," *Raritan* (Fall 1983), pp. 130–49.

7 Judith Newton, paper delivered at the 1983 MLA Feminist Criticism session chaired by Shari Benstock, to which the present essay was also a contribution.

8 Nina Auerbach, *Woman and the Demon* (Cambridge: Harvard University Press, 1982).

9 *Critical Inquiry* 10 (September 1983), and Lillian Robinson, "Treason Our Text: Feminist Challenges to the Literary Canon," *Tulsa Studies in Women's Literature* (Spring 1983): 83–98. See also Paul Lauter's "Race and Gender in the Shaping of the American Literary Canon: A Case Study from the Twenties," *Feminist Studies* 9/3 (Fall 1983): 435–63.

10 Barbara Taylor, *Eve and the New Jerusalem* (New York: Pantheon, 1983); Marta Wiegle, *Spiders and Spinsters* (Albuquerque: University of New Mexico Press, 1982); *Women Poets of the World,* ed. Joanna Bankier and Dierdre Lashgari (New York: Macmillan, 1983).

11 *Inanna,* ed. Diane Wolkstein and Samuel Noah Kramer (New York: Harper & Row, 1983).

12 Feminists should note the reviews of *Inanna* by Piotr Michalowski in the *New York Times Book Review* and Harold Bloom in the *New York Review of Books* (October 13, 1983). Neither man tells the reader what is in the book. Certainly it appears that much more work must be done on the texts. Michalowski actually declares that Wolkstein "has violated the culture that produced the texts in which Inanna appears," and Harold Bloom writes an essay on contemporary attitudes toward the idea of hell. He is defensive about the Sumerians' primacy as writers and thinkers, and distances them as "alien," thus rejecting this most important text for our culture because it is "mythologically bewildering" to him, "an alien vision that has little in common either with the Bible or with Homer." Bloom is most upset when Inanna sends her husband to take her place in hell, and he chastises Wolkstein for praising a goddess "who may not be the best 'role model' for us and our children." He cites this action as "caprice" and "brutality" and urges us to reject Inanna on moral grounds, citing the later patriarchal curse on her in the legend of Gilgamesh.

13 Dale Spender, *Women of Ideas and What Men Have Done to Them,* p. 9.

14 Catherine des Roches (c. 1555–84). Unpublished translation by Tilde Sankovitch, Northwestern University.

15 Silver, *Virginia Woolf's Reading Notebooks.*

16 See Geoffrey Hartman's talk in *The Challenge of Feminist Criticism,* pamphlet, ed. Joanna Lipking, from the School of Criticism and Theory Symposium, The Challenge of Feminist Criticism, November 1981, pp. 23–26 (available from The Program on Women, Northwestern University, 617 Noyes St., Evanston, Illinois 60201). My own essay here "Gunpowder, Treason and Plot," naively asked male critics to read feminist critics. For what happened when they did, see Showalter's "Critical Cross-Dressing." See the papers by Marlene Longenecker and Judith Gardiner in this collection for rejections of formalism and socialist-feminist critiques of contemporary critical discourse, and note as well the interaction of the speakers with each other and with the audience in dialogue.

17 Shari Benstock, "The Feminist Critique: Mastering Our Monstrosity," *Tulsa Studies in Women's Literature* 2 (Fall 1983): 137–49.

18 *Critical Inquiry* 8/2, *Writing and Sexual Difference.*

19 One of the books I attacked was Elaine Showalter's *A Literature of Their Own,* arguing that it was not materialist or historical enough. Given the subsequent almost wholesale shift into psychoanalytic theories by feminist critics, her book now looks like a model of materialist scholarly practice.

20 Gayatri Spivak, "Making and Unmaking in *To the Lighthouse,*" in *Women and Language in Literature and Society,* ed. Sally McConnell-Ginet, Ruth Borker, and Nelly Furman (New York: Praeger, 1980), pp. 310–27.

21 Gayatri Spivak, "Draupadi," *Critical Inquiry* 8/2 (Winter 1981): 380 – 402. It is only in the reading of *To the Lighthouse* that Spivak fails to write theory and practice. See her "Three Feminist Readings" in *Union Seminary Quarterly Review* 35/1–2 (Fall–Winter 1978–79): 15–18.

22 Peggy Kamuf, "Penelope at Work: Interruptions in *A Room of One's Own,*" *Novel* 16/1 (Fall 1982): 5–18.

23 On the footnote, see Shari Benstock's "At the Margin of Discourse," *PMLA* 98/2 (March 1983): 204–25. I have remarked in chapter 8, above, on the peculiar lack of footnotes to feminist critics whose ideas are used in their essays by male critics. See n. 3, p. 233 and 234 of J. Hillis Miller's *Fiction and Repetition* (Harvard University Press, 1982) for an interesting example of the way in which the critic identifies himself by naming all the critics he wishes to be his brothers and equals. Like some tribal ritual, this incantation places his own work among those he respects; he even names the journals whose views he acknowledges, and throughout the text he refers to the fiction he is writing about as "*my* seven novels." Does this represent a kind of crisis or anxiety of authorship/critical identity in the establishment? This minimalism in annotation has the political effect of isolating the critic or theorist from scholars and from the history of scholarship. If present practice in footnoting is a legacy of nineteenth-century capitalist recognition of the ownership of ideas, the minimalism of theorists, as opposed to scholars, represents a new economy of critical exchange in which the work of scholars is fair game (like exploitation of third-world countries), and the big White Men acknowledge only each other. Feminist practice continues to acknowledge students, participants in seminars, casual conversations—one scholar recently thanked Ma Bell for enabling her to discuss her work with her colleagues on the telephone. Nina Auerbach goes so far as to say that a whole chapter of *Woman and the Demon* owes its genesis to Martha Vicinus' opening of her files to a sister scholar.

24 Peggy Kamuf, *Fictions of Feminine Desire* (Lincoln: University of Nebraska Press, 1982).

25 Rachel Brownstein, *Becoming a Heroine: Reading about Women in Novels* (New York: Viking, 1982); Joanna Russ, *How to Suppress Women's Writing* (Austin: University of Texas Press, 1983); and Alice Walker, *In Search of Our Mothers' Gardens* (New York: Harcourt Brace Jovanovich, 1983).

26 Sylvia Townsend Warner, "Women as Writers," in *Collected Poems* (New

York: Viking, 1983). Viking has also published a selection of Townsend Warner's letters, edited by William Maxwell (1983), and *Scenes of Childhood* (1981) is still in print. There is an Academy/Chicago edition of her brilliant feminist novel *Lolly Willowes* (1929). Virago (London) has reprinted two other novels, *The True Heart* and *Mr. Fortune's Maggot.* Townsend Warner deserves a major revival. I have discussed *Lolly Willowes* in "A Wilderness of One's Own: Feminist Fantasy Novels of the Twenties" in Susan Squier, ed. *Women Writers and the City* (Knoxville: University of Tennessee Press, 1984), pp. 134–60.

27 *But Some of Us Are Brave,* ed. Hull, Scott, and Smith.

28 Mary Ellman, *Thinking about Women* (1968; reprint, London: Virago, 1982); Adrienne Rich, *On Lies, Secrets and Silence;* Tillie Olsen, *Silences* (New York: Dell, 1975); Carolyn Heilbrun, *Reinventing Womanhood* (New York: Norton, 1979); Lillian Robinson, *Sex, Class and Culture* (Bloomington: Indiana University Press, 1978).

29 Richard McDougal, ed., *The Very Rich Hours of Adrienne Monnier,* p. 185; quoted and discussed in Shari Benstock, *Women of the Left Bank* (Austin: University of Texas Press, 1986).

30 Colette, *My Mother's House and Sido,* pp. 33–47.

31 Jean Rhys, *Smile Please* (Berkeley: Donald Ellis, 1979), p. 20. I discuss this passage in relation to Freud's "The Uncanny" in "Laughing at Leviticus" in *Silence and Power: Djuna Barnes, A Revaluation,* ed. Mary Lynn Broe (Carbondale: University of Southern Illinois Press, forthcoming).

32 I coined the word *cliterologos* in "Taking the Bull by the Udders."

33 Virginia Woolf, *To the Lighthouse* (1927; reprint, New York: Harcourt Brace and World, Harvest Edition, 1955; page numbers in the text are from this edition). In "Sapphistry," Mrs. Ramsay reading "The Fisherman and His Wife" to James is an almost parodic rendering of Freud's oedipal stage. I am indebted here to an undergraduate Yale essay by my niece, Susan Lubeck, and to a presentation in my seminar in feminist theory by Mary Mathis, as well as to the helpful comments of Angela Ingram.

34 William Empson, "Virginia Woolf," *Scrutinies II,* ed. Edgell Rickword (London: Wishart, 1931), p. 216. I would offer this section as an example of a feminist deconstructive reading. Yet, like other feminist critics, I am cautious about the final turn required by this practice in other circumstances and its tendency to negate the historical justice of feminist interpretation.

Index

Jane Marcus is Professor of English at the City University of New York Graduate Center and the City College of New York. She is the author of *Virginia Woolf and the Languages of Patriarchy, Virginia Woolf and Bloomsbury, The Young Rebecca West, Virginia Woolf: A Feminist Slant,* and *New Feminist Essays on Virginia Woolf.*

The text of this book is set in Caxton Light
by Chappel Typography, Athens, Ohio.

Jacket and text design by Jane Forbes.

DATE DUE

NOV 30 90			
DEC 1 2 1994			
GAYLORD			PRINTED IN U.S.A.